Erin Wheeler

Spring '08

(214) 289-5198

7"0ɔ

<u>Time in the Ditch</u>

Time in the Ditch

American Philosophy and the McCarthy Era

John McCumber

Northwestern University Press
Evanston, Illinois

Northwestern University Press
Evanston, Illinois 60208-4210

Printed in the United States of America

10 9 8 7 6 5 4 3 2 1

ISBN 0-8101-1809-2

Library of Congress Cataloging-in-Publication Data
McCumber, John.
    Time in the ditch : American philosophy and the McCarthy era / John
McCumber.
        p. cm.
    Includes bibliographical references and index.
    ISBN 0-8101-1809-2 (alk. paper)
    1. Philosophy, American—20th century.   2. McCarthy, Joseph,
1908–1957—Influence.   I. Title.
B936 .M36 2000
191—dc21   00-010668

To the memory of Reiner Schürmann
and Louis Comtois

Iassou, phile!
Kai philou!

Atque inter silvas
Academi quaerere veritatem.
—*Horace*

Contents

Acknowledgments

This has been an unusually painful and troubling book to write. Fortunately, I have had the advice and encouragement of an unusual number of wonderful people, including but not limited to Michael Baur, T. David Brent, John D. Caputo, Jonathan Culler, Frank Cunningham, Jude P. Dougherty, Abraham Edel, Arthur Fine, Nancy Fraser, Nelly Furman, Ronald Giere, Gary Gutting, David Hull, Reginald Lilly, Françoise Lionnet, Jeff Rice, Thomas Ryckman, Robert C. Scharff, Ellen Schrecker, Reiner Schürmann, Charles Sherover, Laurie Shrage, Thomas Uebel, Bruce Wilshire, and especially Gerald Graff, Susan Harris, and Jane Winston.

The book was written during my tenure of a faculty fellowship at the Alice B. Kaplan Center for the Humanities at Northwestern University. I am grateful to the center, to its directors, Whitney Davis and Helmut Müller-Sievers, and especially to its assistant director, Elzbieta Foeller-Pituch.

I wish to thank all these people, and many others, and to apologize for the many defects that remain in spite of their efforts.

Portions of chapters 1, 2, 3, and 5 appear in different form in "Time in the Ditch: American Philosophy and the McCarthy Era," *diacritics* 26 (spring 1996): 33–49. Portions of chapter 5 appear in different form in "Reconnecting Rorty: The Situation of Discourse in Richard Rorty's *Contingency, Irony, and Solidarity,*" *diacritics* 20 (1990): 2–19.

Abbreviations

In citing works in the text and notes, short titles have often been used. Works frequently cited have been identified by the following abbreviations and shortened forms:

AAUP
Bulletin of the American Association of University Professors

APA
Proceedings and Transactions of the American Philosophical Association

Bloom
Allan Bloom, *The Closing of the American Mind.* New York: Simon and Schuster, 1987.

Borradori
Giovanna Borradori. *The American Philosopher.* Translated by Rosanna Crocitto. Chicago: University of Chicago Press, 1994.

CAF
Communism and Academic Freedom: The Record of the Tenure Cases at the University of Washington. Seattle: University of Washington Press, 1949.

CIS
Richard Rorty, *Contingency, Irony, and Solidarity.* Cambridge: Cambridge University Press, 1989.

Fine
Arthur Fine, *The Shaky Game.* Chicago: University of Chicago Press, 1986.

Hegel
G. W. F. Hegel, *Phenomenology of Spirit.* Translated by A. V. Miller. Oxford: Oxford University Press, 1979.

Hull
David Hull, *Science as a Process.* Chicago: University of Chicago Press, 1988.

MacIntyre
Alasdair MacIntyre, *After Virtue.* 2d ed. Notre Dame, Ind.: University of Notre Dame Press, 1984.

Rorty
Richard Rorty, *Philosophy and the Mirror of Nature.* Princeton, N.J.: Princeton University Press, 1979.

Schrecker
Ellen Schrecker, *No Ivory Tower.* New York: Oxford University Press, 1986.

Searle
John Searle, *The Campus War: A Sympathetic Look at the University in Agony.* New York: World, 1971.

WD
Martin Heidegger, *Was Heisst Denken?* Tübingen: Niemeyer, 1971.

Wilshire
Bruce Wilshire, "The Pluralist Rebellion in the American Philosophical Association: Eastern Division, 1978–1985." Unpublished manuscript, 1985.

"WM"
Martin Heidegger, "What Is Metaphysics?" In *Basic Writings,* translated by David Farrell Krell, 95–112. San Francisco: Harper and Row, 1977.

Introduction

Philosophers, like academics in other fields, enjoy thinking of themselves as engaged in what one thinker to be discussed in this book calls a "timeless, selfless quest of truth." They view themselves as seeking, and perhaps even finding, truths that are universal and atemporal and that, therefore, hold independently of the conditions under which they are arrived at.

This conceit is not new, for philosophy began when Thales of Miletus dared to look up from the path of his own feet to the stars, which shine forever on everyone. But Thales paid a price for his disinterest: he lost his footing and fell into a ditch. An old woman, seeing this, wondered aloud how he could expect to understand the heavens when he knew nothing about what lay at his own feet.[1] Thales's pride, I suspect, was hurt more than his body; but most damaged of all must have been his investigation of the cosmic order. You can't see many stars from the bottom of a ditch.

Thales was not the last philosopher to lose his footing so badly that his quest for truth was impeded or even ended. Much of the time, the footing involved is political. Socrates, Plato, Aristotle, Abelard, Ockham, Locke, Kant, and Hegel, to name a few, all at one time or another fell afoul of the social, religious, or political powers in their respective societies.[2] Moreover, as any work of Foucault will suggest, political events and pressures may go beyond interfering with individual careers to influence the nature of philosophy itself. In Germany after 1830, for example, reactionary forces purged the Young Hegelians—including such able thinkers as Ludwig Feuerbach, Karl Marx, Max Stirner, and David Strauss—from academic positions. This helped consign the country's universities to a generation and more of the kind of egoistic charlatanry described by Lewis White Beck: "[M]en entered and left the [neo-Kantian] movement as if it were a church or political party; members of one school blocked the appointments and promotions of members of the others; eminent Kant scholars and philosophers who did not found their own schools or accommodate themselves to one of the established schools tended to be neglected as outsiders and contemned as amateurs."[3]

It was not until the end of the century—two full generations later—that respectable versions of neo-Kantianism returned to German universities, in the shapes of phenomenology and logical positivism.

Political interference with philosophy did not end with the nineteenth century, of course. Many Anglo-American philosophers, if they thought about it at all, would say that the rise of the Nazis in Germany allowed Heidegger to chew his way to the top of the German philosophical heap; in more recent images of Germany, Habermas figures as the pet Marxist of the *Bundesrepublik*. In France, the debacle of 1968 clearly called forth irrationalism in the thought of Derrida and Foucault. Britain's Thatcher, apparently unwilling to tolerate philosophy at all, instigated the greatest academic exodus since Hitler.

So much for poor Europe. Fortunately, such things—we Americans like to tell ourselves—do not happen here. Though politics may influence philosophy in the Old World, American philosophy is an autonomous, indeed overwhelmingly tenured, discipline in the freest country on earth. The only important force shaping it has, it appears, been reason itself: the ongoing process of argument and evaluation in which American philosophers excel. At least, that's all we hear about.

But this exemption from politics may be more spurious than real. There is, in fact, a good deal of evidence that American philosophy in the 1940s and 1950s confronted a political movement that threatened its future in important ways. The record suggests that philosophers did not exactly win their battle against that movement, which is usually called McCarthyism. And there is also evidence suggesting that American philosophy largely remains, even today, what Joe McCarthy's academic henchmen would have wanted it to be.

If anything like this is even possible, discussion is long overdue. Giovanna Borradori has argued that American philosophy has in recent years become crucially concerned with its own history (Borradori 3). This currently amounts, she notes, to the history of what is often called "analytical philosophy" (the nature of which I will discuss later). As Borradori, Richard Rorty, and Richard J. Bernstein have all recognized, analytical philosophy—whatever it is—came to dominance in American universities in the early 1950s.[4] None mentions that the triumph was simultaneous with the McCarthy era. Indeed, the whole issue has gone almost wholly undiscussed in the United States and Britain (though not, for example, in France).[5] This silence is remarkable because many American philosophers still active lived through the witch hunts, and presumably have lively memories of them.

In spite of this, the very possibility that the political pressures of the McCarthy era might have skewed the development of their discipline has, to my knowledge, been publicly suggested only once, by a single American philosopher.[6] This silence is, I believe, inexcusable. Consider the parallel with Martin Heidegger's despicable actions as a member of the Nazi Party in 1933 and 1934. By joining the Nazi Party at the same time that he became rector of Freiburg University, Heidegger behaved in a personally reprehensible way and gave crucial credibility to the Nazi cause. Yet serious arguments can be made that we should, to some extent, excuse Heidegger's engagement: the times were confused and dangerous, the full evil of the Nazis was not known until later, and so forth.[7]

However that may stand, it is clearly indefensible that in the ensuing four decades, Heidegger never honestly discussed or apologized for his earlier actions. I find parallels in the McCarthy era. The 1940s, 1950s, and even the early 1960s in the United States were by no means as volatile as the 1930s in Germany, but they certainly were, in their own way, tumultuous and conducive to paranoia. It should not be unthinkable that such social upheaval may have had effects on the academy, even on philosophy's rather arcane corner of it. That philosophy was damaged by McCarthyite forces would, in itself, be no scandal.

Nor would it be scandalous if the damage were not clearly perceived for a while after the fact. Many victories of the anti-intellectual forces were far from obvious, won deep in the legitimately fearful hearts of scholars. A group of professors reporting on the "oath controversy" at the University of California, for example, provides an extravagant but telling analogy: "[W]e felt it necessary to organize the writing of this book as the French organized their *Résistance* during the years of the Nazis . . . with no one knowing all the others who were involved." The writers report that during the controversy, professors did not dare communicate openly over their phones, which seemed to be tapped.[8]

Such fears and perceptions made the truth hard to come by for subsequent inquirers, but they were by no means exaggerated at the time. One purpose of this book, in fact, is to show how legitimate they were. But the McCarthy era was almost half a century ago. Why has silence been maintained for over a generation since?

Given the reluctance of American philosophers to talk, it is fortunate that much information about American philosophy during the McCarthy era has been preserved in a public, written record. My recounting here will be based on that record, which is contained chiefly in the *Bulletin of the American Association of University Professors,* the *Proceedings and Transactions of the American Philosophical Association,* and Ellen Schrecker's book *No Ivory Tower.*

The picture it paints is dismal. American philosophy during the McCarthy era seems to have confronted difficulties well beyond those faced by other disciplines. Philosophy's overall spokesperson, the American Philosophical Association (APA), failed miserably to come to grips with the threat. And the tactics by which the APA sought to avoid confronting the issues of that day turn out to instance intellectual gestures constitutive of much American philosophy since. In the first two chapters of this book, I will argue these points in turn and as strongly as the written record enables me to do. That will not be strongly enough, I think, to establish definitively that the McCarthy era decisively shaped subsequent American philosophy; but then, nothing in history is definitive. What the record does show, and amply, is that the possibility should not be passed over in silence.

Chapters 3 and 4 will adopt a somewhat different method. One way to argue, in the absence of explicit testimony, whether something really happened or not is to build a circumstantial case. If you see bear tracks and a number of dead sheep, you do not need eyewitness accounts to conclude, at least provisionally, that a bear killed the sheep. In chapter 3, I will discuss a number of characteristics of American philosophy today. Those characteristics—the dead sheep of my analogy—are consistent with the view that American philosophy continues to suffer from the wounds inflicted during the McCarthy era as documented in the public record—the bear tracks of my analogy. The data will suggest that the ongoing trauma takes the form of a discipline that is, internally, more tightly controlled by its establishment than are other disciplines in the humanities. Externally, American philosophy is traumatized in that it is far more isolated from other academic discourses, and from American culture in general, than it ought to be.

In chapter 4, I will reflect on some of the effects that this ongoing timidity on the part of philosophers seems to have had on American cultural life. I will argue, in particular, that much important work in the humanities has required either the rediscovery or the reinvention of philosophical traditions and approaches that were banished from most American philosophy departments at the time of the McCarthy era. The famous "culture wars," within the academy at least, have largely been fought between those who are undertaking this labor of rediscovery and reinvention, and those who want to stop it.

Chapter 5 discusses the philosophical payoff. I must admit that I was rather surprised to find such a payoff, since (like many philosophers) I was not educated to regard history as a plausible source of philosophical insight. But though politics cannot determine what is true, as Aristotle noted, it does determine what can be studied in a state.[9] The McCarthy era, it turns out, imposed an important restriction on just what kind of goal philosophers can pursue. It limited them to the pursuit of true sentences (or propositions, or statements). Once chapters 1 and 2 have brought this hidden protocol to light and stated it fully, its philosophical indefensibility will be manifest. Numerous alternatives then suggest themselves, and chapter 5 will sketch a particularly promising one of these—one that, in addition to other merits that I will claim for it, would have been guaranteed to infuriate Joe McCarthy and his academic henchmen.

I will be distinguishing, throughout the book, between two different kinds of history of philosophy. One is the *intellectual* history of philosophy, which is a history of the views philosophers have held, their reasons for holding them, and (most important, as will be seen) of the words in which they have couched them. Although this kind of philosophical history was, as will be seen in chapter 2, tossed out of philosophy by the logical positivists, it is today making a strong return, and I will pursue some of it in chapter 5. The other kind of history of philosophy has yet to return, but it will be central to the first four chapters of this book. It is the *disciplinary* history: the history of the group of people who do philosophy and of the rules by which they do it. Whatever one thinks philosophy is, both types of history are highly relevant to understanding it. This is especially true, I think, today, for the turn of the millennium finds American philosophy in a parlous state. In chapter 3, I will discuss the fact that between 1992 and 1996, the United States closed down philosophy departments at the rate of one hundred per year. During that time—just as the baby boomlet was arriving on campus—the number of philosophy department faculty fell by about 4 percent. For this and other reasons, American philosophy ended the century in serious institutional trouble. But, as I will also document in chapter 3, most philosophers seem to have been unaware of that trouble. Often and sadly enough, this ignorance was entirely honest. American philosophers are simply not used to thinking about the social, historical, and even intellectual contexts within which they work. This renders those contexts difficult to see, even after they become problematic or troublesome. (That, at least, is how I prefer to explain my own astonishment at some of the discoveries I made!)

Another largely unknown problem in American philosophy, to which I will come back briefly in chapter 3, is the migration of prominent and creative philosophers out of philosophy departments into other fields. The toll among continentally oriented feminists is particularly distressing. Such eminent philosophers as Seyla Benhabib, Judith Butler, Drucilla Cornell, Nancy Fraser, Elisabeth Grosz, and Iris Marion Young have all left philosophy departments in the last twelve years.[10] The quiet exit of so many excellent scholars in a single field cannot help but skew the discussion in American philosophy as a whole. Even on the crudest level of financial self-interest, the exclusion of so many prominent voices is no boon to philosophy departments seeking to enhance their resources or, more realistically, to retain the resources they already have.

Moreover, institutional problems of the kind I just mentioned usually percolate up to the intellectual level, and vice versa. Many of the institutional or disciplinary difficulties currently faced by American philosophy spring, for example, from the usual academic competition for resources. Philosophy's ability to compete for such resources is hampered by its inability to put its own intellectual house in order. One particularly striking case of this is the stubborn persistence, after half a century and in spite of much rhetoric to the contrary, of the split between analytical and continental ways of doing philosophy. However open-minded they proclaim themselves to be, hiring records show that most American philosophy departments remain unwilling to allocate significant representation to continental philosophy. A minority appears equally loathe to hire a Davidsonian or a Kripkean.[11] This is nothing new. In his recent sociological history of philosophy, Randall Collins notes that the "unprecedented vehemence" with which both sides of this split have condemned any philosophical approach but their own "has outlasted virtually every other substantive feature of their programs."[12] Strangely, the split itself has proved more basic and durable than the disagreements that originally provoked it.

I will discuss the analytical-continental split in chapter 3, and provide an antidote in chapter 5. One reason an antidote is still needed after so long, and one of the split's most embarrassing features, is that philosophers have not succeeded in construing it in philosophical terms. They seem to be unable to locate specific issues on which analytical and continental philosophers disagree, or to formulate the views of the respective sides on those issues, or to decide the merits of those views.

Unsurprisingly, then, debate has not moved forward. The split endures, and increasingly gets construed in *non*philosophical terms, as an effect of geography, culture, or psychology. Hence the standard caricatures: continentals are from Europe, are usually religious, and cannot learn logic; analysts are from Anglo-Saxon lands, usually worship science, and cannot learn languages. These caricatures are hardly good ways to present philosophy to deans, donors, or trustees, but as long as either important faction of the profession believes them about the other, they are difficult to deflect.

It is perhaps not surprising, either, that neither approach is doing very well these days. Analytical philosophy's core area, the philosophy of language, has run so far out of steam that one of its main recent debates has been whether what is called "The *New* Theory of Reference" was invented in the early 1970s or the mid-1960s.[13] The liveliest fields in analytical philosophy today are those that, like philosophy of quantum physics and philosophy of cognitive science, borrow their interest from other fields. Things are not much better on the continental side. In many ways even more self-protective than their analytical confreres, continental philosophers seem unable to break away from commentary and even, as Reiner Schürmann put it, reportage.[14] Philosophy thus appears as an oddly neurotic discipline: blocked, fearful, and at cross-purposes with itself. No wonder administrations are reluctant to give it new resources, so that philosophy departments remain static (or disappear) at a time when university enrollments are rising and endowments are soaring.

As with neurotics, treatment is likely to include airing the past trauma that helped create the present situation. My focus in this book will inevitably be what, in the pivotal years after World War II, became the dominant American philosophical paradigm: analytical philosophy. But I do not make my criticisms in the name of any allegiance to the other side of the split, to continental philosophy. The names of continental philosophers will figure in what follows, and it is noteworthy that when continental philosophy arrived in America—also after World War II—it was in two decidedly ahistorical and asocial forms: as phenomenological introspection into the structures of consciousness as such, and as an existentialism so radically individualistic that Sartre's Marxian commitments, evident after 1968, came as a shock to many American philosophers.

Nor should my critical focus on analytical philosophy be taken to mean that I think it is a useless or inferior paradigm. I believe that analytical philosophy, with its rigorous (though wrongly exclusive) focus on sentential truth and its exemplary concern with clarity, has made important contributions to philosophy. It was an insightful and productive philosophical project, both in Britain and in Austria, long before the McCarthy era even began. What I criticize in this book, I hope unsparingly, is the undeserved *dominance* of the analytical model over much of American philosophy.

It is not, in short, that the McCarthyites told Americans to do bad philosophy. (Some of them did, but they generally lost the argument.) Rather, it is that they told them to do only one kind of philosophy. Those who pursued that one kind quickly came to portray it, and perhaps even to regard it, as the only kind—or at least the only kind worth knowing about. Unfortunately, when any approach reaches a level of dominance in which most of its practitioners are entirely comfortable in their ignorance of any alternative to it, it becomes something no one can commit to. You cannot, after all, commit to something without intelligently evaluating the alternatives to it. Among the victims of the dominance of analytical philosophy in America, in other words, has been analytical philosophy itself. I hope this book will contribute to its critical renewal.

Finally, I do not wish to assert that accommodation to McCarthyism, as it seems to have occurred, was a wholly bad thing. It is all too easy for later generations to condemn their predecessors for failing to exhibit a courage that, in the actual event, would have been mere foolhardiness. The defensive posture to which I have alluded may well have been a wise and necessary one. It is neither wise nor necessary, however, to prolong such a posture once circumstances have changed.

Time in the Ditch

1

Philosophy's Family Secret

The Nature and Impact of the McCarthy Era

The fiftieth anniversary meeting of the Eastern Division of the American Philosophical Association (APA) was held in Toronto from December 27 to December 29, 1950. It seems to have been an enlightening and successful affair, as well as a rather cozy one. Of the division's 744 members (*APA* 24:55), only a couple hundred presumably chanced the train rides, primitive aircraft, or the two-lane highways required, in those days, to get to the capital of Ontario—and to the redoubtable Canadian winter. Those who did so were amply rewarded. True, they had no choice about what to hear: as befits so small an organization, all ten sessions were plenary and everyone attended them. But those sessions included, among other things, discussions of "Recent Trends in Philosophy," "The Modern Distemper of Philosophy" (with George Boas and Gilbert Ryle), "One Hundred Years of Canadian Philosophy," "Problems of General Systems Theory" (with Carl Hempel and Hans

Jonas), and "Leibniz and the Timaeus." Evenings brought the meetings of no fewer than three associated societies: the Association for Realistic Philosophy, the Personalist Discussion Group, and the Peirce Society.

The traditional presidential address was given that year by Professor Arthur E. Murphy of Cornell University, who had been elected president the year before. Its title was "The Common Good." Murphy analyzed this expression in strikingly contemporary terms, seeing it as both "a term of praise and an instrument of power" (*APA* 24:3). Murphy also took the occasion to reflect on philosophy itself, the discipline and where it was going. Here—along with expressing the typically American inability to acknowledge Canadian sovereignty—he sounded a note of caution: "There are enemies outside and enemies within our national borders. And there is also the enemy within ourselves—the pressure of fear and confusion and partisan advantage to break down those hard-won habits of rationally self-controlled behavior in which agreement is maintained through understanding and freedom actualized in community. A philosophy that can tell us how to make our ideas clear may be an aid to honest speech and wise decision in the years that lie ahead" (*APA* 24:18).

There was, as we will see in chapter 2, much going on at that particular meeting, and the ominous tone of Murphy's comments was fully justified. But I will come back to Eastern Division, for it was not the only part of the APA to hold meetings that year. Eastern Division, in fact, is only one of three separate divisions constituting the American Philosophical Association. This structure is based upon the most philosophically irrelevant of possible criteria: geographic location. Regardless of their interests and approaches, philosophers belonged, then as now, to either Eastern, Western (now Central), or Pacific Division of the APA. Each division has its own officers and holds its own meetings in its own area of the country. Eastern Division is by far the largest and, partly because most job interviews take place at its December meeting, the most important division. But the fact remains that, in all strictness, Murphy was the president of only about half of the APA's membership.

Five months later, at the beginning of May, Western Division held its yearly meeting in Evanston, Illinois. D. W. Gottshalk, from the University of Illinois, was its president, and in his address he too sounded a note of caution. His talk was entitled "Twentieth Century Theme" and, though with the male chauvinism typical of the time, he had this to say about philosophy itself:

> Today, philosophy seems to be in a lull. The greatest living philosophers are venerable old men whose main work is done, and the younger men have not yet grown to greatness. In this situation, amid the shattering perplexities of twentieth-century life, a natural impulse has been to mark off some limited domain for attention, and to concentrate great effort on it. Perhaps the most energized phase of philosophy in the last three decades has been its investigations of language, symbolic systems, and techniques of analysis. . . . But philosophy is more than a technological enterprise. As our whole argument has tended to show, it can reach to the presuppositions of our common life, and submit them to critical examination. (*APA* 24:28)

The same kind of reflection on the discipline of philosophy itself also found its way, if only cursorily, into Pacific Division's presidential address. Speaking on "The Science of Creation" at the divisional meeting, held in Berkeley simultaneously with Eastern Division's meeting, Hugh Miller of the University of California, Los Angeles, pointed out that "the philosopher should learn that *to defend science* he must *defend it in its social-economic consequences*" (*APA* 24:44). Whether this was or was not an accurate reflection on philosophy or good advice to philosophers, it would seem strange to many later philosophers, who held that science was fully legitimated as a quest for truth and were rather dismissive of its socioeconomic consequences.[1]

By 1961, a different format was firmly in place for APA presidential addresses. The three divisional presidents, Carl G. Hempel, C. L. Stevenson, and A. I. Melden, all adhered to this second format, as have most presidential addresses since. Hempel spoke on "Rational Action," Stevenson on "Relativism and Non-Relativism in the Theory of Value," and Melden on "Reasons for Action and Matters of Fact." Each of these papers took a philosophical issue and argued for a thesis that would resolve it. None of them even mentioned philosophy itself. The presidential address, in other words, had become an occasion to do philosophy rather than to reflect upon it. Though a reflective dimension could be found in some later addresses, just as some unreflective addresses could be found earlier, a balance had clearly tipped. It has remained tipped. In 1997, the most recent year available as I write, the three presidential addresses—by Arthur Fine, Philip Kitcher, and Robert Nozick—all involved the notions of objectivity and truth, with Nozick and Kitcher defending and Fine diffusing them.[2] But none of them even broached the relation of objectivity and truth, if any, to philosophy itself.

This change in format went along with a significant change in personnel. Unlike Murphy, Gottshalk, and Miller, the speakers from 1961 whose names I just gave are all still well known today. Hempel was one of the important logical positivists, an approach whose influence today is still enormous.[3] The main claim of the positivists, of which we will hear more, was that if a statement could not be verified, it had no meaning. Though most philosophers would now disagree with this, it remains beguiling in its simplicity and self-assurance, so influential that much subsequent American philosophy since has been informally characterized as suffering from postpositivist depression.

Stevenson was a leading proponent of a related view in ethics, emotivism. He argued that though ethical statements cannot be verified and so do not have meaning (that is, they do not convey information), they are not wholly trivial. They are in fact very important because they recommend attitudes. If I say "Murder is evil," for example, I am not telling you anything about murder. I am expressing an attitude that can be formulated as "I disapprove of murder, and you should do likewise."[4] Melden, though not as clearly identified with a particular approach as the other two, was an influential ethicist and rights theorist and was still publishing in 1988.[5]

The doctrines and approaches of emotivism and logical positivism, however, did not survive as long as their authors' reputations. Indeed, they have largely fallen by the philosophical wayside. Many if not most philosophers today hold views more akin to those of Murphy than to those of Hempel and Stevenson. Yet the names of the two later philosophers remain much more familiar to us today. Why is this? Why are Hempel, Stevenson, and Melden, whose presidential addresses are now almost forty years back, known and remembered today whereas Murphy, Gottshalk, and Miller, only ten years older, are not? Is it possible that the emotivists and logical positivists are on "our" side of some historical break, while their predecessors by a few years are not? What might this have to do with the change in format for presidential addresses? Did the disciplinary mores themselves also change? In short: was the decade of the 1950s a sort of axial period during which a new (and apparently unreflective) paradigm, represented by new people, got put in place for American philosophy?

The answer would seem to be obvious from demographics alone. In 1950, the APA proudly boasted almost 1,400 members (*APA* 24:55). In 1990, it would have close to 9,000 members,[6] and the 1995 membership list (in *APA* 69, no. 2) would run to 145 pages. In part because of the increasing ease of travel, attendance at the Eastern Division meeting, the largest of the three yearly meetings, is now ten to fifteen times as great as it was in 1950. The fact that the overwhelming majority of APA members are teachers in postsecondary education points to something already well known to American academics: that there was an explosive growth in the number of teaching positions in philosophy after 1950. Moreover, given that the philosophy job market virtually collapsed in 1967, that growth lasted for less than twenty years.[7] Hence, the demographic history of American philosophy does not exhibit a steady pattern of retirements and hirings over the postwar period. Instead, it is overpopulated with people who entered the job market between 1950 and 1967.

Though the baby boom generation is working its way through American society at large like an elephant through a python, in philosophy it is the next older generation—often called the silent generation—that has, for the last thirty years, constituted the bulk of the profession. Among them are many former students and junior colleagues of professors like Hempel, Stevenson, and Melden, who remember them well and often fondly (as I remember Stevenson). To put the matter in brief: because of the way the job market has functioned, many American philosophers are about the same age. They have good memories of the people who educated them, but none at all (apparently) of those a few years older, and they have taught their own students accordingly.

What about the disciplinary mores, the nature of philosophy itself? That American philosophy received a new and enduring shape in the years after World War II is confirmed by at least a couple of its most eminent representatives. For in general, American philosophy is what is called analytical philosophy; and both Richard Rorty and Richard J. Bernstein—themselves past presidents of Eastern Division—have publicly noted that analytical philosophy came to dominance in American universities in the early 1950s.[8] This was a major revolution—an influential British anthology of analytical philosophy was even entitled *The*

Revolution in Philosophy.[9] Like all intellectual revolutions, this one made those who came even just before it, like Gottshalk, Miller, and Murphy, seem antiquated and forgettable.

Silence, Isolation, and Secrets

Demographics and meeting programs thus suggest that the postwar years brought two significant developments in American philosophy: an important change in philosophical personnel and a revolutionary change in philosophical orientation. These developments have been maintained since, which suggests that we should take a close look at those years if we are to understand American philosophy today.

Dysfunctional families, however much they may differ from one another, tend to engage in two types of behavior. One is that their talk diverges from their reality: they have a lot of family secrets, such as alcoholism or even incest, which may be very obvious but which, like the proverbial elephant in the living room, are never openly acknowledged. Partly to preserve those secrets, such families often tend to isolate themselves from the surrounding community. Two characteristics of American philosophy today push us toward viewing it, in some ways, like such a dysfunctional family. One, which I have noted above, is the ongoing and *general* absence of reflection on the discipline. The second is philosophy's self-imposed isolation from other fields. Chapters 3 and 4 will discuss both of these phenomena, and some of their consequences, in more detail. For the moment, I am interested in how they may have come about.

Reflective comments on American philosophy, its prospects, and its needs have not merely grown rare at the APA since the days of Gottshalk and Miller, they have become almost completely absent. Even the most specialized discourses in the academy, from time to time, publish work by senior figures reflecting upon where the field is and where it is going. Consider the important 1991 anthology on philosophy of science edited by Richard Boyd, Philip Gasper, and J. D. Trout.[10] The articles routinely rehearse the entire development of the discipline before making their own contribution, and every section of the anthology—except for the final one on the philosophy of psychology—begins with an essay by a logical positivist, that is, by one of the early figures in the field.

But philosophy in general, it appears, feels no such need to confront its own history.

In 1964, for example, the leading American philosopher of his generation, W. V. O. Quine, responded as follows to questions put to him about philosophy by Robert Ostermann, the editor of the *National Observer:* " '[P]hilosophy' is one of a number of blanket terms used by deans and librarians in their necessary task of grouping the myriad topics and problems of science and scholarship under a manageable number of headings. . . . I am not alluding to the fragmentation of specialties; I speak of the insignificance of a certain verbal grouping."[11] Contemporary postmodern proponents of the death of philosophy are thus too late; for America's most prominent philosopher had denied philosophy's existence, as anything other than a *flatus vocis,* thirty-five years ago.

Quine's refusal to reflect on philosophy has since been upheld by his colleagues. One ransacks the pages of the *Journal of Philosophy, Philosophical Review,* and the *Review of Metaphysics* looking for articles that reflect intelligently on philosophy in America, its problems, and its prospects. Largely, though not wholly, in vain.[12]

Absences are of course difficult to demonstrate, but the change in format for APA presidential addresses is telling in itself. Presidential addresses to the APA are not, to be sure, the only places where the need for reflection might be addressed; but if any prominent analytical philosopher has addressed it elsewhere in the last twenty years, I have not found where.[13] As Richard Rorty has written, "Analytic philosophers are not much interested in either defining or defending the presuppositions of their work. Indeed, the gap between 'analytic' and 'non-analytic' philosophers nowadays coincides pretty closely with the division between philosophers who are not interested in historico-metaphysical reflections on their own activity and philosophers who are."[14]

Such absence of critical reflection, we have seen, was not always the rule for American philosophers, at least not for those elected to the presidencies of the APA. And it is certainly not the rule for philosophy in general. Indeed, critical reflection on itself is traditionally one of philosophy's most central and distinctive parts—for philosophers since Plato's *Republic* have been charged with establishing not only the starting points of other disciplines but also of their own (*Republic* 7:533c).

Gottshalk alludes to this at the conclusion of his presidential address to Western Division:

> The truth is, whether we like it or not, philosophers today have a tre-mendous work on their hands. This work is nothing more, yet nothing less, than revealing our civilization in its true light, of depicting its elemental ac-tualities, and its inherent and imperative possibilities. It is the task of *crit-ical, reflective self-understanding.* This task is what the great philosophers have always faced and tried to perform in their own times, in light of the evident features of their existence. It is, as I see it, the obligation and the opportunity that we have in our day, to gain *the greatness that philosophy at its best has always had.* (*APA* 24:30; emphasis added)

The recent silence of philosophers concerning philosophy itself thus amounts to the professional abandonment of what for over two millennia, from Plato to Gottshalk, was central to them: that of seeking critical, reflective self-understanding. That the philosophical profession in America has so largely, and quietly, abandoned this task is certainly odd enough to call for an explanation.

Several are possible. One is that American philosophers are simply too busy doing philosophy to step back and reflect on their discipline. That is, in a way, very true. Philosophers in the United States are also busy teaching and mentoring students, serving on committees, con-ducting relationships, raising children, coping with illnesses, and per-forming the many other chores that fall to human beings. But that the multifaria of life leave little time for philosophizing is nothing new; and that philosophers should be too busy doing philosophy to engage in one of philosophy's traditionally central tasks merely epitomizes the issue I am raising here.

The distinction between reflecting on philosophy and doing philos-ophy may seem, at first glance, utterly specious; but, in fact, there is an honorable philosophical side to it. The refusal of American philosophers to reflect on philosophy can be seen as part of their positivist heritage, for as Habermas writes, "that we disavow reflection *is* positivism."[15] This disavowal is not mere spleen, however. It dates back at least to one of analytical philosophy's founding distinctions, that between language and metalanguage. This was advanced by Bertrand Russell to solve (among other things) what is called the paradox of self-reference, the problem that arises with sentences that proclaim their own falsity: if

"This sentence is false" is in fact true, then that sentence must be false; but if it is false that the sentence is false, then it must be true (and so, once again, false).[16] Russell solves this by asserting as a general principle that any logically correct language has a specific domain of objects it can talk about and that its own sentences cannot be part of that domain. Hence, if I talk about a sentence such as the one above, I cannot be doing so in the language in which that sentence is written, but in another language, or metalanguage. If philosophy is, as it is, a kind of language, then any language that talks about philosophy must not be philosophy but some other discourse. It follows that reflections such as those in Murphy's and Gottshalk's presidential addresses are not philosophy. And since the job of philosophers is to do philosophy, it would be mere laziness or tomfoolery for them to engage in reflection *on* philosophy.

But even if we conceded all this (and the unspoken presuppositions which, as will be seen, it contains), it would not follow that reflection on philosophy should be tacitly banned from its public journals and meetings. Such a ban, in short, is too convenient to be wholly comfortable. For if philosophy professors provide no account of themselves, of how they got to be where they are or of where they are going, then the impression given to their students is inevitably that they somehow dropped from heaven. What drops from heaven is hardly open to discussion, much less to criticism. The usefulness of such a standpoint to the professor can hardly be disputed. But neither can its harm to the student.

Another response, also justified in its way, would be that such reflection has, in fact, begun. The view that the origins of analytical philosophy are in fact relevant to its current situation has come, in spite of its radicality, to be rather widely accepted. Scholars such as Michael Dummett, Michael Friedman, and Peter Hylton have begun to reconstruct the philosophical debates of the early century, when analytical philosophy first arose in England.[17] But even those thinkers are far removed from the kind of reflection we saw in Gottshalk, Miller, and Murphy, for their books focus on the *philosophical* origins of analytical philosophy; that is, they remain within the basic view that philosophy is an autonomous enterprise whose nature, though it changes, is not deeply affected by the kinds of cultural and political factors that all three of the earlier philosophers addressed.

The reasonable next step would be to admit that *some,* at least, of contemporary philosophy's origins may not be philosophical at all but rather lie in the politics and culture of the historical period in which current American philosophy took shape. If so, then those circumstances need to be discussed and understood. Even those who are wholly resolute in their ahistorical view of their discipline—those many who, in the words of Peter Hylton, see analytical philosophy "as taking place within a single timeless moment"[18]—cannot escape this. For in the eyes of such people, political and cultural circumstances are failings and defects that at the very least need to be weeded out. You can't weed them if you don't see them, and you can't see them if you won't look for them.

A third possibility is the one appealed to by Quine in my quotation of him above, from 1964: that philosophy is simply too disparate a set of enterprises to be unified other than nominally. As I mentioned, this view has been maintained in practice since. The subject index for the *Journal of Philosophy* from 1990 to 1996, published annually, does not, for example, contain a single entry for "philosophy," though there are entries for subfields, such as "philosophy of science" and "philosophy of language."

But this appeal to (intellectual) diversity raises two important questions. One is whether mainstream American philosophy really is as diverse as Quine and others suggest. Perhaps its seeming diversity really masks an underlying unity. I will argue later that this is in fact the case. For the moment, let me just note that the diversity in question is simply asserted by Quine, not shown or argued for.

Second, even if the description is accurate, *should* philosophy be left in such a disjoined state? Would it not be worthwhile to try to give it more coherence than it happens, on this view, to have? Is it not precisely the job of the most influential thinkers in a given discipline to give it some degree, though not overmuch, of unity and direction? Is there not a strange abdication taking place in these words from the man who, at the time he wrote them, was America's most influential philosopher?

A fourth possible reason for contemporary American philosophy's neglect of reflection is that philosophers simply do not have answers to the kinds of questions that such reflection poses. The failure of the philosophical establishment, over the last twenty years, to find a persuasive answer to Richard Rorty's critique in his 1979 *Philosophy and the Mirror of Nature* suggests this.[19] But if that is the case, then we need to explain the persistence of an approach that has been unable to respond to such a serious challenge. If Rorty finished them off, why are the analysts still here? Could it be that what holds them in place is political circumstance rather than philosophical merit? Is it possible that analytical philosophy, the most resolutely apolitical paradigm in the humanities today, is itself more a political than a philosophical phenomenon?

There is one more possible explanation. Could it be that open reflection on the history of and prospects for American philosophy would bring something unpleasant to light? Some dark family secret that those in the know are afraid to mention and that those not in the know are afraid to see? Something like little Bertie's strange resemblance to the milkman or Grandpa's year at the Betty Ford Clinic?

All of these explanations probably hold to some degree. In this book I will be primarily concerned with the final possibility: that there is something important buried in American philosophy's not-so-distant past—something that many philosophers do not want to face, even though it explains much about the structure of their discipline.

American philosophy's disavowal of reflection is not the only clue that something is wrong with it. In spite of efforts to break down some of the barriers between philosophy and other disciplines—efforts that are beginning to pay off in philosophy of science—American philosophy remains strangely isolated from other fields, not only in the humanities and the sciences but within philosophy itself. As Richard Rorty writes, analytical philosophy "has pretty well closed itself off from contact with non-analytic philosophy, and lives in its own world."[20] Some of the criticisms of analytical philosophy made by postanalytical philosophers such as Rorty and Stanley Cavell[21] actually suggest a discipline that defines itself as being not merely isolated but under attack.

As Giovanna Borradori summarizes them, those criticisms maintain that analytical philosophy "canonized a philosophical discourse that remains within rigid disciplinary and professional confines, bleakly isolating philosophy from history, culture, and society" (Borradori 20). Rigid confinement and bleak isolation sound, at first hearing, like the defensive posture of a threatened discipline—threatened, presumably, by that from which it seeks to isolate itself: the historical circumstances of the surrounding culture and society. In the case of philosophy this posture is, like the absence of reflection it exhibits, mysterious, for if we look at analytical philosophy today, comfortably ensconced in the best American universities to the virtual exclusion of other approaches, we are at a loss to identify what those threatening circumstances might be.

Surely a country that can tolerate Watergate and *l'affaire* Lewinsky is not going to shower hemlock on a few philosophers!

If we look back fifty years, however, a possible answer emerges. A serious threat *might* have been posed to philosophy by the anti-intellectualism of the McCarthy era, if it were strongly enough directed against philosophers. And if so—once again—it is unlikely that we will fully understand analytical philosophy, or achieve an adequate critical appreciation of it, until we understand how and to what degree it served as a response to such specific historical circumstances. And we cannot understand those circumstances without setting them into a wider context.

. . . as Apple Pie: American Suspicions of Philosophy

As Richard Hofstadter showed thirty-five years ago, hostility to philosophy—as to other manifestations of intellect—is a long tradition in America.[22] The United States was the first country to be founded on a philosophy—a sometimes uneasy synthesis of Locke and the Scottish enlightenment.[23] This places philosophy in a most peculiar position. Because philosophical work underpins the Republic, philosophy is very important. But, for that reason, it is also very important that philosophy be over with, done, its basic issues settled, for any innovation calls old doctrines into question—and if the innovation is in philosophy, those doctrines could be the precise ones that serve as the foundation of the Republic. Under such a regime, philosophy cannot be what most philosophers today think it should be—an ongoing process of critical inquiry that can lead anywhere and overturn anything. Rather, it must present itself publicly, if at all, as a body of established doctrine, like geometry or arithmetic, or as inquiry that, though critical, has somehow been diverted into nonthreatening fields.

American suspicion of philosophy is enhanced by the country's Puritan heritage. Hofstadter has brilliantly traced the evangelical roots of anti-intellectualism in the United States. Puritan ministers, he points out, were by comparison very intellectually accomplished and alive.[24] But it should not be forgotten that the intellect they so admired was quite different from the critical, skeptical modern or postmodern mind that we see today. Puritanism was classically directed, of course, against the temptations of the body. But the mind presents a similar set of dangers: free thinking and adultery went together as early as *The Scarlet Letter*. Hence, those today who think they need to resist, for example, the intellectual seductions of modern science—the fundamentalists—are not simply a deluded tribe of media pulpiteers. They carry forward an ancient and deeply rooted American tradition, one that is as deeply disturbed by the free use of the human mind as by that of the human body.

American suspicions of gratifying either the mind or the body came together over a philosopher in 1940, when Bertrand Russell arrived in the United States to teach at City College, New York. Russell was better known in this country as a libertine atheist than as a mathematical logician, and his pedagogical employment was pronounced by a judge to be dangerous to the public health, safety, and morals. Russell, who was in serious financial difficulties at the time, had to withdraw his acceptance of the post.[25]

World War II made this already chilly climate notably harsher, and five years after Russell's fiasco Brand Blanshard could write: "[M]athematics, physics, engineering, medicine—all the sciences, theoretic and applied, that have to do with the art of war are riding high; the humanities, including philosophy, have gone into temporary eclipse."[26]

Eight years after that, Blanshard himself became an example of American dislike of free-thinking philosophers. He had sent a letter to the editor of the *New York Times* (July 1, 1953) saying that as an American traveling in Europe he found it tiresome to have to apologize continually for Joseph McCarthy. This drew a scorching tirade from William F. Buckley:

> What about Mr. Blanshard—Phi Beta Kappa, senior professor of philosophy in Yale University, sometime co-president of the American Philosophical Association, member of the American Academy of Arts and Sciences? Why Mr. Blanshard is, in respect of . . . McCarthyism, a charlatan. He has, in fact, according to all academic rules, given his university grounds for dismissing him. Not, heaven knows, because he disagrees with McCarthy—in American universities, people are *hired,* not *fired,* because they disagree with McCarthy—but because to make such a statement as that McCarthy is engaged in searching out "men who have dared to utter liberal opinions, even in the remote past, and branding them as Communists," is to say a demonstrable untruth, and the person who utters it, in the teeth of the evidence, demonstrably ignorant or mendacious.[27]

The untruth in Blanshard's statement is not demonstrable. In fact, it is not even existent. Evidence that McCarthy's movement, in many if not all cases, went well beyond merely targeting Communists is overwhelming. I will provide examples and countering testimony shortly. For the moment, I will simply note that Alistair Cooke, no lackey of the Communist line, had predicted four years previously that "once [accused spy Alger] Hiss was put on the stand there would be a movement to bring old and young New Dealers to trial, not literally, but to make them judge their past life in the present hysteria."[28] The views Blanshard expressed, in other words, were widely and respectably shared.

But the implications of Buckley's quote reach far beyond its injustice to Blanshard. The view that ignorance and mendacity—derelictions with respect to truth—should be punished by dismissal from the university will play a long role in American thought policing, which usually presents itself as a defense of truth. Consider the following quote from Congressman Bob Inglis, a Republican from South Carolina and a member of the House Judiciary Committee of the Ninety-first Congress, apropos of the Clinton impeachment, which he had just helped orchestrate: "What we're witnessing here is a conflict, a clash between two very different views. One view is that there is absolute truth; the other view is that everything is relative. [Clinton] is the epitome of someone who says there is no truth, everything is relative. For those of us who believe there's truth, that telling the truth is crucial and that there are right statements and there are wrong statements, it is incumbent upon us to act."[29]

Though the differences are obvious, what Buckley and Inglis share is a view that will be stated repeatedly by McCarthyite forces and that will become constitutive of American philosophy itself: that no professor has a right to speak anything but the truth (or what she thinks is the truth or will lead to the truth). What neither Buckley nor Inglis tells us, of course, is how to go about finding the truth. Inglis, even in 1998, presents absolute truth as an object of belief, a matter of faith—as the sheer opposite, then, of philosophy. The weight of the ignorance in Buckley's book can be gauged from the fact that immediately after what I have quoted, he appeals to Socrates against Blanshard. Buckley seems wholly unaware that Socrates was a skeptic, a self-proclaimed apostle, not of truth but of ignorance—ignorance that he demonstrated over and over again in himself and others!

American hostility to philosophy, then, did not end with the chastising of Bertrand Russell. The cold war extended militaristic practices almost five decades into peacetime and made the "temporary" in Blanshard's judgment, quoted earlier, sound naively optimistic. When, as an undergraduate in the mid-1960s, I took a course in journalism, "philosopher" was on the list of pejorative terms. Who had time for philosophy when there was a war to win, appliances to buy, and a continent with some corners yet untamed?

The McCarthy Era: A Paranoid Jumble

At the cold war's beginning, we have seen, its possible influence on American philosophy did not go unremarked. Murphy's cautionary note of 1950, quoted earlier, is, for example, thoroughly couched in cold war terminology: the "enemies outside our national borders" to whom it refers were, in 1950, the Soviet Union and its satellite states. The "enemies within" were the domestic agents of that conspiracy, including (or so it was believed) most members of the Communist Party of the United States. And the "enemy within ourselves" was the inordinate fear of Communism, a fear that was causing serious problems for civil rights and academic freedom.

Now that the cold war is over, its effects on American culture are at last beginning to be explored in a reasonable and nonpartisan way.[30] There is no doubt that they were massive. Like any war, the cold war was a time of national mobilization. Unlike the other, hotter wars in which the United States has engaged, it lasted—for almost half a century. From 1945 until the collapse of the Soviet Union in 1991, the battle against Communism affected every aspect of American life. Not only the McCarthy era but the civil rights struggle, the Vietnam War, and the Reagan presidency were all decisively marked by, if not wholly results of, the cold war—its needs, its events, and its attitudes. It is no coincidence, to take just one small example, that the National Defense Foundation is a leading source of funding for philosophers.

But when I took my first philosophy course in the 1960s (and, for reasons mysterious to my journalism professor, liked it), no one so much as mentioned the cold war to me. Nor did anyone tell me and my fellow students that just a decade earlier the United States had undertaken what was perhaps the greatest intellectual purge in the history of Western democracy. This purge—carried out as part of the McCarthy era—hit academia around 1949 and did not fully subside until about 1960. It therefore coincides with what I earlier suggested was the axial period of postwar American philosophy. And it constitutes, I suggest, the repressed family secret of American philosophy. Its traumatic events explain why philosophers have isolated themselves within academia and why they are unwilling to reflect in public about their own discipline. More than that: as I will show in the next chapter, the McCarthy era explains some of the key *philosophical* presuppositions of analytical philosophy.

Many views of the McCarthy era tend to minimize its damage to American academic life (as does, of course, the habit of ignoring it altogether). Nathan M. Pusey, president of Harvard University from 1953 to 1971, put it this way: "Admittedly, not all responsible groups stood firm against the storm (we have already seen that some of the Regents of the University of California failed to do so); but a sufficient number did to ensure the vitality of higher education in the United States and to enable it to continue to grow."[31] If we descend further into the Harvardian depths, however, things begin to look a bit gloomier. Henry Rosovsky, dean of arts and sciences at Harvard from 1973 to 1984, summarized the McCarthy era as follows: "During the 1950s a number of Harvard instructors and assistant professors became victims of McCarthy-style political pressures. Some term appointments were prematurely rescinded; a few left 'voluntarily' rather than facing investigation of their political opinions or affiliations. The same was true everywhere else, and I do not recall that their elders organized an effective defense anywhere."[32]

It is generally admitted today that, as Rosovsky says, McCarthy-era political pressures thwarted a number of careers, primarily those of junior professors. This, of course, is bad enough; memorials to the fallen, and public acknowledgment of their elders' failure to defend them, are long overdue. This is particularly true, as will be seen, in the case of philosophy.

Before turning to that, however, a few more general considerations are in order. The instructors and assistant professors Rosovsky refers to were, presumably, not chosen at random to be McCarthyite targets. Why were they struck at? What were the real aims of the people we call "McCarthyites"? Who, and what, were their real targets? How anti-Communist was the McCarthy era really?

According to its most responsible spokespeople, what I call "academic McCarthyism" aimed at removing Communists from teaching positions. That in itself held great dangers for both intellectual and personal freedom, because it elevated association into guilt. The Communist Party, after all, was not illegal. Many Americans believed that joining it should not be criminalized into grounds for dismissal from employment and that such sanctions should be based on independent evidence of malfeasance.

On the other hand, the Party was clandestine: its membership was not publicly known. As writers such as James Bryant Conant, Sidney Hook, and James Rorty (father of Richard) argued, those who seek to impose their ideas in secrecy, by force rather than open argument, cannot consistently give allegiance to the community of scholars and have no place in it (Schrecker 105–9). According to this view, no ideas should be forbidden, and advocacy of even the most unpopular of them should be protected. But open advocacy was just what Communism was opposed to, and so it, alone of all approaches, should be forbidden. As the title of one of Hook's books had it: "Heresy, yes—conspiracy, no."[33]

This argument is not only standard but also respectable: if the Communist Party on campus was really such a clandestine conspiracy, then Communists were not true academics. Ellen Schrecker, in *No Ivory Tower,* argues at length that the Party was not conspiratorial, but we can always supplement Hook's argument to note that anyone who was so naive as to think that the Communist Party of any country was a helpful engine of constructive social change simply did not have the brains to be a teacher of any kind. (Both versions of the argument overlook the fact that most academic departments are traditionally full of secret forces seeking to impose their will without open discussion, and also have their share of brainless people against whom no national outcry is raised.)

Whether there was a core of legitimacy to the McCarthyite movement will probably always be debated.[34] What almost no one denies is that the movement quickly fell victim to excesses, both in the targets it chose and in the methods it used to pursue them. My concern here will be exclusively with those excesses, for I do not know of a single clandestine Communist philosopher who was legitimately exposed in the service of his or her Soviet masters.

Targets of the McCarthyites, in philosophy and beyond, can be divided into three groups. Some, though apparently not many, really were Communists (and may have been subversives). Others, such as Martin Luther King Jr., were not Communists but were wrongly given that label. But surprisingly many victims—perhaps most of them—were never asserted to be Communists at all. After all, accusations as specific as membership in the Communist Party were not easy to make stick, particularly when they were false, as they so often were. Those wishing to gain partisan or personal advantage from such accusations therefore resorted to various forms of double-talk, invoking such wraiths as "fellow travelers," "sympathizers," "pinkos," "paid agents," and my own personal favorite (once used by my mother): "anti-anti's." These epithets, and more serious sanctions, were applied to a breathtaking diversity of people, including Groucho (not Karl) Marx.[35] On what grounds?

It is difficult to say. The evidence against Groucho, for example, hardly makes sense to us today. According to FBI files, he had "never forgotten his origin" as a poor Jew from New York's East Side. A listener to his radio show reported that he seemed once to refer to the United States as the "United Snakes." And it was also reported to the FBI that he wrote affectionately of Charlie Chaplin.[36]

We will see more of this diversity of targets and of the irrational ways in which they were targeted. Taken together, the diversity and irrationality actually make it questionable whether McCarthyism is best construed as anti-Communism at all, rather than as an exercise in semifascistic conformism with (like Fascism itself) a core rhetoric of anti-Communism. Certainly, as my examples will show, people who were very far removed, both intellectually and socially, from the Communist Party USA had good reason to feel themselves in danger. Equally important, they had good reason to be confused about *why* they were in danger. Just who were the McCarthyites really after, if so many of their targets were not Communists? More urgently, if one thought one might become a target oneself, what did one need to do to escape McCarthyite cannonades?

The answers to these questions were not clear. True to what I have suggested was one of the heritages of Puritanism, the McCarthy era saw a good deal of ire, not only against Communists but against *any* untrammeled use of the human mind. Examples abound. Gerard Mertens, a professor at Livingstone College in Salisbury, North Carolina, lost his job for being not a Communist but a Unitarian (*AAUP* 44:188–91). John Greenway, an anthropologist, was dismissed from the University of

California, Los Angeles, in 1961 for asserting that the Roman Catholic Mass contained vestigial elements of cannibalism. However offensive, the claim is not notably Marxist.[37] In Michigan, according to anecdote, a state legislator demanded the abolition of all philosophy courses in the state universities except for those in symbolic logic and advanced symbolic logic. Their course descriptions, luckily, mentioned computers.

Not even a genius of the stature of Albert Einstein was safe. His last years were deeply troubled by investigations of his possible Communist sympathies/activities/subversions, conducted by both the FBI and the Immigration and Naturalization Service. Their efforts led him to characterize the American scene as "everywhere brutality and lies" and to complain, in a letter, "The German calamity of years ago repeats itself: people acquiesce without resistance and align themselves with the forces for evil. And one stands by, powerless." As a German Jew, Einstein knew only too well what he was talking about and could not have expressed himself more emphatically about the temper of the times. Among the "evidence" against him was testimony that he had joined with ten former Nazis to witness a beam of light melt a block of metal.[38]

Einstein and the Nazis? Light melting metal? Groucho and the United Snakes? We are in a bizarre world here, and not always a funny one. In the bitter winter of 1947–48, government relief was denied to the Navajo Nation, facing starvation, because their communal way of life was "un-American."[39]

The Puritan background of McCarthyism is also evident in the fact that almost as important to it as Communism was, of all things . . . sex. Kenneth Starr's obsessive pursuit of President Bill Clinton from 1998 to 1999 has been characterized as "sexual McCarthyism."[40] But the original McCarthyism was quite sexualized enough. The sociologist Robert Bellah tells of what happened when, in the spring of 1955, he was nominated for a one-year instructorship at Harvard, where he was a graduate student. Bellah was somewhat surprised by the nomination, because his membership in the Communist Party while a Harvard undergraduate had led to difficulties the previous summer with McGeorge Bundy, dean of the Faculty of Arts and Sciences. Now,

> Bundy made a further request of me, which I found strange but with which I complied. This was a request to visit an official at the Harvard Health Service.

My interview with the official of the Health Service was the strangest event in this strange story. Even in the extraordinary atmosphere of that period when many strange things seemed ordinary that interview was bizarre. He began after a few pleasantries with a story about someone who worked for the State Department who decorated his apartment with pictures of naked women to hide the fact that he was a homosexual. I listened in amazement, wondering what this had to do with me. He became less indirect and began asking whether I had ever engaged in sexual acts for which I could be blackmailed. I was trying desperately to understand what was happening when I remembered that six or seven years earlier when I had been an undergraduate I had consulted a doctor in the psychological clinic of the Health Service about feelings and anxieties not uncommon to college undergraduates. . . . I cannot help but wonder what would have happened had I been a practicing homosexual. Did Harvard's willingness to exert political pressure extend to sexual persecution as well?[41]

Bellah's portrait of a terrified Harvard graduate student bears small resemblance to the dismissive serenity of Harvard's President Pusey, quoted earlier, and puts desperate flesh on the facts so baldly stated by Dean Rosovsky.

In addition to anti-intellectualism and sexual obsession, another important component of McCarthyism was racism. It is no accident that Albert Einstein and Groucho Marx were both Jewish. In addition to the problems encountered somewhat later by Martin Luther King Jr., W. E. B. Dubois and Paul Robeson both had their passports revoked.[42] As I will discuss in the next chapter, one of the most famous cases in philosophy was directed against the first African American to hold a regular position at a major American university, Forrest Wiggins of Minnesota. Other strands in the McCarthyite tapestry included anti-Catholicism (though McCarthy himself was no less Catholic than Roy Cohn was Jewish),[43] homophobia, and general anti-intellectualism. As one writer put it in 1955, "It soon became clear that, whatever the ostensible goal of the early stages of this restrictive movement, its later intent was the achievement of a settled, conservative orthodoxy in the political, economic, and general social opinion of America. The evidence for this conclusion is overwhelming. . . . What we face is a general reaction . . . against the more humane, idealistic, and internalistic tendencies of the past few decades."[44]

This is still too narrow, I fear. Remarks such as Greenway's association of Catholicism with cannibalism hardly qualify as humane, idealistic, or "internationalistic." They are merely provocative and tendentious, and according to Sigmund Diamond that was enough: "Alternatives to existing policies, whether those alternatives were in fact Communist inspired or not, were stigmatized as subversive. Opposition could be treated as treason. It was a remarkably effective strategy, so effective that it would be a mistake to think that only McCarthyites joined in. So did others, university presidents and deans among them, sometimes out of agreement, sometimes hopeful that display of bloodlust would buy immunity for them."[45] Richard Hofstadter and Walter P. Metzger concluded that in almost two-thirds of the cases that came to the American Association of University Professors (AAUP), the causes turned out to be not ideological at all, but personal: a professor or administrator used charges of Communism, or the much vaguer ones available, to make trouble for an unloved colleague.[46] Hofstadter later put it as follows:

> The real function of the Great Inquisition of the 1950's was not anything so simply rational as to turn up spies or prevent espionage (for which the police agencies are presumably adequate), or even to expose actual Communists, but to discharge resentments and frustrations, to punish, to satisfy enmities whose roots lay elsewhere than in the Communist issue itself. That was why it showed such a relentless and indiscriminate appetite for victims and why it seemed happier with respectable and powerful targets than with the occasional obscure Bolshevik it turned up. . . . Had the Great Inquisition been directed only against Communists, it would have tried to be more precise and discriminating in its search for them. . . . In this crusade Communism was not the target but the weapon, and it is for this reason that so many of the most ardent hunters of impotent domestic Communists were altogether indifferent to efforts to meet the power of international Communism where it really existed—in the arena of world politics.[47]

We thus find Communism functioning in what postmodernists might call a rather complex interplay of signifiers. Membership in the Communist Party *infallibly* signified the repudiation of truth and, it followed, unworthiness of academic appointment. But since the Party was (or was believed to be) a secret organization, one could not directly tell who was and was not a Communist. The signifier, in other words, was invisible.

This was a difficult but convenient position to be in. Other signifiers were needed that could, in turn, signal membership in the Communist Party. And those signifiers-of-signifiers were conveniently elastic. They included not only race, ethnicity, and sexual orientation but also behavior: acting, talking, thinking, and feeling like a Communist. And as Harold Taylor, president of Sarah Lawrence College, put it, talking like a Communist could include saying almost anything "provocative, unorthodox, or interesting" (Schrecker 109). While such bad behavior was not an infallible sign of Party membership, it could indicate sympathies that anyway had no business, many felt, in the academy.

This sounds extreme, perhaps paranoid. In fact, however, intellectual carpet bombing, mostly though not always from right wingers, was—like hostility to philosophy—a well-established tradition in the United States long before the McCarthy era. Listen to Frank Hague, the mayor of Jersey City, New Jersey, in 1938: "You hear about constitutional rights, free speech, and the free press. Every time I hear those words I say 'That man is a Red, that man is a Communist.' You never hear real Americans talk like that."[48]

A personal example may help show the depths to which it all sank. When I was eight years old, growing up in a Midwestern university town, I had a number of faculty brats as friends. I heard somewhere that the father of one of them—Andy's daddy—was being accused of being a Communist. I asked my father what Andy's father had done to provoke such an accusation, and received as an answer that Andy's father was very intelligent. Some people were jealous of his intelligence and so said bad things to try to hurt him. I have no idea today whether being intelligent was Andy's father's only sin. But I do know that one eight-year-old learned that day that merely being intelligent was enough to get you into serious trouble—better to go out for football instead! What graduate students in their twenties, and junior professors in their thirties, figured out from Andy's father's misfortunes I can only surmise.

In short: though anti-Communism and even antileftism were important components of McCarthyism, especially on the rhetorical level, they were by no means the whole. Rather, they coincided with, and served to legitimate, a much broader convulsion in which, as Paul Lazarsfeld and Wagner Thielens Jr. write, "what was really under attack (academically) was the quality of American education."[49]

Striking at Philosophy

How did all this apply to American philosophy? How strongly did it come under attack? Did the attacks on it focus merely on various individuals, or did they coalesce to target the discipline itself? Against what—beyond the inevitable anti-Communist rhetoric—were they directed? What were American philosophers entitled to think might get them into trouble? What did they think they should do to stay out of trouble? Did numbers of them do it? Is it, in short, possible that the McCarthy era not only thwarted a number of budding careers but affected the development of American philosophy itself—perhaps even down to the present day?

Philosophy was not knowingly singled out as a target by the vigilantes of the 1950s. The coalition of anti-intellectual forces that came together then was, almost by definition, too untutored, diverse, and confused to have any clearly defined targets. Many of its members doubtless had only the murkiest notion of what a philosopher is. But there is little question that philosophers, among the freest spirits in the academy, managed to attract more than their share of anti-intellectual wrath. Schrecker's book identifies by discipline 98 professors at liberal arts institutions who were either targets of investigation or hostile witnesses at government hearings. Of those, 9 were philosophers—far more than belonged to most fields, ranking behind only English (15) and physics (12).

Philosophy, in fact, may be in first place in terms of the *percentage* of its practitioners who fell afoul of right-wing vigilantes, because philosophy departments are often only half the size of those of English and physics. In 1957 the AAUP counted 4,239 English professors among its members, of whom the 15 Schrecker mentions constitute a mere .035 percent. There were 1,160 physicists, and their 12 troubled professors amount to a little more than 1 percent of the profession. But there were only 742 philosophers, of whom 1.2 percent got into trouble: 4 times the percentage of English professors, and 20 percent above the physicists (*AAUP* 43:57). Unless a smaller proportion of philosophers belonged to the AAUP than did members of the other disciplines—which would, if true, require some explanation of its own—we are left with philosophy in first place.

The figures from the AAUP itself are even grimmer. Among 48 professors at liberal arts institutions identified by discipline in its Committee A reports, 6 are in philosophy, which is tied for the lead with English and economics. Economics departments, again, tend to be larger than philosophy departments; in 1957 the AAUP listed 1,557 economists among its members. Philosophers, it seems, were 6 times as likely to be attacked by witch-hunters as English professors, and twice as likely as economists. As far as the AAUP figures indicate, no other discipline except physics comes close.

We must distinguish the injustices done to individual professors from the effects of these cases on the discipline. An amount like 1.2 percent sounds small, but it means that virtually every philosopher in the country either knew someone who got in trouble or had a friend who knew such a person. Word of mouth alone would carry the stories of those people to every philosophical community in the country.

The agonized gossip would have spread all the more quickly because of the prominence of many of the cases in which philosophers were involved. Four of the nine cases against philosophers mentioned by Schrecker are treated at length in her book. Barrows Dunham, chair of the philosophy department at Temple University, was subpoenaed by the House Committee on Un-American Activities (HUAC) in February 1953. Though the Temple administration encouraged him to cooperate with the committee, he gave only his name, age, and home address before taking the Fifth Amendment. He was tried for this, and was acquitted in 1955. But Temple had already fired him in September 1953, restoring him only in 1981 (Schrecker 209–12).

William Parry, of the University of Buffalo, appeared before HUAC in May 1953, three months after Dunham. He had already stated publicly that although he was willing to talk about himself, he would not give the names of other people. The only way to accomplish this without being cited for contempt was to take the Fifth Amendment, which he did. That unfortunately violated the university's policy—issued on the very day Parry received his subpoena—that faculty members should "testify fully and frankly" if called upon by a legislative committee. Parry managed to keep his job, but his tenure was revoked the next month (Schrecker 205–7). It was later restored.

Stanley Moore had joined the philosophy department at Reed College in Oregon after a job offer from Brooklyn College was rescinded because one of his letters of recommendation called him "a fanatical Marxist, both in theory and in practice." He thought that Reed's reputation for tolerance would help him when he appeared before HUAC in June 1954. But the toleration was extended, it turned out, only by the faculty. Moore was fired by the board of trustees in August. The faculty's opposition to this, according to Schrecker, was rare: "[A]t every other school the faculty was willing to impose some sort of political test on itself. At schools like Rutgers or the University of Michigan, where administrators and trustees fired teachers whom faculty committees had wanted to retain, the committees had voted to retain these faculty members because they had passed a political test, not because those tests were irrelevant. Reed's may have been the only faculty in the country that refused to administer those tests" (Schrecker 240). Reed's board of trustees, the clear villain in this famous case, would admit that its action with respect to Moore had been wrong—in 1978 (Schrecker 236–40).

Preceding all those cases was what Schrecker calls "in many ways the most important academic freedom case of the entire cold war" (Schrecker 320). Herbert Phillips was fired from the philosophy department at the University of Washington, along with two other professors, in January 1950 (Schrecker 94–108). Phillips's sole offense was membership in the Communist Party. It was not even a clandestine membership: Phillips routinely told his students that he was a Marxist and that they should assess his lectures in light of that (Schrecker 44–45).

He was fired anyway, on the recommendation of the university's president, Raymond B. Allen. With a candor that we shall see again, President Allen wrote that Phillips and his colleague Joseph Butterworth, an English professor, "by reason of their admitted membership in the Communist Party . . . [were] incompetent, intellectually dishonest, and derelict in their duty to find and teach the truth" (*CAF* 40). As a result of this case, Allen became a national spokesman for academic Red hunting. Phillips spent the rest of his life working at odd jobs (Schrecker 44–45, 104).

These incidents, as may well be imagined, were only the tip of the iceberg. Most people who were suspected of Communist sympathies during the McCarthy era never became famous and did not draw the fire of such august agencies as HUAC. Rather, as Seymour Martin Lipset and David Riesman put it, they quietly left the country, or "simply trembled, aware of their hidden stigmata, and hoped that no one would notice them."[50] But the cases I have mentioned all became nationally known—Phillips's not only made Allen's reputation but helped precipitate the California oath controversy, when the UCLA graduate students association unwisely invited him to give a paper there (Gardner 14–21). Unlike merely local incidents, these cases could serve as warnings to philosophers all over the country. And because the accusations were usually so confused, phantasmagoric, and often downright incomprehensible, no one knew for sure what had gotten all these people into such trouble, or what one should do to stay out of it.

On this topic, unclarity was endemic. On the one hand, membership in the Communist Party—even if far in the past—was clearly forbidden. Taking the Fifth Amendment, or even being called before HUAC, also usually meant trouble. But for Allen, and for the many whom he influenced, membership in the Communist Party was not evil because it was clandestine—Phillips's membership was not clandestine. According to the quote above, it was evil because of what it *signified:* incompetence, intellectual dishonesty, and the dereliction of academic duty to the truth.

The net, we have seen, was even wider than that. Albert Einstein was hardly incompetent or intellectually dishonest; his life was devoted to finding and teaching the truth if ever a life was. But his well-intended criticism of the hydrogen bomb got him into trouble. Silliness about the Catholic Mass did it for John Greenway. As I have noted, merely antagonizing a colleague could do it too.

As we will see in the next chapter, American academics were eventually told quite explicitly what to avoid in their professional lives, and in a way that held direct relevance for philosophy. For the moment, it is clear that the McCarthyite assault on philosophers was unique, not in the vagueness of the charges but in the number and prominence of the resulting cases.

In addition, two factors within the discipline itself made it particularly susceptible to such attacks. One was the activity of several of its prominent members in *support* of the witch-hunters. William Barrett wrote vehemently against Communism in *Commentary* and *Partisan Review,* while Sidney Hook and Arthur O. Lovejoy traveled the country as expert witnesses for the inquisitors.[51] Though all disciplines had members who supported both sides in the anti-Communist struggles, no other field seems to have combined so many victims of the purges with such prominent supporters of them. The diversity this bespeaks is, in and of itself, enviable, and in the climate of the times, reasonable people could feel that there were good and urgent reasons to exclude Communists from academia. But the conspicuous divisions in their own field cannot have made it easier for philosophers to defend themselves.

The other factor was structural. Given the relatively small size of the discipline, successful graduate education—that which places its students in good jobs—was concentrated in relatively few schools. The almost 1,400 members of the APA in 1950 would, if all were academically employed and were distributed evenly along career paths lasting an average of just thirty years, produce fewer than forty-seven vacancies per year—a demand low enough for just a handful of graduate programs to fill. Troubles at even one or two such schools, then, might prejudice the education of much of the next generation of philosophy professors. And according to Paul Lazarsfeld and Werner Thielens, attacks on academic freedom were more numerous at the "better" schools.[52] The South, they found, had a surprising tolerance for intellectual diversity and, on the eve of the civil rights revolution, a different set of social problems: McCarthyism found little response there. The same was true on Catholic campuses, where Communist subversion was close to unimaginable.

Lazarsfeld and Thielens conclude that, though professors at "higher-quality" institutions attracted more fire than those at less-favored places, the superior ability of their administrations also gave them more protection. This has been challenged by the more recent work of Lionel Lewis, who summarizes: "It has become a cliché that during the Cold War years faculty at undistinguished, parochial institutions were at greater risk than those at more prestigious, visible institutions. This belief seems to be a conceit fostered largely by alumni and employees from more renowned institutions who have had access to publishers and the pages of magazines and journals."[53]

The higher-quality, more prestigious schools, of course, tended to be those with graduate programs. Any inclination of McCarthyite forces to focus on leading institutions would thus increase future problems for philosophy in general, which drew its personnel largely from graduate programs at those same institutions.

Finally, philosophy faced special challenges to its status *as a discipline.* Attacks on any number of English professors, physicists, or economists could never add up to an attack on English itself, or physics, or economics. All but the most benighted Americans knew that they needed what those disciplines produced: people who could speak and write the English language, build atom bombs, and run the economy. But philosophy trained no one to do anything productive and was, in an accusation as old as Thales, useless. Hence the plausibility of my earlier anecdote about the Michigan legislator who wanted to shut down all philosophy courses except those in symbolic logic. Hence also the decision of the president of Marietta College, in 1953, to close the philosophy department altogether—a decision entirely due, he assured a relieved APA, to financial considerations alone (*APA* 27:94).

But philosophy was worse than unproductive. It had disciplinary links to subversion. For what was Marxism, basically, but a kind of philosophy? Simply by being the genus of which Marxism was a species, philosophy was intrinsically open to suspicion. So, at any rate, believed the professorial investigators at the University of Washington. In the cases of Joseph Butterworth and Herbert Phillips, they dismissed out of hand the claim that Butterworth's membership in the Communist Party had influenced his teaching of Old English literature. Phillips the philosopher, the investigators wrote, had no such protection: "As a teacher of philosophy, it might be suggested that, without specific proof, his objectivity as a teacher would necessarily be impaired by his strong bias in favor of a doctrinaire political philosophy" (*CAF* 36–37, 45).

The investigators go on to mention evidence that Phillips was not in fact subversive in the classroom, but it is revealing that evidence was necessary at all. Being a philosopher, as opposed to a teacher of Old English, clearly brought a presumption of guilt that allowed charges to be made without specific proof. The burden of proof for Phillips was, indeed, the reverse of Butterworth's: for the English professor, it would have to be proved that he was, somehow, subversive in the classroom. The philosopher had to prove he was not.

We now have a partial answer to the question of what, behind the paranoid jumble of fantasy and jargon that characterized the McCarthy era, could bring suspicion on a philosopher: simply being a philosopher. (Quine's view, quoted above, that philosophy was a mere *flatus vocis,* a breath with voice, looks very different indeed when seen in this context—and all too understandable.)

On the eve of its greatest expansion in history, then, American philosophy was in deep trouble. Individual philosophers were being purged, rightly or wrongly, and other philosophers were helping to purge them. Attacks were skewed toward institutions with graduate programs, in ways that could foment lasting damage to the profession. Philosophy itself was perceived as possibly subversive, and in any case a mere frill in the cold war economy of ideas.

This all called, one would think, for a response.

I Philosophy Search about the for truth?

We're All Scientists Here

Early Effects of the McCarthy Era on American Philosophy

Philosophy's vulnerability to anti-intellectual threats was also enhanced by the unwieldy structure of its main professional group, the American Philosophical Association (APA). Though, as I noted in chapter 1, Eastern Division is *prima inter pares,* each division has its own officers and holds its own meetings in its own area of the country. Resolutions passed by one division are not binding on the others. This means that just reading the minutes of the APA's meetings, published in *APA,* is an irritatingly unwieldy chore. Even if the prominence of philosophers among both the leaders and the victims of the purges had not prevented it, the structure of the APA would have made it very difficult for American philosophy to speak with a single voice as one after another of its members came under attack.

The story told by the minutes of the various divisions runs as follows. The first great academic freedom case of the McCarthy era involved, as I have noted, a philosopher—Herbert Phillips of the University of Washington, who was fired in January 1950. Following the lead of the APA's Pacific Division, the business meeting of Eastern Division adopted a resolution supporting Phillips on January 13, 1950. This was subsequently confirmed by a mail poll of the entire membership (*APA* 23:88–89). Six weeks later, on March 17, Raymond B. Allen, president of the University of Washington, responded by letter to Eastern Division. In terms that can only be described as contemptuous (as well as ungrammatical), he informed the association that it had not investigated all the facts. He concluded by challenging the APA's professionalism—its raison d'être: "In light of your organization's failure to examine into [*sic*] both sides of the question . . . it would seem to me that there is considerable question as to whether your organization can presume, as it does in the last paragraph of your resolution, the position [*sic*] as [*sic*] 'professional colleagues best qualified to pass on his professional integrity' " (*APA* 24:64).

This letter was read out at the Toronto meeting—the same meeting at which Arthur Murphy gave his prophetic presidential address (*APA* 24:64). Despite its grammar, it seems to have achieved its purpose: it took the APA out of the business of defending philosophers attacked by McCarthyites. With the exception of a 1953 endorsement of the general American Association of University Professors' principles on academic freedom (*APA* 27:87), Eastern Division in particular made no further recorded efforts to deal with infringements on academic freedom. The whole issue simply vanished. Eastern Division's only other foray into *any* political matter during the 1950s was the unanimous passage, in 1956, of a resolution introduced by Sidney Hook in support of the Hungarian freedom fighters (*APA* 30:98).

Pacific Division did a little better: in addition to its resolution supporting Phillips, it would also, at its business meeting of December 30, 1955, adopt one protesting Reed College's treatment of Stanley Moore (*APA* 29:110). But the only division to address recurrently the damage being done to philosophers by McCarthyite forces was Western Division. On May 6, 1950, six weeks after Allen's letter to Eastern Division and presumably informed of it, the executive committee of Western Division reported on a resolution calling for a committee to be set up to investigate cases of philosophers targeted by the McCarthyites. This resolution had been voted down by Eastern Division simultaneously with passage of the one supporting Phillips. Eastern Division's report gives no reasons for the resolution's rejection, but the executive committee of Western Division—clearly not favorable to the resolution—mentions a couple. One particularly instructive one is that the American Association of University Professors (AAUP) has undertaken to investigate individual cases of professors in trouble. The APA must refrain not only from duplicating the efforts of the AAUP, but from even *embarrassing* the AAUP in its quest for the truth, "to our mutual disadvantage" (*APA* 23:97).

Though Western Division favored, in the executive committee's words, "offering such assistance as it could to members under attack on the score of academic freedom, it seems inadvisable at present to set itself up as an investigating committee." What Western Division openly stated it was doing, then, was also done in silence by the other two divisions. In effect, they assigned responsibility for academic freedom to the AAUP and placed themselves above the fray.

There is no record that any of the assistance promised in Western Division's resolution was actually given. On Schrecker's account, philosophers amounted to perhaps 9 percent of the professors at liberal arts institutions under investigation by the witch-hunters or called by them as hostile witnesses; AAUP figures indicate that about 12 percent of the cases reported to the AAUP (and identified by discipline) involved philosophers. Taking the smaller figure and generalizing it to all 399 of the cases reported to the AAUP between 1949 and 1958 (most of which do not identify the discipline), we can conclude that as many as thirty-six philosophers *may* have found themselves under fire from Red hunters during that time. Only eight were mentioned in resolutions from the APA, and six of those were mentioned by Western Division alone. One was Forrest Wiggins of the University of Minnesota,[1] the first African American ever hired as a full-time instructor by a major state university—and the first fired. The others were five professors fired in 1959 from the University of Arkansas.

Even a case as famous as that of Barrows Dunham of Temple University, mentioned in chapter 1, brought no supporting resolution. Nor did those of Jakob Loewenberg and Marcus Singer. Loewenberg, a Hegel scholar, was fired after thirty-five years of service to the University of California, Berkeley, because he refused to take the loyalty oath—apparently the only philosopher there to be so dismissed. (Berkeley has since gotten along without Hegel scholars in its philosophy department.) Loewenberg, having reached retirement age, was eventually restored to emeritus status (Gardner 229, 268). At Cornell, Marcus Singer refused to name names to HUAC and was suspended with full pay. He eventually regained his job (Caute 151, 551).

The APA's silence meant that it now had the best of all worlds. It had made a high-minded pledge to offer assistance to philosophers in trouble—but the pledge was in practice meaningless, since no action could be taken by the APA in any given case until the AAUP had completed its investigation. And the AAUP, most conveniently, was not completing much of anything. In 1951, when Western Division formulated the idea of leaving all concrete investigations to the AAUP, the latter organization's inability to fight effectively on behalf of threatened professors was not known. But, as Schrecker has documented, that inability became more and more obvious over the next few years.

One of the people who found out about it the hard way was Barrows Dunham, chair of the philosophy department at Temple. In March 1953, he and the Temple chapter of the AAUP tried in vain to get Ralph Himstead, general secretary of the national AAUP, to conduct an investigation of Dunham's case. Their requests went unacknowledged for weeks. Himstead eventually claimed that he could not find qualified professors willing to conduct the investigation, but it is not clear how hard he tried to do so (Schrecker 325–26).

Himstead's bizarre lethargy on this and other such matters finally led, in 1955, to a virtual revolt by the membership that forced his resignation (Schrecker 315–37). During those years of inaction by the AAUP—and in spite of the problems Dunham encountered—no division of the APA ever publicly reconsidered its policy. The issue of protecting philosophers under unjust fire from intellectual vigilantes simply never surfaced again.

It is hard to say how all this affected the development of American philosophy itself. We will probably never know, except in a few exceptional cases, who was quietly passed over in the *sancta intima* of hiring and tenure committees, who got confidential warning from a chairman or president that things might get rough unless he or she was careful,[2] who went off and started a new career, and who was able to buy space for private radicalism by restricting his or her professional interests to safe fields. The envelope of secrecy, once sealed, is hard to open. In 1977,

Sigmund Diamond, who had had problems as a history graduate student and junior administrator at Harvard in 1954, was still trying to get that university to answer the following questions:

1. How many faculty members were fired by Harvard or forced to resign during the McCarthy era?
2. How many people were refused appointments at Harvard because of "derogatory information" about them?
3. Were graduate students asked about their political beliefs and associations?[3]

Almost a quarter of a century later, he did not get answers.

A Discipline Distorted?

In spite of the envelope of secrecy, three things suggest that the intellectual climate of the McCarthy era had substantial effects on philosophy at that time. One is the public record itself, as I have recounted it here. It clearly indicates that philosophy was the most heavily attacked of all the academic disciplines. It also shows that philosophy was attacked *as* a discipline and that the attacks were focused to some degree on its institutional crux: the relatively few institutions with effective graduate programs. Those programs would supply most of the philosophy teachers who found jobs during philosophy's subsequent population explosion, which as I noted in chapter 1 occurred in the years from 1960 to 1969, just after the McCarthy purges had been completed.

The second telling factor is the complete absence of discussion of that historical record ever since. Philosophers who entered the field after 1960 usually have no idea of the intensity and importance of the conflict, which, as one eyewitness told me, simply overwhelmed philosophy. Why do philosophers not talk of those struggles? That philosophy was so much a target of the McCarthyites *should* be a badge of honor; why is it not worn?

Finally, the McCarthy era seems to have skewed other disciplines in ways that would hardly have spared philosophy. As Ellen Schrecker points out, in investigating the long-term effects of McCarthyism, we must look not only for the scholarship that was not done but also at that which *was* done. It is probably not coincidental, she notes, that "the fifties were . . . the heyday of consensus history, modernization theory, structural functionalism, and the new criticism. Mainstream scholars celebrated the status quo, and the end of ideology dominated intellectual discourse" (Schrecker 339). Since American philosophy seems to have had even greater problems during the McCarthy era than the disciplines to which Schrecker alludes, it is plausible that such effects extend to it as well.

If the effects were as substantial as these three considerations suggest, what were they? In what directions did the political attacks from inside and outside the academy skew American philosophy?

Consider, first, what Western Division said about the AAUP. The AAUP was to investigate the truth or falsity of charges made against philosophers. The APA was to stay away from such investigations, allowing them to proceed unhindered. The possibility that they might not be proceeding at all went unnoticed, and officially so. For the APA did not, we have seen, want to embarrass anybody.

This division of labor strikingly parallels the general view of the time concerning the relationship between philosophy and science. On that view, it was the job of science to discover truths about the universe. Philosophy, as a second-order discipline, was to reflect on the nature and conditions of that enterprise, whose validity—like that of the AAUP's investigations—was simply assumed. The confinement of philosophy to such second-order inquiry was also carried through in ethics. Philosophers of the day were not to take ethical stands or give moral advice but simply to reflect on the meaning of ethical terms (as did C. L. Stevenson, whom I mentioned in the previous chapter). Similarly, at least in the view of those who called themselves "ordinary language philosophers," for "ordinary language" itself. It was quite in order as it stood. The point of analyzing it was not to make it function better but to cure ourselves of our misunderstandings concerning it. Wittgenstein was fondly quoted: philosophy "leaves everything as it is."[4]

Political philosophy, for its part, disappeared from the American scene altogether, until reintroduced by John Rawls in 1971. Rawls's book, *A Theory of Justice,* thus performed, and performed brilliantly, an extremely important philosophical service. But even in 1971 it seems to have been limited by the context of its times. Anyone who reads it in light of the current investigation will certainly be unsurprised to find that one of its early moves is to place all concrete social arrangements, and hence all concrete social issues, behind what it famously calls the "veil of ignorance."[5]

The very gestures with which the APA absolved itself of fighting the witch-hunters thus came to structure philosophy itself: get other people to do the dirty empirical work, and stay well above the battles. The boundary between what I call disciplinary and intellectual history, always doubtful, begins to fray as one sees how the career choices of individual philosophers were shaped by a hostile political climate.

Philosophers, Truth, and Sentences

But the most important link that can be drawn between the politics of the 1950s and the internal development of American philosophy concerns truth. "Truth" is not just another term for philosophers, because it traditionally designates the goal of their discourse: it is what philosophers have always been after. Hence, as Roger Scruton has written, "in philosophy . . . truth is all-important, and determines the structure of the discipline."[6] It is not too much to say that whoever controls the philosophical definition of truth controls philosophy itself.

This casts a special light on the following passages, written by none other than Raymond B. Allen—president of the University of Washington, foremost articulator of academic McCarthyism and, not incidentally, grand nemesis of the APA. They set forth some of the McCarthy era's own peculiar logic:

> For centuries universities have survived in the Western world, not without difficulties and serious attacks from both without and within, primarily because of their impartiality, objectivity, and determination to seek truth and not be propagandists in partisan political, economic, and other debates. . . . Clandestine activity . . . in the Communist Party means that [professors] have forsaken their duty to protect the University's integrity and to pursue an objective quest of truth in favor of a propagandistic mission entirely unrelated to real educational and scholarly effort.

Quoting from his own inaugural address (but adding italics), Allen continues:

> If a University ever loses its dispassionate objectivity and incites or leads parades, it will have lost its integrity as an institution and abandoned the

timeless, selfless quest of truth. . . . It is for this reason that a teacher has a special obligation to deal in a scholarly and scientific way with controversial questions. . . . Fortunately few faculty members make this mistake [of not being scholarly and scientific]. If they do make it, the institution from which they come will lose its academic standing, *as they will lose their security.*[7]

Two different positions are expressed here. One is the standard argument, associated primarily with Sidney Hook, that the problem with Communists is not their Marxism but the clandestine nature of the Communist conspiracy (Schrecker 105–9). Those who seek to impose their ideas in secrecy, by force rather than open argument, cannot consistently give allegiance to the community of scholars, and have no place in it.

The other position is considerably more sweeping. We have seen it in chapter 1—in Allen's own view that Herbert Phillips, who had made no secret of his Communist Party affiliation, should nonetheless be fired because "by reason of [his] admitted membership in the Communist Party . . . [he is] incompetent, intellectually dishonest, and derelict in [his] duty to find and teach the truth."[8] We also find it in William F. Buckley's view that Brand Blanshard was "demonstrably ignorant or mendacious," a mere "charlatan."[9] This second view says nothing about secrecy, advocacy of violence, or the imposition of views by force. It relies instead on a simple dichotomy: intellectual life is either a scientific quest of truth or a mere propagandistic mission. Scholars must avoid not only conspiracies but even open commitment to positions on controversial questions, except where they can take such positions on the basis of dispassionate objectivity. The possession of objective, scientific knowledge, and that alone, entitles them to a hearing—or a job. The raison d'être of the university is not open discussion but the timeless, selfless quest of truth.

Such a quest, of course, has always been central to philosophy. But philosophy has also, traditionally, included other things: objective truth, always a goal, has not always been the single legitimating criterion that Allen makes of it. Allen's argument would, for example, prohibit virtually all the tentative, open, skeptical discussions that, from Plato's aporetic dialogues on, have constituted much of the philosophical life— but that have, even indirectly, produced no objective truth. It would exclude the kind of moral betterment that Kant extracts from metaphysics in his "Transcendental Doctrine of Method" at the end of the *Critique of Pure Reason,* because such betterment cannot be reduced to truth. It would rule Kierkegaardian and existentialist perspectives out of ethics altogether, because they are wholly personalized and subjective. And it would exclude critical reflection on the social and institutional conditions of one's own discipline. For in such matters scientific distance is lacking, passion abounds, and objective rigor is compromised.

To make truth into the single goal of rational investigation is a falsification, for it misrepresents the human mind itself. Richard Hofstadter put the point well in 1963: "Ideally the pursuit of truth is said to be at the heart of the intellectual's business, but this credits his business too much and not enough. . . . Truth captured loses its glamour; truths long known and widely believed have a way of turning false with time; easy truths are a bore, and too many of them become half-truths. Whatever the intellectual is too certain of he begins to find unsatisfactory. *The meaning of the intellectual life consists not in the search for truth but in the quest for new uncertainties.*"[10]

The most important resonance that Allen's insistence on timeless, selfless truth found in American philosophy of the day, however, concerned pragmatism. A significant role in this was played by the English version of Rudolph Carnap's 1936 article "Truth and Confirmation," which appeared in 1949—the same year that Allen wrote the passages above and the year before his letter to the APA. In it, Carnap neatly formulates *some* of the middle ground that Allen's dichotomy between the quest of truth and propagandistic missions had omitted. He argues that the pragmatists had confused "truth" and "confirmation": "The difference between the two concepts 'true' and 'confirmed' . . . is important and yet frequently not sufficiently recognized. 'True' in its customary meaning is a time-independent term. . . . 'Confirmed,' however, is time-dependent. When we say that 'such and such a statement is confirmed to a high degree by observations' then we must add: 'at such and such a time.' This is the pragmatical concept of degree of confirmation" (Carnap 119).

It is confirmation, not truth, that science achieves; the truth of empirical sentences is, in fact, undecidable (Carnap 123–24). At the very time that Allen was associating science with the timeless, selfless quest of truth, then, Carnap was distinguishing between the two: while agreeing that truth is timeless, he is claiming that we can never achieve it because scientific inquiry unrolls in time. In this, he appears to be reinstating a looser model of scientific inquiry: one which, as Aristotle puts it at *Nicomachean Ethics* 1.3, does not demand more rigor than the subject matter allows.

But Carnap (hardly an Aristotelian!) is going only halfway beyond Allen. For what gets confirmed or disconfirmed are the same *sorts* of things that can be true or false: statements (propositions, sentences, and the like). Statements, for a logical positivist like Carnap, fall into two sorts: analytic, which are true in virtue of their meanings, and synthetic, which must be verified—or confirmed—by experience (and by consistency with other confirmed statements). Hence, truth and confirmation, while distinct from one another, are not radically so: confirmation, we may say echoing Plato's *Timaeus,* is the moving image of truth. Or, as Carnap puts it, it is our knowledge of the truth (Carnap 120).

What Carnap adds to Allen's basic scheme are two kinds of precision. First, he specifies that what is timelessly true are propositions (*Sätze*) rather than, say, Plato's Forms or Augustine's God. Allen, with his emphasis on science, might well have agreed—had he been smart enough to pose the question. Second, Carnap separates what Allen runs together: empirical science and the quest of timeless truth. Hence, Carnap denies the conflation of the quest of timelessly true propositions and scientific practice. But they remain for him the only two options. This places before philosophy a choice: it can either pursue Allenian truth or relegate itself to Carnapian confirmation. In the former case, it becomes a second-order discipline concerned primarily with analytical truths and logical syntax. In the latter, it gets naturalized into an empirical science. In either case, however, philosophy will be scientific. And in either case, it will be a timeless, selfless quest. Its goal will either be timeless, selfless truth or the closest possible approximation to it, empirical confirmation.

We thus arrive at the following inference: truth (or confirmation) is a property of statements. Philosophy seeks truth (or confirmation). Therefore, philosophy seeks a certain sort of statement. The second premise of this syllogism is, at least in sound, quite traditional. But the first is an innovation, perhaps the most radical innovation analytical philosophy ever made, for while philosophers have traditionally agreed that the name of their goal is "truth," they have had wildly divergent views on its nature, and many of them did not restrict it to statements at all.

Plato—to begin with him—continually uses *t'alêthê*, "the true things," to refer to the Forms, to which the Platonic philosopher seeks proximity. Platonic Forms, of course, are unchanging essences, not sentences or propositions. Aristotle, though he begins philosophy's tradition of correspondence theories of truth, has several mysterious discussions of the sense in which things, rather than propositions, are true.[11] Augustine, in his *Soliloquies*, goes so far as to say that truth is being—in which Anselm's *De Veritate* follows him.[12]

Despite Proclus's use of an apparently mathematical procedure in his *Elements of Theology*, and some of his formulations of the nature of truth,[13] we find a rather different view in his commentary on Plato's *Parmenides*. There he comes to distinguish falsity from error: if S is P, and I say "S is not P," I have asserted a falsehood, because S is P. But *both* "S is P" and "S is not P" are in "error," because in them the mind moves (*errare*) from the subject to the predicate of the sentence. Neither true nor false statements are adequate to the unity of the One, and that unity is the truth toward which Proclean inquiry moves.[14]

Question I, Article II of Thomas Aquinas's *De Veritate* begins with the assurance that truth is located not in things but in the intellect as it properly perceives reality. But the intellect may be God's, in which case a thing is true insofar as it "fulfills the end to which it is ordained by God."[15] A statement which accurately depicts reality will be true in this sense, but so will a great many nonstatements. With respect to the human intellect, truth is indeed found in the conformity of intellect to thing; but something's being true in this sense, Aquinas teaches, follows from its being true in the other sense: "Since everything is true according as it has the form proper to its nature, the intellect, insofar as it is knowing, must be true according as it has the likeness of the thing known, which is its form as a knowing power. For this reason truth is defined as the conformity of intellect and thing; and to know this conformity is to know truth."[16]

Truth is primarily in the intellect—because it is the form of the intellect itself. When the human intellect has its proper form, to be sure, it contains propositions it knows to be true, but that state, as far as truth is concerned, is derivative.

The first definition of truth in Spinoza's *Ethics* is "adequate to its object," which again sounds traditional enough. But "adequacy" turns out to mean not "corresponding to an object," but "existing as in the mind of God."[17] This brings us back to a view somewhat similar to Aquinas's (the main difference being that Spinoza emphasizes that God knows an object in relation to its entire causal context, which is ultimately the entire universe: to know anything adequately is to know everything adequately). Kant, in his first *Critique,* granted the view that truth is correspondence, but the grammar of the sentence, as Gerold Prauss has shown, is complex; Kant really means to say that the old definition is no longer adequate.[18]

I will not go into Hegel's complex definition of truth, which I have discussed exhaustively elsewhere; but he is right to assert that it is completely different (*ganz andere*) from the propositional or correspondence view, partly because it assigns truth to things such as words and experiences rather than merely to sentences or propositions.[19] Heidegger, too, criticizes sentential truth in favor of a complex alternative that makes it a property of our encounters with things, rather than of sentences.[20]

Examples could be multiplied of philosophers who held that truth is not merely a property of sentences, propositions, statements, and so forth. I will conclude with the very people that Carnap—in the received English version of his essay—was trying to refute: the pragmatists. They tended, it is true, to speak what sounded to analytical philosophers like an older language—a language of ideas rather than propositions—but they spoke it on principle. As Bruce Wilshire puts it with reference to Richard Rorty: "[F]ollowing a great crowd of analytical philosophers, [Rorty] limits truth to some (adulatory) property assigned to *sentences* or *statements.* In the earlier [pragmatic] tradition's light this appears artificial and thoughtless. It . . . masks out the palpable fact that it is not just true sentences that navigate us through the world. Silences of certain kinds, images, icons, bodies, scenes, art-works, music, perhaps mystical experiences amplify, clarify, and reveal the world, and can be true in their own ways."[21]

Hilary Putnam has written of the strangely uncritical way in which logical positivism was received in this country. The central positivist claim that the meaning of a sentence is its method of verification itself fell on neither side of Carnap's distinction: it was neither analytically true nor empirically confirmable. The point was obvious. But, as Putnam notes, "strangely enough this criticism had very little impact on the logical positivists and did little to impede the growth of their move-ment."[22] With similar strangeness, no one appears to have noticed that Carnap's essay treated the pragmatic theory of truth as if it were a theory of true sentences, when in fact it was something quite different. In spite of this important misreading of pragmatism, Carnap's article played a key role in the defeat of pragmatism and the subsequent triumph of analytical philosophy.[23]

It should go without saying that I am not accusing Carnap of *personal* complicity with McCarthyism. His article, I have noted, was originally published in 1936 in France. Its intellectual context at that time was not pragmatism at all, but Tarski's restoration of "truth" as a semantically respectable term. The very term "pragmatical" in my first quote from Carnap does not refer to the American pragmatists, as it was taken in this country to do, but to the pragmatic dimension of language, that which concerns the relation of language to its users and which is distinct from language's syntactic and semantic sides. Carnap himself was no McCarthyite. A refugee from the Nazis, he refused a position at the University of California because of the oath controversy—showing a courage rarely found among native-born American philosophers.[24] His behavior, in the midst of so much accommodation and even cowardice, was close to heroic. But history has its cunning, and trips up even geniuses if they do not keep an eye on it.

A Path through the Jumble

One reason that American philosophers were so oddly uncritical of logi-cal positivism, I take it, was that it gave them something they needed. In chapter 1, I pointed out that philosophers, just by being philosophers, were potential targets of McCarthyite paranoia. I also discussed the problem that such potential targets had of knowing just what, amidst the arbitrary play of signifiers, might be a sign of Communism that could get them in trouble. But now, thanks to no less an authority than Raymond B. Allen, they had an answer, for they had been told what, in the climate of the times, they needed to avoid: anything unscientific or subjective. Logical positivism provided a philosophical framework for doing this. If they wanted to be really safe, they could accept the Allen-ian view, finding intellectual respectability for their political prudence by claiming to deal with timeless truths. If that was unpalatable, they could see themselves as similar to empirical scientists, borrowing a timeless, selfless respectability that even Allen recognized.

In either case, they had found a way through the paranoid jumble that I discussed in chapter 1. One way to indicate that one was not a Communist, or a fellow traveler, or a sympathizer (and so on) was to engage in a quasi-scientific pursuit of truth, for, as we saw Sidney Hook argue, no one could simultaneously give allegiance both to Communism and to the quest for truth—or, if that was too much to stomach, to the search for confirmation.

The debate between those two alternatives seems to have been played out, on its philosophical level, in the confrontation between philosophers who held that philosophy dealt with analytical (and hence timeless) truths of meaning, and thinkers like W. V. O. Quine, who held that it should be "naturalized" into something differing from science only in degree of generality.[25] Quine, of course, won—few American philosophers today admit to believing in a priori truths, even analytical ones. But the view of philosophy as pursuing a sciencelike form of truth has remained in force, to the extent that Steve Fuller has written that "the legitimacy of philosophy and the human sciences still very much depends on imitating the natural sciences, even if only at a verbal level."[26]

The instatement of scientific truth as philosophy's only goal represents, I think, not only one of analytical philosophy's most radical innovations but also one of its principal undetected dogmas.[27] It is formulated, with Quine's customary integrity and lucidity, in the first sentence of every edition of his *Methods of Logic,* from 1959—written as the McCarthy era was winding down—through 1982, when the battles of those days were largely forgotten: "Logic, like any science, has as its business the pursuit of truth. What is true are certain statements; and the pursuit of truth is the endeavour to sort out the true statements from the others, which are false."[28]

To be sure, the truth to which Quine thus relegates logic—and by extension philosophy, whose intellectual place is for him taken by logic and science—is not, at first glance, timeless. For what is true, strictly, are (Quine writes in *Methods of Logic*) not "statements as repeatable patterns of utterance, but individual events of statement utterance."[29] An utterance, in other words, is made on a specific occasion, and its truth

Heidegger

Aletheia is the shining of being

must be evaluated relative to that occasion. But this move in the direction of temporality is retracted before we are out of the introduction: "Strictly speaking, as urged earlier, what admit of meaning and of truth and falsity are not the statements but the individual events of their utterance. However, it is a source of great simplification in logical theory to talk of statements in abstraction from the individual occasions of their utterance; and this abstraction, if made in full awareness and subject to a certain [technical] precaution, offers no difficulty."[30] The simplification not only offers no difficulty but also avoids quite a few, for it erases from the logical/scientific/philosophical consideration of a statement all the social, historical, and cultural factors that contribute to its utterance, including even those relevant to its Carnapian confirmation. From the point of view of its truth, the utterance of a statement occurs in a personal and social vacuum. Quinean truth becomes selfless, and to all intents and purposes, timeless as well, for if we abstract from all occasions of utterance, we get something that might be uttered, though not always truly, on *any* occasion. That comes fairly close to being timeless.

His own words to the contrary notwithstanding, Quine does not make this particular move in anything like full awareness. This can be seen by noting that the view thus expressed is not new with him. The relegation of philosophical inquiry to the single goal of scientific truth had been stated, with equal integrity and lucidity, by at least two earlier analytical philosophers: Gottlob Frege, in 1918, and Alfred Tarski, from 1943 to 1944. But Frege had acknowledged other, nonscientific senses of truth—especially artistic truth—and had consciously excluded them for purposes of his own investigation. His treatment is explicitly stated to be of "what I want, in this context, to call true. Uses of our word which lie beyond [*abseits*] these may then be rejected. . . . What is meant here is the truth, cognition of which is set before science as its goal."[31]

Tarski is even more emphatic: "I hope nothing which I said here will be interpreted as a claim that the semantic conception of truth is the 'right' or indeed the 'only possible' one. . . . Personally, I should not feel hurt if a future world congress of the 'theoreticians of truth' should decide—by a majority of votes—to reserve the word '*true*' for one of the non-classical conceptions, and should suggest another word, say '*frue*,' for the conception considered here."[32]

What is new in Quine's 1959 formulation, and what gives it a
dogmatism of which Quine himself is apparently unaware, is the utter
absence of any qualification, justification, or explanation. Nonscientific
and nonsentential senses of truth simply go unmentioned; their exclusion is presented unargued, as what Gerold Prauss has called a "commonplace":[33] as an uncontroversial insight into the nature of truth.

The commonplace, in fact, is momentous. When Quinean truth is
made philosophy's only goal, philosophers are directed away from reflecting on the historical conditions of their discipline, and toward
uncovering the logical conditions of the quest of truth; away from social
or pragmatic construals of meaning, and toward a conflation of it with
reference and truth-conditions;[34] away from investigation of the social
work and complicities of philosophical approaches, and toward issues
concerning the scientific justification of beliefs in general.[35] Gottshalk's
words from 1950, which I quoted in chapter 1, begin to ring rather
hollow: "The truth is, whether we like it or not, philosophers today have
a tremendous work on their hands. This work is nothing more, yet
nothing less, than revealing our civilization in its true light, of depicting
its elemental actualities, and its inherent and imperative possibilities. It
is the task of *critical, reflective self-understanding*" (*APA* 24:30; emphasis
added).

What, in Carnapian or Quinean terms, is the true light of a civilization? It is certainly not merely a set of sentences true of that civilization:
we know a number of such truths about ancient Sumer, for example, but
it would be hard to say that we therefore understand Sumer the way
Gottshalk asks us to understand America.

In its contrast with Gottshalk's view, Quine's pursuit of truth, in
fact, looks much like Allen's quest of it. That such a momentous doctrine should be advanced unargued by a thinker as scrupulous as Quine,
that he should apparently be wholly unaware of its controversial relationship to earlier formulations, and that these things should remain
unnoticed for long are matters at least as stunning as the uncritical
reception of logical positivism had been earlier. Something so invisible
is, one presumes, deeply rooted indeed. When the roots are philosophically unseen, they can lie only in the surrounding culture and its recent
history—in this case, I suggest, in the view that adopting the mantle of
science could help philosophers find their way through the paranoid
jumble of McCarthyism.

A New Age for Philosophy?

Whether what was left to philosophy by all this laid the groundwork for a golden age, or a dark one, or something in between, is still undecidable. There is no question that, as I noted in chapter 1, philosophy's new age was a lonely one. Excluded from the quest of truth by both Carnap and Allen, as well as by Quine, were forms of inquiry that appeal to nonscientific criteria of validation, such as faith, tradition, or aesthetic insight; that use those criteria to illuminate, however fallibly, our lives and engagements; and that draw our allegiance from that very capacity. Along with them, of course, went the diverse, contextualized, and subtle considerations of social benefit advanced by the pragmatists. Also eliminated were views like Hegel's, which see truth as emerging not from a disinterested, scientific attitude but from the dialectical clash of a variety of committed standpoints. Among such standpoints, of course, are literature and religion, which could thenceforth be no more than objects of dispassionate investigation on the part of philosophers.

The pursuit of quasi-scientific truth also alienated philosophy from its own history. The mechanism of this is shown by Hans Reichenbach's *The Rise of Scientific Philosophy,* which was published in 1951 and so, presumably, was in preparation during the California oath controversy. In it, the UCLA philosopher "insists" (that is, does not argue) that "the question of truth must be raised within philosophy in the same way as in the sciences,"[36] which means as a matter of empirical confirmation. This enables Reichenbach to excise the history of philosophy from philosophy itself: "I do not wish to belittle the history of philosophy; but one should always remember that it is history, and not philosophy. . . . There is more error than truth in traditional philosophy."[37] As the rest of the book shows, little is possible on such premises except caricature and dismissal.[38]

Philosophy's alliance with science, in itself a source of vitality (as even Hegel recognized), thus became exclusive. But in a final irony, philosophy's timeless quest succeeded in alienating it even from its hoped-for allies, the scientists. As the distinguished philosopher of science David Hull has written: "The chief weakness of the logical empiricist analysis of science has been the emphasis of its advocates on inference to the near total exclusion of everything else about science, especially its temporal and social dimensions."[39] Philosophy's idealized view of science as timeless, disinterested truth seeking was far from reality, even in the 1950s. It rendered philosophers unable to understand science, the one enterprise with which they felt affinity, in any but the narrowest of ways.

As I will argue later, analytical philosophy is far from being a mere artifact of the McCarthy era. Its *dominance* in America, however, is I think precisely such an artifact, and an unfortunate one. When other voices are no longer heard, the ability to understand them atrophies, and the rise of a new approach turns into a triumph in which alternatives are forgotten. Thus, says Hilary Putnam, one became an analytical philosopher in the 1950s by learning "what *not* to like and what not to consider philosophy. . . . I think that is a terrible thing, and that it should be stopped in all schools, movements, and philosophy departments."[40]

But it did not stop. When I first began to get acquainted with the American philosophical scene, in the mid-1960s, it seemed to me to resemble American race relations of the day. The analysts, nine-tenths of the philosophical population (or so it seemed), enjoyed almost all the power and prestige. The continentals, as they were beginning to be called, were like an oppressed minority asking only for equal rights and the chance to be heard.

In 1976, when I attended my first Eastern Division meeting, the situation was unchanged. Except for three sessions—one on hermeneutics, one on Charles Taylor's recently published *Hegel,* and one on the phenomenology of naming—the entire program was strictly analytical. Two of those three continental sessions, moreover, were held at the same time—during the final time slot—on Saturday afternoon. I attended the session on Taylor, and suddenly everything was different. The speakers and the audience, in some indefinable way, no longer looked the same (though they still looked awfully white and awfully male). It seemed to me that it was clearly time for the continentals to creep out from the burrows where they had been hiding the previous two days—now that all the real philosophers had gone home!

But philosophy's new age—at least insofar as it was predicated upon the uncontested dominance of analytical philosophy—was not to last. The marching started in 1978, just a couple of years after that Eastern Division meeting. To be sure, the APA, in the words of Bruce Wilshire, was still "dreary" and "unpardonably parochial" (Wilshire 256). American philosophy in general was similarly parochial: "Persons outside this field may find it difficult or impossible to believe, but by the late 1970s nine out of ten newly minted Ph.D.'s in philosophy could not speak intelligently for two minutes on the work of the nineteenth- and twentieth-century philosophers that the rest of the world deems important, e.g., James, Emerson, Dewey, Thoreau, Whitehead. Many had never read cover to cover a major treatise in the history of philosophy" (Wilshire 257–58).

American philosophers had thus managed, twenty years ago, what the most extreme postmodern theorists can only hope for today: they threw out the canon. With that, there was no one for them to read except each other. So they did, sometimes at least. A weird forerunner of more recent identity politics began to run wild in, of all places, philosophy departments.

This provided another, more timely motive for anguish among the people who met in January 1978 in the Manhattan apartment of Charles Sherover, a professor at Hunter College. An accrediting committee of the state of New York—its personnel supplied by the APA—had just visited the philosophy department at the New School for Social Research. The committee had recommended that the program be disaccredited, on the grounds that it was so far removed from the mainstream of American philosophy as to be overspecialized and sectarian.

I arrived at the New School as an assistant professor in September 1980 and was personally informed about all this. Though the New School had serious problems, caused by retirement, death, and financial difficulties, the unfairness of the APA inquisitors was obvious. Far from being sectarian, the New School was one of the few places where one was free to study such figures as Adorno, Benjamin, Hegel, Heidegger, and Marx, along with nonanalytical approaches to Greek philosophy and to the history of philosophy generally (that is, approaches that do not begin and end with a search for true sentences in the texts considered, a search that somehow always fails). When the APA said that this kind of identity was sectarian, they merely meant that it wasn't Us. The New School had run afoul of identity politics, APA-style.

The unfairness assumed lunatic proportions in the case of Hannah Arendt, whom the inquisitors (I was told) deemed an unproductive drone because her works were not cited in important journals such as the *Journal of Philosophy* and *Philosophical Review*. Of course, she published regularly in the *New York Review of Books* (no obscure venue), had

been on the cover of *Time* magazine, and was one of the most famous
political thinkers in the world. Too bad that she hadn't done anything
philosophically important! (As with Wilshire's statistic about the nine out
of ten newly minted Ph.D.'s, quoted above, this kind of reasoning may
seem to be too bizarrely parochial to have actually occurred. I can only
say, from my knowledge of the situation, that I had no trouble believing
it at that time, and accept it still.)

The story of the "pluralist rebellion" is a long one and should be
told elsewhere.[41] Suffice it that attention soon focused on the nominating committee of Eastern Division. Though divisional officers were
elected by the membership at the yearly business meeting in December,
all the members ever did was approve the single slate proposed by the
nominating committee. The way to get around this, the pluralists decided, was to take advantage of the requirement that the nominating
committee solicit and receive suggestions for nominations from the
membership at large. Rumor had it that the nominating committee in
fact paid little attention to such suggestions, instead selecting its candi-
dates from a small clique of analytical philosophers employed at prestigious universities. The rumor was proven true at the 1979 business
meeting. Monroe Beardsley, chair of the nominating committee, was
forced to read out, for each position, the names of the five people who
had received the most suggestions from the membership for that position. Not one of them, for any position, had actually been nominated by
the committee.

This exposes a degree of control—and of intellectual sclerosis—that,
like so many things in American philosophy, is stunning to outsiders.
The American Philosophical Association, America's national organization for philosophers, is as I mentioned in the previous chapter divided
into three divisions: Eastern, Central (formerly Western), and Pacific.
Eastern Division is by far the largest; of the APA's members, half traditionally belong to it. Eastern Division's yearly meeting, because of its size
and because it includes the job market, is de facto the only "national"
meeting of American philosophers: the only one regularly attended by
philosophers from across the country. This means that Eastern Division,
to be blunt, *is* the APA, somewhat as Paris is France; the fraction of the
membership that belongs to other divisions is relegated to the provinces.
And Eastern Division, in turn, was—through its nominating committee—controlled by a few senior professors from prestigious schools: the

same schools that had been most viciously attacked twenty years before, when those very professors were beginning their careers. The gist of it was that a very small, clubby, and intellectually homogeneous group of people—Wilshire estimates it at no more than sixty (Wilshire 261)—determined things for American philosophy as a whole.

The Committee on Pluralism continues to work to get nonanalytical philosophers elected to positions within Eastern Division, and with a good deal of success. But the successes are intermittent, and are confined in any case to Eastern Division. Many things in American philosophy, as I will argue in the next chapter, remain unchanged today. In any case, winning battles at the APA is not exactly the way to open up the profession. As one prominent logician informed the pluralists after their 1978 victory, "You keep the conventions; we'll keep the graduate schools" (Wilshire 274).

Conclusions

I am not arguing that the McCarthy era is somehow responsible for the existence of analytical philosophy. Such philosophy hardly began with the arrival in America of the logical positivists. It has a longer and honorable history, beginning well before the McCarthy era with the work of Gottlob Frege in Göttingen, and passing over to the Cambridge of Bertrand Russell at the close of the nineteenth century. But it never had the kind of dominance in its homeland—Germany—that its transplanted varieties enjoyed elsewhere. And it is worth noting that its rise to such dominance in England betrays some similarities with the American scene.

The McCarthy era itself, of course, found no resonance at all in British society. Many Americans who were attacked by McCarthyites found refuge there (though not, so far as I am aware, a single philosopher). But analytical philosophy's rise in Britain began earlier, during the run-up to World War I. The national paranoia in Britain at that time in fact sounds quite familiar to anyone acquainted with the McCarthy era in the United States. Consider this writing, from the newspaper of Noel Pemberton-Billing, a "prominent demagogue in Parliament" (though perhaps never as successful in causing trouble as Joe McCarthy). It concerns the infiltration of Britain by German agents called "urnings": "All I can do is point out to those who find their spiritual home in Germany that a great cancer, made in Germany, is eating at the heart of England and civilization. . . . When the blond beast is an urning, he commands the urnings in other lands. They are moles. They burrow. They are hardest at work when they are the most silent. Britain is safe only when her statesmen are family men and use the . . . power of England to starve the urning nations."[42]

If for "Germany" we substituted "Russia," and for "urning," "Communist," we would have a vintage document from the McCarthy era. But this was written in England in 1918, not in America in the 1950s. And it concerned not Communists but urnings. These fantastic creatures were a fifth column of homosexuals believed to have been sent from Germany to seduce young Englishmen into sodomitic service to the Kaiser. They were every bit as dangerous as Communists: "Londoner urnings," went the article I have just quoted, "have much more in common with Teuton urnings than their own countrymen." Just like New York Communists. What American McCarthyites would decades later call "fellow travelers" were also a problem for Pemberton-Billings: all who "find their spiritual home in Germany," even if heterosexual, were part of the problem.

Of course, the substitution of "Communist" for "urning" is hardly necessary to bring out the resemblances between American McCarthyism and its British forerunner. Robert Bellah, whose encounter with homophobia at Harvard I mentioned in the previous chapter, would not be surprised to learn that homosexuals were spoken of in pre–World War I England much as Communists were in America during the McCarthy era. Homosexuality, like Communism, does not display itself in physical features, and is thus apt for the confused interplay of signifiers that constituted American anti-Communism.

Pemberton-Billing's kind of thinking was powerful enough to help give rise to the Official Secrets Act, which by 1920 forbade British subjects to communicate with foreign agents. A foreign agent, in turn, was anyone reasonably suspected of being engaged by a foreign power, directly or indirectly, to commit acts prejudicial to British state interest—"reasonably," "indirectly," "prejudicial," and "interest" all being defined by the state.[43] In the climate of the times, it is easy to see why the first translator of Hegel's *Phenomenology,* J. B. Baillie, never checked his translation with a German speaker, with the result that his translation is a laughable disaster—and makes Hegel look like one.[44] How far the

Official Secrets Act has gone in general to foster the notable insularity of
British philosophy in the twentieth century is not for me to speculate
upon here. The parallels between the two main cultures in which analytical philosophy came to dominance, however, are worthy of further
investigation by others.

Analytical philosophy is certainly not *merely* a defensive reaction
against political threats, wherever and whenever it should appear. In its
early decades it had a great deal to recommend it: openness to new tools
and to reformulated issues. True, those issues, though reformulated,
were not exactly new. Most of analytical philosophy's inventory of problems comes from the seventeenth century. Such "perennial" issues as the
mind-body problem and free will would have been recognizable to
Descartes and Locke, but they would have been unintelligible to philosophers from the twelfth century, and uninteresting to many from the
nineteenth.

American philosophy's orientation toward science, if conveniently
uncritical and far too exclusive, has been extremely important and fruitful in its own domain. Indeed, the rise of science, independently of the
McCarthy era, was sure to have effects on philosophy, and this is as it
should be. There *is,* somehow, such a thing as the truth about things,
and science *is* our only organized way of finding it; science richly deserves the kind of concrete and informed discussion philosophers are
now giving it. But why did it not receive such discussion earlier? Why
were philosophers content for two decades with general gestures in the
direction of an idealized science, the concept of which they themselves
had largely constructed?

The history of philosophy, for its part, has never been well taught in
America, where at midcentury it was still possible for Plato scholars to
know no Greek. Its abandonment may result, to some degree, from simple ignorance of what it contains. But more may be at stake. Like philosophy itself, from which it can be only tendentiously distinguished, the
history of philosophy is oddly threatening to America's self-image. Not
only may pursuit of it undermine the foundations of the Republic,
which, as I argued in chapter 1, is the case for philosophy in general, but
even when that does not happen, study of the history of philosophy is a
dangerous thing for Americans, for it inevitably jeopardizes America's
status as a new beginning in world history. If our ideas come from
philosophers down through history, then the basic tools of our minds—

including, for example, words like "life," "liberty," and "the pursuit of happiness"—were formed by some of the most elitist and undemocratic people ever to walk Western earth. What happens to the originality of the American way?[45] It is small wonder that the United States, a country that has many fine centers for the history and philosophy of science, and can even afford one for the study of the Belgian endive (at the University of Massachusetts, Amherst), remains without a single one for the history of philosophy.

Granted all this, however, the question remains: why did philosophy so definitively abandon its own history just when it did? And whence the strange view, still found in philosophy departments, that although no one can think intelligently about science without sustained investigation of its disciplinary and intellectual history, philosophers can do precisely that when it comes to philosophy itself?

Finally, the defensive posture American philosophy adopted after World War II actually had some good results. It was only after the McCarthy era, with its obvious anti-Semitism, that Jews were really free to pursue careers in American philosophy departments. One wonders how soon that would have happened if philosophy had continued to be the sort of value-bound enterprise it tended to be earlier—bound in part, inevitably, to the higher wisdoms of the small-minded America of which Bertrand Russell, and not only he, had run afoul.

The McCarthy era also brought universities some practical benefits. The dominance of a single paradigm meant that philosophy departments could be small and cheap, as befitted a possibly subversive frill in a country whose chosen mission was the preservation of global free enterprise. Genuine and fecund pluralism, were it ever to arrive in the New World, would require far larger and more expensive departments, and there is no evidence that American universities are ready to support them.

This is in contrast to other countries, where philosophy departments—at least some of them—are far larger than they tend to be in America. Thus, according to the *International Directory of Philosophy and Philosophers, 1997–98,*[46] Oxford has 88 philosophers and the University of London 62, while the University of Paris has 108 philosophers among its five campuses. In West Germany, the Free University of Berlin has 39 members of its philosophy department, and Bochum, 33. In Italy, Bologna has 37, and Turin, 29. Closer to home, the National

Autonomous University of Mexico has close to 50 members, and the University of Toronto has 58 (plus 10 emeriti). Plenty of foreign philosophy departments are much smaller than this, and some foreign universities are much larger than their American counterparts (the National Autonomous University of Mexico, for example, has approximately 270,000 students). Philosophy departments with more than 20 faculty members, though quite common in other countries, are almost unheard of among American secular universities. According to the *Directory of American Philosophers, 1998–99*,[47] Columbia has 15 faculty members (and 6 emeriti); Harvard, 13 (and also 6 emeriti); Michigan, 20 (and 4 emeriti); Princeton, 19 (and 4 emeriti); Stanford, 28 (and 3 emeriti); and UCLA, 12 (and 8 emeriti). Numbers do not guarantee quality, of course (though large numbers of emeriti hint at a need to rebuild). But they do bespeak an ability to garner resources that are denied to American philosophy departments, even those at universities as wealthy and prestigious as those just mentioned. And one guesses that those large foreign departments fill some sort of purpose: why else have them in countries that are often notably less wealthy than the United States?

It seems possible, in other words, that the choices American philosophy made in the 1950s enabled it to survive the McCarthy era. But they may have allowed it to survive only as a reduced and reticent discipline, able to see just a few stars in an intellectual firmament that was once much wider and more interesting. It is not obvious that those advantages from forty years ago justify perpetuating the present situation much longer.

3

Has It Stopped Yet?

The McCarthy Era's Lasting Effects on American Philosophy

In the two previous chapters I argued that American philosophy went through serious trauma in the 1950s. The force of the McCarthyite attacks seems to have affected philosophy substantially at that time and led indirectly to the pluralist rebellion of the early 1980s. Is there any reason to think that its effects have persisted down to the present day?

Anyone who thinks that the McCarthy era is over and done with, that the purges are merely a matter of history, and that American philosophy has returned to a path of normal and healthy intellectual development is invited to contemplate the fact that eleven years after the 1987 breakthrough anthology *Feminism as Critique* none of its contributors was still in a philosophy department.[1] This includes the names I mentioned in the introduction: Seyla Benhabib, Judith Butler, Drucilla Cornell, Nancy Fraser, and Iris Marion Young.[2] Other prominent gender theorists who have left philosophy departments include Allison Brown,

David Goldberg, Lewis Gordon, Elizabeth Grosz, Sandra Harding, and Linda Nicholson. The combined departure of such well-known figures from any discipline would be cause for concern—especially because it cannot be coincidental. Though each case is different, the common threads are only too obvious: feminism and continental philosophy. (The difficult story of American philosophy and feminism, as well as that of minorities in American philosophy, can be better told by others; I will discuss the case of continental philosophy later in this chapter.)

American philosophy has hardly stood still, of course, since the days of Joe McCarthy. But on both its disciplinary and its intellectual levels, it remains today in part a legacy of the junior senator from Wisconsin and his academic allies. This chapter will concern itself with some aspects of that legacy. It will contain, I am afraid, some very critical reflections on the present state of American philosophy. The criticisms will be of two quite distinct types. On the disciplinary level, I will discuss evidence that philosophy in America remains dysfunctional in ways already suggested by chapter 1. It does not reflect upon itself, it remains isolated from other disciplines, and its main institutions— departments, conferences, journals, and the APA itself—are under a tighter establishment control than are comparable institutions in other fields. The controls have the effect of fostering the continued dominance of analytical philosophy, which seems to be the main legacy of the McCarthy era. That dominance, I will argue, is not merely a matter of emotional commitment or ignorance of alternatives on the part of individual philosophers. It has become institutionalized in ways that point back to the difficulties of forty and fifty years ago.

Though this institutionalized dominance cannot help but affect the intellectual content of American philosophy, that is a separate set of issues. I do have what I think are serious criticisms of the dominance of analytical philosophy, and indeed of such philosophy itself, on the intellectual level. Those criticisms are related to the disciplinary history I am reconstructing here. I will discuss them in chapter 5, along with the somewhat milder criticisms I will make of continental philosophy. The dominance of analytical philosophy has, in fact, been bad for *both* analytical and continental philosophy. Neither can go forward alone. For philosophy itself to make progress, serious dialogue between the two approaches has to become a main concern of each.

In chapter 1, I noted the isolation of American philosophy from other academic discourses and its strange inability to reflect on its own history. I argued in chapter 2 that the McCarthy era fostered those characteristics. As a preliminary to my main discussion, I will present here some anecdotal evidence suggesting that the exclusionary attitudes of the McCarthy era toward other disciplines and toward the history of philosophy remain in place on the disciplinary level. The anecdotes come from the Ivy League, which, when it comes to American philosophy in general, is hardly an unrepresentative fringe.

Universities, to begin with, are supposed to be open communities where intellectual discussions are publicly advertised so that anyone, and certainly any members of the university community, can attend them. But as recently as 1988, the philosophy department at one Ivy League university where I was a visitor refused to inform nonmembers of invited papers. Announcements of visiting lecturers were posted only in the mailroom, access to which was limited to those with departmental mailboxes. There was a mailing list, but in spite of the efforts of a full professor in the department, I—at that time an assistant professor of philosophy at Northwestern University—was unable get my name on that list.

If we ask what could provoke such a remarkably stringent secrecy, we are at a loss (certainly my friend was unable to understand it). But it is noteworthy that if this policy had been in effect forty years previously at the University of California, the oath controversy would never have taken place. As I noted in chapter 1, that cataclysm was triggered when it became publicly known that a Communist philosopher had been invited to speak. No such publicity was in store where I now found myself, at least as far as the philosophy department was concerned, because invited talks were virtual departmental secrets. But if McCarthy-era fears were indeed responsible for the policy that I found in place in 1988, then the policy was, to say the least, sorely outdated. Powerful McCarthyites had long disappeared from government and were only beginning to move into their current redoubts on private foundations. The only people the policy could have been designed to protect against were, perhaps, literary theorists and their embarrassingly messy questions.

When, at about the same time, another Ivy League department hired a Plato scholar, one of its senior figures was alleged to complain that there was no need to hire someone to "teach the mistakes."[3] This complaint promulgated unchanged the views of Hans Reichenbach, which I discussed in chapter 2 and which had themselves been published in 1951.

Finally, a third Ivy League department was publicly described by its own dean in 1990 as "in imminent danger of becoming a club of old gentlemen, more exclusive with every retirement and death. In my imagination I picture the department with only one member: a patriarch holding a gigantic bag of black balls in his hand" (Rosovsky 48).

The Ongoing Absence of Reflection in American Philosophy

In chapter 1, I brought up the fact that discussion of where American philosophy is and where it may be going has virtually disappeared from the scene. I suggested one reason was that such discussion risked revealing where American philosophy had come from, which turns out to be a very unpleasant place indeed. But the absence of professional self-knowledge among American philosophers has had other manifestations and effects on both the disciplinary and the intellectual levels, manifestations which suggest that such reflection is not only avoided but resisted.

The present research is a case in point. The executive director of the APA is also the editor of its main publication, *Proceedings and Addresses.* I first wrote to him in November 1989, to inform him of the basics of what I had uncovered regarding American philosophy and the McCarthy era. Noting that the available record was highly critical of the APA, I suggested that publication in *Proceedings and Addresses* would testify to the APA's open-mindedness, and so would be good for the organization. I received no reply for three years, until that editor was leaving his position with the APA. On November 4, 1992, he wrote to tell me he had come across my material while cleaning out his office and suggested that I send it to his successor. I did, but this time noted in my letter several reasons why *Proceedings and Addresses* might not want to publish anything so critical. The successor responded on March 9, 1993. Clearly anguished, he declared that the research could not be published in *Proceedings and Addresses* because "it does not fit our format" and belonged in a real journal. But real philosophy journals, as I noted in chapter 1, do not publish even intellectual reflections on philosophy, let alone disciplinary ones. (The format of *Proceedings and Addresses,* by the way, can accommodate letters to the editor demanding that all philosophy professors be required to take oaths that they are not homosexual; *APA* 67, no. 4: 132.)

When I served on the program committee for the APA's Central Division in 1996, I discussed the material with the committee's chair. He informed me, on January 8, 1996, that in his view it would be highly inappropriate for members of the program committee to schedule themselves for any sessions. He suggested that if I wanted to have the material discussed at the next meeting, the following spring, I should send it either to the chair of the Committee on the Status and Future of the Profession or to the chair of the Committee on the Defense of the Professional Rights of Philosophers. Those two committees had the power to hold sessions of their own at the meetings outside the aegis of the program committee.

Both generally and in view of the controversial nature of this specific material, the chair's reservations and suggestion made excellent sense, and I sent the material off to the two philosophers he had suggested. Neither responded, and the following year—once I was off the program committee—an invitation was at last tendered. Interested members of Central Division finally heard some of my material at the division's annual meeting in Chicago in May 1998—eight and a half years after I had first contacted the APA. No one who has read the preceding chapters can be surprised that the invitation was from Central Division (or that Eastern Division, as I have been told, simultaneously refused to issue one). But no one will be surprised, either, to learn that my paper was scheduled as the last paper given at that meeting, or that its title was—though at least partly through my own fault—left off the program.[4]

Of seven efforts, then—not all made by me, and perhaps not all there were—one had finally succeeded, after a fashion. The story is not one that philosophy should be proud of. With the single exception of the chair of Central Division's program committee, the philosophers in question—all of them holding positions of trust in the APA—showed various mixtures of trepidation, hostility, and lassitude. More important, the story also shows that American philosophy is a long way from where it should be with respect to this kind of work. Research into the history of one's own field, on both its intellectual and its disciplinary sides, ought to be a matter of course, and forums for it should be routinely provided.

American philosophy's indifference and hostility to reflection on the discipline go well beyond the issue of the McCarthy era. The logic of repression itself dictates that they must, for repression cannot be limited to just one theme without, perversely, awakening it. If philosophers were to refuse to discuss only the McCarthy era, it could hardly remain hidden. The repression of a specific topic always and necessarily requires larger failures of historical memory, so it is not surprising that there are other aspects to the recent disciplinary history of American philosophy that do not get the open discussion they deserve.

One of those topics is the emigration of distinguished philosophers from the profession. In addition to the distinguished feminists I have mentioned twice before, Richard Rorty and Stephen Toulmin have left, apparently permanently (as have I). Martha Nussbaum and Robert Pippin, among others, left at least temporarily. At the University of California, Irvine, four philosophers of science (Gian Aido Antonelli, Jeffrey Barrett, and, on a more senior level, Penelope Maddy and Brian Skyrms) have left to form their own department; David Malament, from Chicago, is expected to join them.[5] Are there common factors to these different cases? How extensive is the trend? Does it hold among less-famous figures as well? What are the reasons for it? We do not know, and will not, because the issue is not discussed: *de nobis ipse silemus,* as Kant said.

Another case of cultivated self-ignorance concerns the overwhelm- ingly disastrous job market. The onset of what is usually called the "job crisis"—though something that lasts for thirty years is not normally called a "crisis"—was recorded in the report of the chair of the Commit- tee on Placement, Ruth Barcan Marcus, to Eastern Division's business meeting of December 28, 1968. She noted ominously that the ratio of job seekers to jobs had doubled since the previous year (*APA* 42:136). Matters quickly got worse, and at the 1977 Western Division meetings in Chicago, I and other job seekers were told by the APA's Committee on Non-Academic Employment that the number of completed philoso- phy Ph.D.'s who would ever have tenure was . . . 5 percent. Only 10 per- cent of new doctors would find tenure-track positions, and only half of those would get tenure. Since the late 1960s, then, with the recent exception of Yale and a couple of other places, there has been only spot hiring in American philosophy.

The agony this has caused was obliquely recognized, but in no way halted, by the APA's formulation of a statement to be given to those admitted to graduate programs. The statement, available through the APA's Web page, informs prospective students that although graduate study in philosophy is an admirable undertaking, it should not be expected to lead to employment.[6] This strategy, like the APA's actions with respect to the AAUP fifty years ago, conveniently shifts the moral burden, in this case onto the student. Anyone who comes to graduate school after reading the statement now knows what he or she is in for. The professoriat is not responsible if such people waste several years of their lives pursuing professional degrees that cannot possibly lead to places in the profession.

In fact, the APA statement never deterred anyone I know from pursuing such degrees. Perhaps we were just stupider than the APA thought, but the possibility of running into serious job trouble at the other end of an eight- to ten-year program meant little to us. How long was the "crisis" going to last, anyway? Crises don't last long—that is what makes them crises. Maybe I'll be among the lucky ones. Maybe my genius will get recognized while I am still in graduate school. And so on. As Harvard English professor John Guillory put it at a congress on doctoral programs sponsored by the Modern Language Association (MLA)—a conference without any analog, so far as I know, in philosophy: "Human beings in general overestimate their chances of success—state lotteries depend on this, and graduate students are no exception. . . . Our students persist in wanting to pursue an academic career even after hearing the worst from us."[7]

It should be no surprise, then, that graduate student enrollments have continued to rise since the APA's statement. Further action might be in order. But the responsible path of admitting that many graduate programs in the United States are simply superfluous and the painful path of cutting them back have not been addressed on a discipline-wide basis, though individual departments (such as Northwestern's, which I left in 1997) have behaved admirably in this regard.

What is interesting about the estimates concerning the job market that I quoted earlier, apart from their gloominess, is who issued them and when. One will search in vain for a more recent sustained discussion of the toll the lack of jobs has taken on the discipline. In yet another move reminiscent of the McCarthy era, the APA seems to have shoved the whole issue off onto the Committee on Non-Academic Employment and has itself stayed above the fray.

The APA's efforts to shield itself from the suffering of recent Ph.D.'s can verge on the ridiculous. In the 1978 Central Division, held in Denver, which I attended as a job seeker, one found the placement center in the following way: One took the elevator down to the hotel's shopping arcade, one floor below the main lobby. One then took some stairs down to a lower level of the arcade. This lower arcade was entirely deserted, the storefronts empty. It bore somewhat the look of an Old West ghost town, though underground. Proceeding out the back door of this arcade, footsteps echoing, one found oneself in a covered bay for taxis and limousines, none of which ever showed up because the arcade (now at one's back) was completely empty. Directly across the traffic lanes, still under the hotel roof, one confronted a buttress containing a single unmarked elevator door. One crossed to this elevator and took it down two flights. The door slid open, and there they were: the tired, the poor, the huddled masses, yearning to be paid. . . . The message could not have been clearer: *de vobis ipseis silemus.* . . .

But American philosophy's inattention to itself can go beyond the ludicrous to become truly alarming. One example of this concerns the most important disciplinary level of philosophy: the individual department, within which those philosophers lucky enough to get hired at all pass their working lives. As I noted in chapter 2, American philosophy departments are relatively small in comparison to many of those in other countries. Even those with graduate programs are usually far too small to develop credible pluralism, even if they wanted to. They tend to consist, as one eminent American philosopher put it to me in a conversation, of grab bags of people whose only common denominator is a rigorously analytical education.

Not only are American philosophy departments small and homogenous, but they are also decreasing in number. On December 26, 1997, an article appeared on the first page of the business section of the *New York Times* concerning the large numbers of philosophy Ph.D.'s finding jobs in the computer industry. The article pointed out that such jobs were necessary because the United States was getting out of the philosophy business: it had closed or amalgamated 100 departments *per year* for the preceding four years, and only 650 or so still offered majors. The source given for this information was the *Directory of American Philosophers, 1992,* together with its 1996 counterpart. The statistical pages in the 1996 volume alone clearly showed it: 2,110 departments listed in 1994, as opposed to 1,723 in 1996.

That no philosophers had ever noted this astonishing fact about their own profession was itself astonishing, because many of them (including, I admit, myself) make regular use of the directory to get addresses and phone numbers. In spite of this, the information came as enough of a shock to provoke APA inquiries to the directory. These resulted in the publication, in *Proceedings and Addresses,* of a letter from George Leaman, director of the Philosophy Documentation Center, which publishes the directory (*APA* 71, no. 5: 157–58).

Leaman made three basic points. First, he suggested that the departments that had been closed down were at small colleges and community colleges. This raised a few questions, such as: Why is the loss of a department even at such a college not cause for concern? How did those departments become so vulnerable in the first place? Is this merely a result of the perennial belt tightening that goes on in the humanities in the United States, or is philosophy being singled out? (Leaman assumed the former but offered no evidence.) Should we be happy with the survival of some of the large, flabby departments that abound and, as I have noted, year after year send forth graduate students to be slaughtered in a job market with no jobs?

Leaman also pointed to several signs of "widespread growth across the profession." One was that the number of Ph.D. programs in philosophy had increased from 106 to 114. But this is not exactly a healthy sign, since as I have suggested the degrees most of these new and unknown programs provide will likely be professionally worthless. The approximately 150 jobs that came on the market in a typical year of the 1990s could be filled by the graduates of, say, twenty good graduate programs. We could double that figure, and double it again, without getting near the actual number of graduate programs in operation. An increasing number of graduate programs, in short, is *not* a sign of health.

Three of Leaman's other examples—increases in the number of philosophy centers, societies, and journals—point to widespread health in the egos of philosophers, and to some ability to raise small amounts of money, but to little else (a center can be merely a filing cabinet; a journal can cost less than $5,000 a year to produce). Finally, and in his own view most important, Leaman noted that the number of individual philosophers had actually gone up during the four years in question, from 10,640 to 11,248. What he did not say is that the 1996 figure included a total of 1,015 faculty listed as adjunct or of unknown status, but the

1994 figure did not. If we adjust for that, the number of philosophers *fell* from 10,640 to 10,233, or by about 4 percent.

Leaman then fell on his own sword and admitted that the figure of approximately 100 departments a year was merely worked up from what had been reported to the Philosophy Documentation Center and might not have any relationship to reality whatsoever. But the sword, alas, was pointing *away* from him. Start-ups seek publicity far more than do terminations, and the tendency would be for the demise of philosophy departments to go underreported. So it is quite possible that if the center's figures need correction, it would be downward. Any discrepancy between the facts and what was reported to the directory could well be in the direction of understating the problem.

Like Allen's letter of forty-eight years before, which I discussed in chapter 2, this one seems to have worked: there has been no further discussion of the matter in *Proceedings and Addresses.* Never broached was what many outsiders would think to be crucial: why did American philosophers have to read about such a prima facie important development in the *New York Times?*

This lack of reflection is not confined to the disciplinary side of American philosophy. It extends to the intellectual side as well. Most philosophers, for example, consider analytical philosophy to be a species of empiricism. They thereby locate it in a British tradition of intelligent and unpretentious skepticism about reason, coupled with unreserved admiration for science. But true empiricists, such as Hume and Mill, hold that all knowledge comes from the senses. Mathematical knowledge is no exception. Mathematical necessity for Hume testifies, at best, only to the propensity of the understanding to move from one idea to another—to what Hume calls "custom."[8] From Russell and Frege at least until Quine, by contrast, most analytical philosophers believed that mathematical and logical truths were necessary and universal (because tautological, which was not what Kant thought they were). This in effect made much analytical philosophy either Leibnizian or what Alasdair MacIntyre calls a "reformulation" of Kantianism in response to empiricist challenges, rather than a genuine empiricism.[9]

After an apparent brief flirtation with genuine empiricism in the case of Quine, analytical philosophy returned to its idealist nature with Donald Davidson.[10] But this facet of Davidson's work cannot be appreciated unless we understand how deep the traditional differences are between analytical philosophy and empiricism. Hence it is that people are unnecessarily surprised by discoveries such as Simon Evnine's on Davidson:

> [Davidson's views] developed out of an empiricist, and generally anti-metaphysical tradition, and are often framed in the vocabulary of this tradition. . . . But in fact . . . Davidson has now stepped entirely outside this empiricist tradition. It is far more useful to see him in the company of Plato . . . and Hegel, with all their metaphysical baggage, than in the company of the Vienna Circle and Quine, with their austere, anti-metaphysical scientism. . . . Davidson's problems are of a piece with the problems that have always afflicted rationalist idealists such as Plato and Hegel: how can people, as finite, limited, and material creatures, participate in an ideal?[11]

Analytical philosophy's failure to locate itself correctly within modern philosophy is not just historically misleading. It fosters problems, I think, with the way such philosophy has made the linguistic turn. In this respect, the linguistic revolution in philosophy was not as revolutionary as has been thought.[12] It was in fact more like a refocusing of interest within a basically modern framework of viewing language.

That framework was at bottom, for both rationalists and empiricists, one of distrust. In Descartes's *Principles of Philosophy,* for example, language is a sort of subrepository into which drip cognitive evils, already several times distilled.[13] It is not merely an impediment to thought but also its deepest enemy, for it refines prejudice and permits the weight of the past to bear, prejudicially, on the present. Always present to us as a medium for our thought, language for Descartes is—like his famous evil demon—a continuous deceiver.[14] For the empiricist Locke as well, "the very nature of words makes it almost unavoidable for many of them to be doubtful and uncertain in their significations."[15] Thus, Locke's chapter "Remedies of the Foregoing Imperfection and Abuse of Words" in the *Essay concerning Human Understanding* contains a number of strategies for making words dependably subordinate to ideas.[16] Leibniz, a rationalist of course, sought to dispense with language altogether in favor of his *ars characteristica,* and Berkeley could write: "It were, therefore, much to be wished that everyone would use his utmost endeavours to obtain a clear view of the ideas he would consider; separating them from all that dress and incumbrance of words which so much contribute to blind the judgment and divide the attention. . . . We need only draw the curtain of words, to behold the fairest tree of knowledge, whose fruit is excellent, and within the reach of our hand."[17]

Even the empiricists, then, did not view language very empirically. Like the rationalists, they approached it armed with the preconception that it is, and can only be, a tool of something nonsensible, and so decidedly unempirical: thought itself. This view, common to both main branches of modern philosophy, was decisively challenged by the later Wittgenstein, who argued in the *Philosophical Investigations* that "thinking is not an incorporeal process which lends life and sense to speaking, and which it would be possible to detach from speaking."[18] But apart from the (later) Wittgensteinians, analytical philosophy's linguistic turn generally retained the view that language needed to be subordinate to thought. Like many modern approaches to language, this one is in some ways not so much a turning *to* language as a turning *on* language. As Gilead Bar-Elli puts it:

> Contrary to a common view, the great analytic philosophers were so concerned with language not because they believed that "everything is linguistic" and that "language is the key to truth," but for quite the opposite reason: they believed that language, i.e., natural language, can be quite misleading and that we must free ourselves from its bonds. The idea was not that language is misleading in its regular capacity as a tool of communication. The idea was rather that some features of language—particularly logical and grammatical features—may suggest wrong and misleading philosophical . . . conceptions. And that is how logic came to acquire its central role. Logic was held to be the route to freedom—the means of escaping the misleading bonds of language.[19]

Wittgenstein was not the only opponent of this view. It is precisely what Heidegger warns against when he says, "We do not wish to assault language in order to force it into the grip of ideas already fixed beforehand." Among those ideas Heidegger identifies three: (1) that language is expression, that is, that in it something internal is uttered or externalized; (2) that speech is an activity of man; and (3) that human expression is a representation of the real and unreal, that is, truly or falsely depicts the world.[20] These views are mainstays of American philosophy of language, with (1) its recurrent debates about speakers' intentions, (2) its endless efforts to attain clarity, and (3) its overwhelming concern with truth and reference. They are also encapsulated in Bar-

Elli's quote. For (1) the claim that language's regular capacity is as a tool for communication invokes the standard model of a human being putting her thoughts into words for the sake of sharing them with others. That language ought not to mislead us presupposes (2) that it should be the dependable instrument for our linguistic activity. And language misleads us (3) by misrepresenting certain basic truths about the world.

In Heidegger's view, all these preconceptions see language not in its own right but as subservient to something else—to our thoughts, our linguistic activity, or the states of affairs language should represent. They embody for him the kind of assault Bar-Elli describes in its analytical form: "But language, it was believed, can be fought against from within, so to speak, by rejecting, correcting, and improving the pictures and preconceptions it suggests. It has often been assumed and asserted by the great champions of analytic philosophy that modern logic, and the logical analysis of language, are the main weapons against this misleading 'bewitchment by language.' "[21]

Heidegger, like the later Wittgenstein, thus makes a more radical linguistic turn than does classical analytical philosophy. Such a radical turn to language requires us to dispense with the view that the sole legitimate purpose of language is to depict the world truthfully. Though that view was present in modern philosophy generally, it was reinforced by what I have suggested was the restriction of philosophy to truth during the McCarthy era. Good work on the relationship of language to truth is, to be sure, being done, but a lot of good work on other important philosophical issues concerning language, especially its ethical and social dimensions, is not being done.[22]

As a Heidegger-inspired philosopher myself, I can testify that the quasi-scientific concept of truth to which philosophy was relegated during the McCarthy era remains in the psyches of many American philosophers today, too deeply rooted even to be stated, let alone challenged. I have listened to many analytical philosophers of goodwill confess their bafflement at the writings of Jacques Derrida, for example. Derrida's essays, like those of other postmodern philosophers, do not center on theses he is trying to prove but finish, typically, on the brink of a number of unasked questions. The idea that such a thing could even be worth doing, let alone that it could have any right to be called philosophy, continues to be foreign to most American philosophers.

Meantime, philosophers who do not seek a quasi-scientific type of truth continue to be excluded from philosophy departments—including not only our homegrown continental philosophers and pragmatists, but such major thinkers as Hegel, Marx, and Nietzsche, not to mention Derrida, Foucault, and Heidegger. Though philosophy of science has grown closer to the actual scientific communities and practices on which it reflects, analytical philosophy in general remains largely isolated from the rest of the humanities. Richard Rorty's point that it "has pretty well closed itself off from contact with non-analytic philosophy, and lives in its own world," which I quoted in chapter 1, is no ancient insight; it was first published in 1986 and republished in 1991.

A Discipline under Control

As any practitioner of identity politics can testify, an isolated community is more easily controlled than one in which people, or ideas, move freely to and from the outside. So it is no surprise that above the departmental level, American philosophy's disciplinary structure exhibits a degree of establishment control unusual in today's academia. The structures facilitating such control have been in place since the McCarthy era, and in some cases before. Some of them were doubtless innocuous in the small, clubby discipline that philosophy used to be, while others were perhaps necessary when the ill-informed and vicious attacks of the McCarthy era demanded discretion; but they have little business on the contemporary scene. Were it not for the self-perpetuating absence of professional self-knowledge on the part of American philosophers, most would probably have been changed long ago.

One is the divisional structure of the APA, which, as I noted in chapter 2 (following Bruce Wilshire), not so long ago allowed the main organization of American philosophers to be controlled by about sixty well-placed people, and which still relegates half of the APA's membership to something less than full participation.

Another, retained both by the APA and to some extent by its continental counterpart, the Society for Phenomenological and Existential Philosophy (SPEP), is increasingly unusual among academic professional organizations: the centralized program committee. Organizations such as the Modern Language Association and the International Association for Philosophy and Literature allow groups and individual members to propose and organize sessions. Once such a session has been approved—the main constraint is often just the space available—the appointed organizer calls for papers and does the rest. The APA, by contrast, does not trust its members nearly to that extent. All papers are submitted to a single program committee for each division. Members of the committee read them, rank them, and group those that survive the process into sessions.

It is odd that a discipline as self-consciously subspecialized as philosophy, where no public reflection on the entirety of the discipline goes on, should place such emphasis on the centralized selection of papers for its main meetings.[23] In fact, the process is not overly credible. The program committees are usually chaired by and composed of highly intelligent, honest, and dedicated people. Papers in the mainstream areas in which they work receive informed judgments. But offbeat efforts often do not. I remember my own bafflement at some of the papers I was assigned to read as a member of Central Division's 1996 program committee. Anything groundbreaking, of course, will by definition be offbeat, and it is noteworthy that, as Jaako Hintikka has recently complained, APA program offerings are characterized more by safety than by anything else (*APA* 72, no. 5: 51–52).

The idea that any group of (relatively) senior figures, no matter how ramified and dedicated, has the expertise to separate the good from the bad in all fields of philosophy is perhaps suitable for a discipline with few members, a single paradigm, and relatively few new ideas. In a field as large as American philosophy is now, it makes little sense. This has been obliquely recognized by Eastern Division, which has set up an advisory committee to the program committee consisting of three experts in each of twenty-four fields. But this metacommittee is confined to advising the program committee about invited papers. Submissions are still actually judged by the program committee itself.

In recent years, the APA has also increasingly opened its meeting rooms to other groups, such as the Society for Ancient Philosophy and the Society for Symbolic Logic. Those groups run their own meetings, which therefore work somewhat like the regular sessions of other academic associations. In the beginning, they met in the evening and were commonly called "pariah groups." Since 1968, they have been allowed to schedule sessions during the day (though most of them still meet in the late afternoon or evening), and the politically correct term for them has come to be "associated groups." But any APA meeting retains an oddly two-tiered structure: there are those papers that have been judged, by the divisional program committee, to be worthy of APA endorsement and those that have not.

Cronyism also remains a problem at the APA. Its divisional structure continues to privilege Eastern Division, a state of affairs that could begin to be fixed by rotating the all-important December meeting, with its crucial job market, among the three divisions. (Abandoning the divisional structure altogether might be less complicated.)

The pluralist rebellion, which I discussed in chapter 2, has concentrated on the offices of the APA itself, especially that of divisional president. Its effect was to open those offices to people who previously would have been mere outsiders. But the APA's various committees, some of which are quite important, are still generally staffed by the APA Committee on Committees. And as a letter from Felicia Ackerman to *Proceedings and Addresses* points out (*APA* 71, no. 5: 158–59), the committee does not abide by National Endowment for the Humanities (NEH) conflict-of-interest rules: members are free to select their own colleagues and former students for committee service. Under the NEH rules they would not even be allowed in the room when colleagues or former students are discussed for such positions.

Nor is there any limit to committee service: nothing prevents someone from serving on more than one committee simultaneously, or from serving a number of successive terms, even when there are other qualified people who have not recently served. Ackerman concluded by noting that "[s]ome APA members suspect that the APA board is an old boy (and old girl) network that is difficult for outsiders to penetrate." Henry Rosovsky, the Harvard dean suffering from his nightmare of blackballs, would presumably agree. So did the APA's Committee on Committees, which in a response to Ackerman acknowledged that "there is a history which seems to confirm" her point, while also asserting that "progress has been made toward greater openness" (*APA* 72, no. 5: 133–35).

Finally, it is by now standard in most fields for the main journals to be peer reviewed. In philosophy, however, most of the grand old journals—including the *Journal of Philosophy,* the *Philosophical Review,* and the *Review of Metaphysics*—have seen no reason to change their policies of decades past. Editorial decisions on submitted articles are therefore made primarily by the editors themselves rather than by experts in the articles' fields. Philip Gossett, dean of humanities at the University of Chicago, ran up against this in a tenure case when he told the philosophy department that books accepted by major presses and articles in independently reviewed journals were necessary for tenure. The philosophy department asked that this policy not apply to them, and the dean agreed: "While my statement to the Department of Philosophy . . . would have seemed quite normal to Departments of English, History, Art, Music, Romance Languages, Germanic Studies, etc., I can understand that it may be inappropriate to a discipline in which publication patterns differ from those prevailing in other humanistic disciplines" (*APA* 70, no. 5: 168–69). Peer review is not, of course, limited to other humanistic disciplines; it is basic to the sciences as well.

The dean's lack of favor toward such venerable and uniquely philosophical practices as unrefereed journals and invited papers was enough to lead Howard Stein, a professor in the Chicago philosophy department, to request reduction in rank to the level of associate professor. The dean told Stein that there was nothing to stop him from calling himself an associate professor if he wished but that there was no formal procedure for such reduction. Stein thereupon began to call himself an associate professor, thus expressing his chagrin at the dean's attack on the structure of his discipline (*APA* 70, no. 2: 160–61).

These practices—centralized program committees for the most important conferences, APA committee cronyism, and unreviewed journals—do not function in isolation from one another. Together, they constitute an apparatus of control over philosophical institutions above the departmental level that begins to look positively Foucauldian. The usefulness of such control in a time like the McCarthy era speaks for itself: philosophy needed to avoid public embarrassment at all cost. But it is long outdated and comes at a high price, for disciplinary control fosters intellectual exclusion, which leads, in turn, to intellectual sterility, collegial disrepute, and administrative disfavor.

After the Soviet invasion of Czechoslovakia in 1968, the philosophy department of Charles University in Prague was transferred from the humanities faculty to the journalism school. This seemingly odd move actually made a good deal of bureaucratic sense. The Communists had already installed a full apparatus for surveillance of journalists, and the prominence of philosophers in support of the Dubček regime certainly showed that they needed to be watched. Fifty years after the attacks of the McCarthy era made care and discretion necessary, American philosophy continues to police itself.

Analytical and Continental: Heidegger versus Carnap

The most intellectually crippling characteristic of American philosophy today is without doubt the ongoing split between its analytical and continental dispensations, for it means that philosophy is divided into two groups that have little understanding of or sympathy with one another. That this situation has now been in place for almost half a century also bespeaks a certain inability on the part of American philosophers to sort out their issues and get their own intellectual house in order. Since philosophy is supposed to be all about getting your intellectual house in order, this failure to do so leads, like so many others, to credibility problems with administrators, trustees, and the general public. As Jorge J. E. Gracia put it in a 1998 report published in *APA:* "And never mind that some efforts have been made by members of both camps to bring about a rapprochement. In fact, these two groups consistently and regularly disparage each other, undermine the credentials of each other, and seldom, if ever, engage in serious dialogue. A house so bitterly divided cannot justify a positive attitude toward itself by those who do not live in it."[24] I will argue here that this split is in large part a relict of the McCarthy era.

As with the job crisis, the analytical-continental split has been given the wrong name: it is not really a split, but a distribution, an assignment of complementary values. The two sides of a split are, after all, more or less equal. But that is not the case with analytical and continental philosophy, which seem to have been assigned the status of "essence" and "accident," respectively. Hegel argued in his *Logic* that when one thing establishes itself as the essence of something else, as the fixed and definitive formula for what that something else is, there is always in that latter something a residuum that, since it is excluded from the essence, can only show up (*scheinen*) as a passing play of accidents.[25] Thus, it is not surprising that in the United States analytical philosophy, which has become the essence of philosophy in general, has stood on its own internal resources and developed from them for more than fifty years.

Continental philosophy, its philosophical Other, has assumed a variety of identities.

In the beginning, in the Germany of the 1930s, the logical positivists—true to their Kantian origins—pitted themselves against the metaphysicians. The polemics were, as polemics are and often ought to be, acute. In my own opinion, the positivists won an important and resounding victory. But in the climate of the 1950s in America, they—and their victory—were often poorly understood.

In 1932, Carnap published his essay "Überwindung der Metaphysik durch logische Analyse der Sprache"; translated by Arthur Pap, it received its first English publication in A. J. Ayer's 1959 anthology, *Logical Positivism.*[26] In this essay, Carnap includes a quote from Heidegger's "Was ist Metaphysik?" This quote, as Carnap gives it, became rather famous. One of the phrases it contained became a virtual catchword for the kind of muddleheaded pseudoprofundity that analytical philosophers rightly wanted to avoid: *das Nichts nichtet,* often translated as "the Nothing nothings." Because of this, Carnap's quote from Heidegger provides a good example of the way American philosophers (I among them) failed to understand *either* Carnap *or* Heidegger. I will, therefore, discuss it in some detail.

In Carnap's rendering, Heidegger says the following:

> What is to be investigated is Being only and—nothing else; being alone and further—nothing; solely being, and beyond being—nothing. What about this Nothing? . . . Does the Nothing exist only because the Not, i.e., the Negation, exists? Or is it the other way around? Does Negation and the Not exist only because the Nothing exists? . . . We assert: the Nothing is prior to the Not and the Negation. . . . Where do we seek the Nothing? How do we find the Nothing? . . . We know the Nothing. . . . Anxiety reveals the Nothing. . . . That for which and because of which we were anxious was "really"—nothing. Indeed: the Nothing itself—as such—was present. . . . What about this Nothing? The Nothing itself nothings.[27]

Carnap quoted this, he notes, at a time when Heidegger was the most influential philosopher in Germany. Anyone who read Carnap's article could be expected to have at least a passing familiarity with Heidegger's essay, which had been delivered as his inaugural address in Freiburg and had first been published in 1929, three years before Carnap quoted it. But though Heidegger's essay had been given an English translation in 1949, ten years before the English appearance of Carnap's article, it was not well known in this country (an adequate translation, by David Farrell Krell, first appeared only in 1977).[28]

The translation of Heidegger published in Carnap's article, to begin with, is often tendentious. The German version of the first sentence, for example, does not refer to Being at all (*das Sein*) but to beings (*das Seiende*); Pap's English version thus violates one of Heidegger's most basic distinctions, the ontological difference between Being and beings. Moreover, the bizarre capitalizations in the translated text are not Heidegger's, who capitalizes in accord with standard German usage (I will follow Krell in capitalizing my own discussions of this text in the standard English way).

More important than these problems, however, is that the first and last words of Carnap's quote are, in Krell's translation, some eight pages apart. The elisions (". . .") are therefore massive. German readers of Carnap's essay would have been acquainted with the essay in toto; they would know what had been elided. American readers (I was among them) did not.

Let me give *some* of the elided material.

The first elision ("What about this Nothing? . . .") omits, along with much else, the following:

> Our first approach to this question has something unusual about it. In our asking we posit the nothing in advance as something that "is" such and such; we posit it as a being. But that is exactly what it is distinguished from. Interrogating the nothing—asking about what and how it, the nothing, is—turns what is interrogated into its own opposite. The question deprives itself of its own object. ("WM" 98)

Carnap's quote suggests that Heidegger moves directly from one question ("What about this nothing?") to a second, which, asking about the nothing's ground, presumes the nothing's existence. But Heidegger does not do this at all. Instead, he calls his question itself into question. This questioning of his own question continues in a second passage, also elided by Carnap:

> For the nothing is the negation of the totality of beings; it is nonbeing pure and simple. But with that we bring the nothing under the higher de-

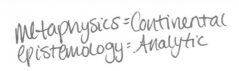
Metaphysics = Continental
epistemology = Analytic

termination of the negative, viewing it as the negated. However, according to the reigning and never challenged doctrine of "logic", negation is a specific act of the intellect. How, then, can we . . . wish to brush the intellect aside? Are we altogether sure about what we are presupposing in this matter? ("WM" 99)

    The question about the relation between the nothing and the not comes, in Carnap's quote, entirely out of the blue. But Heidegger in fact introduces it via a rather clear distinction: the not is the result of negation, which as logic tells us resides not in things but in our thought about things. If I say that the stop sign is not green, I am not saying that a property called "not green" inheres in the stop sign in the way that red does but that the predicate "green" does not apply to the stop sign. That the sign is not green is thus a result of my thinking about it, in a way that its being red is not. Is the not-greenness of the sign, then, the same thing as the nothing? If so, then the nothing must also be a result of my thought. This is the presupposition that Heidegger wants to question. He wants to consider the possibility that we do experience lacks in the world, lacks that are apparent to us before we think about things so explicitly as to deny various predicates of them. And he also wants to question (once again) his own questioning of this.

    The second elision (following "Does Negation and the Not exist only because the Nothing exists? . . .") is, in its entirety, of the following: "That has not been decided; it has not even been raised expressly as a question." Heidegger then, in words that Carnap does quote, goes on to "assert" (*behaupten*) an answer to that question. It seems, then, that Heidegger is just blurting dogma with this assertion. But given that he has just said that the question has not been raised, much less decided, and given that the words immediately following Carnap's quote, also elided by him, are "If this thesis is right," it would not be out of line to translate *behaupten* as "suggest."

    Heidegger does not then plunge into a headlong quest of the nothing, as Carnap's text suggests. The third elision (following "How do we find the Nothing? . . .") omits the following:

    But if we do not let ourselves be misled by the formal impossibility of the question of the nothing; if we pose the question in spite of this; then we must at least satisfy what remains the basic demand for the possible advancing of every question. If the nothing itself is to be questioned as we have

Object essentially

Can't be made into an object/subject it's only negation

been questioning it, then it must be given beforehand. We must be able to encounter it. ("WM" 100)

Heidegger here openly concedes that his question is formally impossible according to logic, that is, is logically ill formed. And he is claiming that to formulate something so absurd, even if as a question, there must be some sort of experience that leads us to do so. This claim, of course, is nothing other than the Meno paradox, first advanced by Plato in the dialogue of that name: we must know something to some extent and in some way even to ask about it. Hence, Heidegger's next quoted claim—"We know the Nothing"—is not the dogmatic asseveration that Carnap's text makes it sound. Nor, in fact, is it very strong: it is saying simply that for us to ask the logically ill-formed question "How is it with the nothing?" we need to have some *experience* that pushes us to do so.

The sentence from which the words "we know the Nothing" are taken immediately continues:

if only as a word we rattle off every day. For this common nothing that glides so inconspicuously through our chatter, blanched with the anemic pallor of the obvious, we can without hesitating furnish a definition. The nothing is the complete negation of the totality of beings. ("WM" 100)

There then follows a discussion of anxiety, which relies largely on the phenomenological account Heidegger has given of anxiety in *Being and Time* and which I will not go into here.[29] Our experience of the nothing—that is, for Heidegger, the nothing itself—is defined as an ingredient in this experience, an ingredient that he calls "nihilation" (*nichten*). And so we get "the Nothing nothings" (or, as Krell has it, "The nothing itself nihilates" ["WM" 105]).

Finally, the view expressed in the first sentence of Carnap's quote is *not* Heidegger's, even when we allow for the mistranslation. It is a view that Heidegger attributes to the metaphysically guided scientist, that is, to someone who sees the overall scientific task as accounting for all that is—and leaving "nothing" out. The entire essay, then, is a critique of the metaphysical claim to give "theories of everything"—a critique with which, one suspects, Carnap had sympathies. Carnap, of course, misses this dimension of the essay altogether and takes Heidegger to be exemplifying metaphysics rather than criticizing it.

The main problem with the English version of Carnap's essay is that it makes what is actually a rather subtle and interesting, if ultimately unconvincing, argument look like a string of dogmatic assertions. Heidegger begins with what he sees as science's claim to explain everything. Scientific explanation thus, in the ideal case, leaves out nothing. But how, then, can we say that "nothing" lies beyond science's explanatory powers? Heidegger admits, we saw, that this way of putting it amounts to an illegitimate reification. Nonetheless, he presses on because, he argues, there is an experience at the bottom of that claim: an experience that metaphysical science wants to occlude by explaining it, so to speak, away. As philosophers often do, Heidegger then turns to ordinary language, to the "anemic pallor of the obvious," for a clue. The clue is that the experience in question is not cognitive (and hence does not come under the rules of logic) but emotive in nature: anxiety. And so on. All of this is elided by the selection of quotes Carnap gives, leaving the impression for an English-speaking reader (I was one) that Heidegger is an absolute buffoon who attempts to philosophize without knowing the first thing about logic.

What remains of Carnap's polemic against Heidegger when all this is recognized? Astonishingly, the answer is "everything." When read in the light of Heidegger's actual essay, Carnap's article turns out to be clearly directed, not against someone who presumes to do philosophy without knowing logic but against someone who does know logic (Heidegger's doctoral dissertation was on logic) but is turning away from it.[30] Carnap thinks Heidegger is a turncoat. But in the minds of many Americans who read the essay, Carnap thinks Heidegger is a fool. Both sides of the Carnap-Heidegger polemic completely escaped those American readers, who did not understand Carnap any better than they understood Heidegger.

Analytical and Continental: Subsequent Developments

In such fashion, the logical positivists carried the day against the metaphysicians. They also, as I noted in chapter 2, carried it against the pragmatists. Moreover, both victories were, at least in the minds of the victors, complete: there was nothing, or nothing much, to be salvaged from either of the two vanquished approaches. The pragmatists, pursuing not truth but confirmation, were in competition with empirical science. The metaphysicians, pursuing truth but without benefit of logic, were as well. The latter group was illogical and hence unphilosophical; the former mistakenly took philosophy for a first-order enterprise. The only point of reading the writings of either metaphysicians or pragmatists was to search for those few nuggets that may have found their way into those writings, either independently of the intentions of their authors or against them. But why, in the words of many analysts in the 1960s, bother with that? Why not rather spend one's time reading people who did not begin with major confusions? Why, in the words of the later analytical philosopher mentioned previously in this chapter, teach the mistakes?

The next incarnation of analytical philosophy's Other, in the 1960s, was as phenomenology and existentialism. Those approaches generally avoided pursuing truths about nonempirical realms, and so could not easily be discounted as metaphysical. Phenomenology was the brainchild of the German philosopher Edmund Husserl, Heidegger's erstwhile mentor. He gave it birth at the turn of the century, from the same broadly neo-Kantian ferment that produced the logical positivists.[31] Its basic move was to "bracket" the actual existence of objects, which cannot be known to us with certainty, and to describe only the appearances of objects to us (whence its freedom from metaphysics).

The word "appearance," of course, is ambiguous (in English as in German). It can mean either the act or the process of appearing itself, of which phenomenology would investigate the modes and structures, or it can simply mean the way something appears, that is, looks, to me. Left at the latter level, as it all too often was, phenomenology was little more than an excuse for self-indulgent blather. Husserl himself, a mathematician, took it at the former level. He believed, roughly put, that the kind of introspection championed by intuitionistic philosophers of mathematics such as L. E. J. Brouwer could be expanded into accounts of the appearing of objects. I personally find this view unpalatable and probably wrong, but it is neither implausible nor an abandonment of rigor.

Husserl's sometime protégé, Martin Heidegger, sought another kind of discipline for phenomenology. He believed that the basic structures and modes of appearing were constitutive of our lives on a very basic level: we are, in sum, how things appear to us (nihilation being, in his view, one of those ways). This meant that those structures and modes were not susceptible to any kind of mathematical treatment, since not all appearing-to is even, strictly, cognitive in nature. When I use a hammer, for example, the hammer appears to me, but not in such a way that I am explicitly aware of it; if I am, I will never hit the nail. Mathematics and logic were of little help in understanding this sort of thing. For a control on his own interpretations, Heidegger turned instead to history, and in particular to the history of philosophy. In the first phase of his philosophical work, he advanced a phenomenological account of human life, or existence, in close connection with Aristotle's *Nicomachean Ethics*.[32] Published in his magnum opus *Being and Time*, this account of human life is often called the "analytic of Dasein," using Heidegger's untranslatable word for the kind of being that we are.

When the analytic of Dasein arrived in France, Heidegger's approach lost most of its historical grounding and encountered the literary interests and political commitments of thinkers such as Simone de Beauvoir, Albert Camus, and Jean-Paul Sartre. The result was existentialism, an approach in which philosophical writings allowed themselves to be judged more on the acceptance they found from readers than on their own methodological rigor. (This does not of itself make phenomenology unscientific, except to people like logical positivists. Many philosophers of science today—I will discuss a couple in chapter 4—take a similar view: beliefs, or theories, are scientific when a community of scientists evaluates them.)

Those approaches migrated to America in the late 1950s and 1960s in two decidedly ahistorical and asocial forms: as an introspective phenomenology and as a radically individualistic existentialism. Their shared quietistic individualism, as might be expected, served phenomenology and existentialism well in their new land, where they supplanted metaphysics and pragmatism as the privileged Others of analytical philosophy.

But analytical philosophy had by now both achieved its dominance and forgotten how that achievement had come about. This meant that there was no need to reopen old questions about its justice. So phenomenology and existentialism did not receive the kind of vigorous polemic that metaphysics and pragmatism had enjoyed. Instead, they were just assumed to be either metaphysics under a new name, or mere subjective prattle.

This was the sort of atmosphere that gave birth to SPEP, the Society for Phenomenological and Existential Philosophy, in 1961. The Hegel

Society of America was founded seven years later, and other societies of the sort proliferated, devoted to thinkers such as Heidegger, Husserl, Merleau-Ponty, and Sartre. They were accompanied by such further groups as the Society for the Advancement of American Philosophy, which is devoted to pragmatism, the Society for Phenomenology and the Human Sciences, and the International Association for Philosophy and Literature.

None of these societies was originally intended to be a place from which analytical philosophy was excluded, but they all sought to accommodate work that was outside what they saw as its unjustifiably narrow parameters. Hence the founding myths of these societies tend to begin with a group of philosophers who were tired of being laughed at and derided (not polemically refuted, as earlier) and who decided to get together in a space apart to discuss their interests without the restraints imposed by their analytical colleagues.

But this strategy had its downside as well. Gathering the members of any discursive community together so they can meet face-to-face is in general a good thing. It is especially good when, as was (and is) often the case with phenomenologists and existentialists, they are the sole representatives of their approach in their home departments and have no one to talk with there. But when the members of a discursive community encounter each other *only* in the absence of outsiders, their insularity grows, and this has been the case (for example) with SPEP. Philosophers older than I am have bemoaned to me, in recent years, the dwindling sense for analytical philosophy on the programs (and among the members).

Such intellectual self-isolation also fosters ignorance among the majority. Many analytical philosophers, for example, continued to assume through the 1980s that Hegel was well and safely dead, when, in fact, his thought was undergoing a kind of renaissance in North America. I once astonished a young analytical philosopher by informing him that the Hegel Society of America had almost four hundred members. "We're so provincial!" he exclaimed.

The proliferation of philosophical societies in the 1960s was an early sign that phenomenology and existentialism were not the whole of continental philosophy. By the end of the decade, European philosophy had begun to shake off both the strictures of phenomenology and the concerns of existentialism. Its representatives in North America, and the Other to analytical philosophy, were again redefined—or at least renamed. The chosen word this time was "continental." Like the divisions of the APA, then, analytical philosophy's most recent privileged Other is now characterized solely by geography. On the one hand, this is good, because since geography is, or should be, completely irrelevant to philosophy, a movement named for a region cannot be very exclusionary. Continental philosophy today is a charming, motley collection of everything analytical philosophers dislike. Not only existentialists and phenomenologists of various sorts, but also numerous varieties of deconstructionists, genealogists (both Nietzschean and Foucauldian), theologians, dialecticians, literary theorists, and historians of philosophy, jostle companionably in the hallways and lobbies of its various meetings.

But there are also some problems with this nomenclature—and with what it names. The intellectual diversity in which continental philosophers rightly glory (declaring that the only real opposite of "continental" is "insular") hides a provinciality of its own, for the continent after which these philosophers are named, and to which they therefore look, is Europe. There is an underlying feeling that continental philosophy's true home is there, whereas the American version is a transplant, a colony, or even a bush league. Hence the eagerness with which continental philosophers, come summer, abandon the United States for institutes and programs in Europe, or (at any time of year) for study at archives and universities in Belgium, France, Germany, and Italy. (I once had a continental philosopher explain to me, not implausibly, that the reason analytical philosophers dominated his home department was that they were always on campus and ready to vote, having nowhere interesting to go.)

There is, in turn, a certain hero worship of Europeans at the larger conferences, such as SPEP, where of the two plenary sessions one traditionally goes to a woman and the other to a European. Hence, as Reiner Schürmann has noted, where analytical philosophers increasingly argue like lawyers, their continental counterparts increasingly behave like journalists, reporting to the world what Jacques or Jürgen wrote last year—or, if one is *bien branché*, what he said last week.[33] This makes it rather difficult for American continental philosophers with something original to say to gain a hearing: not only are they ignored by the analysts, but also they must fight against the Eurocentric prejudice of their own confreres.

The situation is increasingly difficult because Europe, intellectually, is not really doing very much. The great chance to build a truly European philosophy was to open a critical dialogue between Jürgen Habermas and Jacques Derrida. No such dialogue even remotely came to pass, and in the epoch of the European Union, French and German philosophy have gone separate, Balkanized ways. In France, the first generation of postmodernists—Derrida, Foucault, and others—is giving way to epigones, as might be expected, to more traditionalist thinkers such as the Catholic philosopher Jean-Luc Marion, and to historically informed versions of analytical philosophy such as those pursued by Jacques Bouveresse, Pascal Engel, and Antonia Soulez.[34] In Germany, philosophy has always been dominated by historians such as Dieter Henrich and Michael Theunissen. The main exception, the neo-Kantian critical theory of Karl-Otto Apel and Jürgen Habermas, is producing epigones of its own. In short, nothing new and interesting is presently on the horizon as viewed from North America, which makes it increasingly difficult to draw inspiration from the Continent.

The label "continental" is deeply misleading in another way. A large and important component of SPEP consists of pragmatists, who have emerged from the eclipse they went into during the McCarthy era and are reasserting the merits of their approach. But they are not "continental," because they are not from Europe. In spite of the importance of William James for phenomenology and of Charles Sanders Peirce for the critical theory of Karl-Otto Apel, for example, a line tends to be drawn between them and their continental descendants. (At the 1998 SPEP meeting, the program announced the formation of a Society for Continental and American Philosophy to overcome the growing estrangement of the two fields.)

Through all this, the defining and enduring feature is the analytical-continental split, with analytical philosophy serving as the stable essence and continental philosophy constituting a passing and motley play of accidents. Though well-intentioned rhetoric about bridge building and openness abounds, the reality is quite different. When analytical philosophers talk about being open to other traditions, they usually mean that they are willing to accept that those other approaches may have interesting theses and useful arguments to offer. The idea that continental philosophy could, and should, consist in something other than theses and arguments was not even broached for an analytical audience until Richard Rorty's 1979 *Philosophy and the Mirror of Nature*.[35] Rorty's insight led to no discernible changes where it counts—in the hiring practices of philosophy departments. According to a 1995 survey, continental philosophy provided 9 percent of job applicants, but only 4 percent of the jobs were in that field—the largest oversupply in any field of philosophy.[36]

This shortfall is perhaps a result of the fact that the situation in American philosophy today is basically the one expressed by the logician I quoted in chapter 2: continental philosophy gets the conferences (some of them); analytical philosophy keeps the major graduate programs. Coming (by definition!) out of less-than-favored programs, continental philosophers find it more difficult to get jobs, and the exclusion persists. I have quoted Hilary Putnam's testimony that one became an analytical philosopher in the 1950s by learning "what *not* to like and what not to consider philosophy." Putnam continues, "I think that is a terrible thing, and that it should be stopped in all schools, movements, and philosophy departments."[37] But his call, like Rorty's and the increasingly numerous calls of others, goes largely unheeded, at least when it counts—at hiring and tenure time.

As I will argue in chapter 5, if we ask what sort of philosophical differences can be found between the two traditions, we find ourselves right back in the McCarthy era, for philosophers such as Hegel, Nietzsche, Heidegger, Derrida, Foucault, and Deleuze all reject the timelessness of sentential or propositional truth as their goal. Analysts continue to accept it as their only goal, just as they were told to do fifty years ago. As Reiner Schürmann has written, the long-awaited dialogue between analytical and continental philosophy is taking place in Europe, not in America.[38]

Conclusions

The primary reason all these institutions and attitudes persist appears to be demographic. Consider, to begin, the situation of American philosophy in 1960, at the end of the McCarthy era. The discipline had been under attack for about twelve years. Since the average philosophical career is about thirty-five years (assuming a Ph.D. at age thirty and retirement at age sixty-five, which was standard in those days), a third of the profession active in 1960 would have been hired during that period of time. Their education would naturally reflect the prejudices and fears of those days, which, as the previous chapter has argued, would bias them toward viewing philosophy as a sort of scientific enterprise. Some of their older colleagues would have had such interests and approaches all along, and would be allied with the younger set. If we imagine a department of fifteen people—not an unusual size—about five would have come of age during the McCarthy era. Another three or so would be older: kindred spirits who now found themselves no longer a minority but the senior figures in an emerging majority interested in scientific approaches to epistemology and second-order approaches to everything else.

What about those among the remaining seven who had interests in such fields as problems in ethics or social and political philosophy, or in approaches inspired by literature and religion rather than science? What about those who were pragmatists or whose work was inspired by the history of philosophy? Presumably, if they were still around at all, they would to some extent have shelved or curbed those interests and approaches for the previous twelve years. A conference on symbolic logic, for example, would have been much safer and easier to organize in 1957, or even in 1967, than one on dialectics. To an incoming student, the fields and approaches favored by such philosophers would have looked like antiquated areas in which nothing much had happened for quite a long time. The students would have been right in their judgments, of course—but for different reasons than they supposed.

The intellectual havoc wrought by the McCarthy era was thus unevenly distributed: nonscientistic approaches were at a significant disadvantage. In addition, the younger generation of philosophers—both analytical and continental—happened to be on an exclusionary warpath unprecedented, according to the sociologist Randall Collins, in the entire history of philosophy.[39] Finally, as I have suggested, McCarthyite attacks were stronger at universities that housed graduate programs. If the students in question were graduate students, they would naturally gravitate to the younger professors in the seemingly more dynamic fields, as well as to their older allies. Thus, the real fears and necessary accommodations of the McCarthy era—converted into prejudices by being left unspoken—seem to have transformed themselves into permanent features of the philosophical landscape.

As always, there are other explanations for some of these characteristics. The prestige of science, for example—though admittedly floating on an ocean of money provided by the government and private industry—is no invention of the logical positivists, and fully merits the serious philosophical reflection it now gets. As I suggested in chapter 2, a sort of fear of the history of philosophy is deeply American.

And there are other possible explanations. The failure of continental philosophy to break into the American mainstream, at least in the more prestigious locales, may have been encouraged by the fact that many developments in recent European philosophy have been brought to this country by priests and have found homes at Catholic universities. This plays into what has been called the "last respectable prejudice" in America—anti-Catholicism.[40] But is that prejudice really so strong? Are not many able practitioners of mainstream American philosophy Catholic themselves, or of Catholic background?

The stasis in American philosophy can in part be explained by the fact that, since 1967, the job market has been virtually nonexistent: relatively few new people have joined the profession, and the baby boom generation is only now coming to provide the critical mass in some departments. These facts are painfully undeniable, but they can only be responsible for the recent stasis if we accept that new ideas will flourish only among new people, that older philosophers are somehow unable to criticize or revise their basic perspectives. This invites us to view most American philosophy professors, themselves quite senior, as members of a sort of Brezhnevite generation, unwilling to reexamine the views they adopted during the "Stalinist" purges of another era.

A more complex alternative explanation is cultural diffusion. American philosophy in the 1950s came to resemble rather closely the philosophy of two tired empires: Great Britain, where as I have noted philosophy had fallen into xenophobic doldrums in the years preceding the Official Secrets Act, and Austria, where open discussion of political and social issues was virtually impossible.[41] This is at least partly explainable on cultural and historical rather than political grounds. Britain and America, already speaking a common language, had cooperated in the World Wars, while Europe remained largely cut off. The logical positivists were mainly Austrians forced from their homes by Hitler. In contrast to the phenomenologists and critical theorists, who tended to come from Germany, they felt themselves committed to the American context. Unlike the critical theorists, for example, they did not leave to reestablish themselves in Europe after the war, and unlike the phenomenologists they did not cluster in Teutonic enclaves (such as the New School for Social Research at that time). But this account cannot explain such things as the rapid eclipse of pragmatism after the war; the failure of ordinary language analysis, itself a British import, to flourish on our shores;[42] the strange persistence of the 1950s consensus, like a neurotic symptom that suggests that something important is being repressed; or the even stranger silence of American philosophers with respect to the whole issue of the McCarthy era.

Except for the model of cultural diffusion, none of the competing explanations I have discussed—the prestige of science, fear of the history of philosophy, anti-Catholicism, the job market—suffices to explain even one of the features of American philosophy I have discussed here, much less all of them. This does not mean that they, and probably other factors, did not contribute to the current situation. What we can say is that the McCarthyite hypothesis has as much empirical plausibility as, and more explanatory power than, its competitors and deserves at least to be discussed.

Such discussion is, I suggest, absolutely necessary if American philosophers—and intellectuals in general—are to enjoy intellectual freedom today. For freedom from political interference not to be a chimera, it cannot be won by fiat. We cannot simply do against the McCarthyites what Lyndon Johnson was urged to do in Vietnam—declare that victory has been won and leave the field. True intellectual freedom must be fought for, not assumed, and the fight must include two things that American philosophy studiously avoids: critical examination of its own historical roots and open dialogue with outsiders.

4

Culture Wars, Culture Bores

Philosophy's Absence
from American Academic Culture

I have argued not only that the McCarthy era affected American philosophy at the time but also that some of its effects have been ongoing. One of those effects, I suggested, was the isolation of philosophy both from other academic disciplines and from American culture at large. What effects has this sort of isolation had? What is missing, as a result of it, from American culture and, in particular, from the American academy?

Absences, I have said before, are difficult to document—but sometimes they become ludicrous. Two recent examples of philosophical ignorance on the part of educated Americans illustrate this. First, Harvey Cox has demonstrated the oddly theological language in which supposedly tough-minded businesspeople think about the market: "[I]n fact there lies embedded in the business pages an entire theology, which is comparable in scope if not profundity to that of Thomas Aquinas or

Karl Barth. It needed only to be systematized for a whole new *summa* to take shape."[1]

That people wish to deify the market is a psychological or a social problem; that they do it unknowingly is, or ought to be, a philosophical problem.

Another example of the insouciance with which even American intellectuals can maintain the most amazing ignorance of philosophy came to the fore in a *New York Times* article of February 2, 1999.[2] The article recounted findings by psychologists at the University of Rochester and Knox College to the effect that people who seek "extrinsic goals" such as money, fame, and beauty tend to be less happy than people who value "intrinsic goals" such as self-awareness and close relationships. The psychologists were unable, however, to say why this is so.

Nowhere in the article was there the slightest awareness, either on the part of either the journalist who wrote it or the scientists who figured in it, that in fact that very question had been thoroughly argued out by Greek philosophers two millennia earlier. Aristotle, for example, pointed out that the bestowal of fame depends on the bestower more than the person to whom it is given, and so fame can be easily lost.[3] The life of moneymaking, he says, is cramped and compelled, and no one really wants money anyway: they want what it can buy.[4] Many arguments, says Aristotle, have been thrown away on this subject; but he probably did not expect his own to be among them.[5]

It is not as if this material were buried in some arcane manuscript under lock and key in the Vatican libraries; this kind of thing is usually covered in introductory philosophy courses. When a friend of mine, who teaches such a course in the city college system of Chicago, showed the *Times* article to his students—who had just finished studying Aristotle—they burst out laughing.

The absence of philosophy from American cultural life has not gone unnoticed, however. In an article in the *Baltimore Sun* of January 12, 1999, *Sun* reporter Michael Hill wrote:

> In the last week of December, some of the top names in philosophy gathered here for the annual meeting of the Eastern Division of the American Philosophical Association. Were such a gathering to have taken place in a city in Europe . . . the media would have trained their attention on the affair, eager to learn the thoughts of the educated elite.

But this convention passed, as it does most every year, with hardly any-one outside the prescribed limits of professional philosophy paying any at-tention. . . . Whatever these philosophers are saying, they are saying it only to one another.[6]

Laments about this state of affairs have occasionally come from within philosophy itself. Jorge J. E. Gracia, in a 1998 report published in *APA,* writes:

> Philosophy has no place in American public life. There are no discus-sions of public policy which include philosophy. Philosophers are generally excluded from policy-making bodies or posts in which they can have se-rious influence on the development of public policy. . . . The cold shoulder that philosophers get . . . is not to be perceived as part of an overall attitude toward academics. [The hostility of some politicians to academics in gen-eral] has not deterred academics in fields other than philosophy—law, po-litical science, economics, art, sociology, medicine, engineering, or the sciences—from being appointed to important posts in the government or from having their opinions on important matters of public policy sought and considered by the country's political leadership.[7]

Gracia's complaints were somewhat overdrawn—William Bennett, the former secretary of health, education, and welfare, was trained as a philosopher, for example—but they were not off the mark. They were seconded, in the same issue of *APA,* by Robert Audi:

> Consider national panels, programs on TV and radio, and large com-missions established by governments to explore major social problems. In the U.S. at least, philosophers and their works appear far too infrequently relative to their pertinence to the subjects at hand. . . . Few foundations substantially support basic philosophical research and I believe that colleges and universities across the country and perhaps worldwide are tending to provide less and less research support in the form of, for instance, internal fellowships and replacement funds for faculty going on leave.[8]

Audi presents no evidence that the problems with philosophy are world-wide. In fact, in other countries—countries such as France and Ger-many, which did not have a McCarthy era or an analog to it—philoso-phy is, as Hill notes, a much more forceful presence on the cultural scene than it is in America.

General Effects of the McCarthy Era on American Culture

Nicholas Rescher wrote in 1993 that insofar as American philosophy has any influence at all beyond its own borders, that influence is confined to academics in other fields.[9] In the rest of this chapter, I will simply assume the basic absence of American philosophy from the culture in general, as illustrated and bemoaned above. My focus will be on philosophy's absence even from those areas where Rescher thinks it may retain some influence—from the recent history of the university as an institution (particularly during the protest movements of the 1960s) and from certain aspects of the contemporary academic intellectual community.

First, however, some contextual sketching is in order. It is beyond dispute that the McCarthy era had enormous and lasting consequences for American culture in the broadest sense. The effects of McCarthyism on Hollywood alone, to take one example, were clearly considerable. The Hollywood Ten, a group of blacklisted screenwriters, were among the most famous martyrs of the times, and there is little doubt that their absence from active screenwriting affected the development of the American movie industry in important ways. Moreover, though the tumult of the McCarthy era hurt certain careers, it helped others. Ronald Reagan, to name just one, began his political career by introducing a loyalty oath for the members of the Screen Actors Guild.[10]

But beyond such famous cases as these, the cultural effects of the McCarthy era remain almost unknown. On the one hand, they tend to involve absences—the absences of certain people from their professions or the absence of certain ideas and discourses from the academy.[11] We will never know what movies the Hollywood Ten might have written had they been free to work openly, or what novels, plays, and poems might have come to be if other authors had not been frightened by their example. On the other hand, the fact that certain careers were also *helped* by the McCarthy era often compounds the ongoing ignorance. Those whose rise to success began with political cowardice and accommodation are unlikely to want the matter discussed.

Certain general features of the contemporary American cultural landscape seem, however, clearly to continue trends established during the McCarthy era. One is the gulf that even today divides art from politics much more thoroughly in America than elsewhere. Though there are valiant counterexamples, the United States does not in general have committed novelists like Günter Grass and filmmakers such as Jean-Luc Godard, and (outside of hip-hop) it produces relatively few politically controversial performers such as Sinead O'Connor. When artists do have political commitments, they tend to keep them out of their art. Barbara Kingsolver has suggested that this situation dates from a massive "cave in" to McCarthyism on the part of critics in the 1950s.[12] Novelists, filmmakers, painters, and singers whose political commitments were evident in their work found it harder to get good reviews.

The McCarthy era is doubtless not the sole reason the United States has not produced any George Bernard Shaws or Aleksandr Solzhenitsyns—authors Kingsolver refers to—to say nothing of Grasses or Godards.[13] Indeed, art with overtly political themes has never had an easy time of it in the United States, perhaps because Americans do not respect politics enough to make the political sphere a plausible setting for the great and momentous action dear to traditional artists. But it is a fact that artists of a certain important sort cannot easily coexist with the kind of gulf Kingsolver laments, a gulf that leaves little even to serious novelists except the private themes usually explored by popular music: love and violence.

Some effects of the McCarthy era, to be sure, are specific enough to be readily visible today. Many of the tactics of the McCarthyite cultural police have been retained and expanded, in quite specific ways, by more recent American inquisitors. The FBI's tactics with Robert Bellah in the summer of 1954, to which I referred in chapter 1, read uncannily like a low-budget version of a more recent, and more famous, interrogation of a young American by government agents: "One week after meeting with [Faculty of Arts and Sciences Dean McGeorge] Bundy, I was picked up on the street by two FBI agents and taken to the Boston office for interrogation. I suppose that technically I went voluntarily but it did not feel very voluntary. . . . Most of the meeting and one subsequent meeting were devoted to more or less intense psychological pressure to get me to name other people. I insisted resolutely on my moral position but I was impressed that they came up with names and events I had long forgotten. Indeed I wondered whether the real purpose of all this was not information, which they seemed to have in superabundance, but some further form of cooperation."[14]

Bellah's account foreshadows, in detail, the way Special Prosecutor

Kenneth Starr treated a similarly youthful and uncertain Monica Lewinsky almost fifty years later. The main difference is that whereas Bellah's interrogators took him to FBI headquarters, Lewinsky's took her to a room at the Ritz-Carlton.[15]

Much as postwar Poland could exhibit what was sometimes called "Anti-Semitism without Jews," blaming Jews for all of Poland's problems decades after the Polish Jewish community had been virtually destroyed, so post-Communist America developed various forms of McCarthyism even without Communists. The House Committee on Un-American Activities itself found eager successors, decades later, among those whom Robert Hughes in 1995 called "the young velociraptors in Congress"— the ones who gutted affirmative action and tried to end funding for the arts and humanities.[16] The fact that by then the Communist world no longer even existed hardly deterred them, or the press, which—as it had forty years before—gave them the publicity they needed to succeed.[17]

Against this background, it is not surprising that the views of Raymond B. Allen—the claim that only their possession of truth entitles scholars to speak out on socially controversial issues, and that only their pursuit of it entitles them to anything at all—should be found in the culture wars of the 1980s and 1990s, sometimes in surprising ways. In 1956, for example, Edward Shils could write feelingly of the "depredations of Senators McCarthy and McCarron."[18] But in 1993, no less a journal than the *American Scholar* could publish his thoroughly Allenian reduction of free inquiry to the pursuit of truth: "Academic freedom is only justified if it serves the causes of the discovery and transmission of truth by scientific and scholarly means. . . . The theory of academic freedom rests on the view that the truth can be achieved."[19] Shils's 1983 attack on those who "derogate or even . . . dissolve the idea that truths can be discovered and taught" was approvingly quoted by none other than Lynn Cheney, in her final report as chair of the National Endowment for the Humanities. The report was entitled *Telling the Truth*.[20]

In this way, McCarthy's heirs at century's end trumpeted their devotion to truth while dishonoring it in practice, much as McCarthy himself had done with freedom fifty years before. Artists and writers still get penalized if politics transgresses too deeply into their art, and the postmodernists, though successful on campuses from coast to coast, cannot get their provisional and contextualized insights to travel past the ivory gates. Hence, in addition to the "sexual McCarthyism" unleashed upon politicians after the Clinton-Lewinsky scandal, we have the "pomo Mc-Carthyism" to be found in the academy itself. As Jeffrey Wasserstrom put it in 1998: "Some people are flinging the term 'postmodern' around much as Joseph McCarthy hurled the epithet 'Communist'—to smear a broad range of people whom a scholar deems objectionable, and to do so in a way that makes it hard for the accused to mount a defense."[21] If the overall picture is not the same as during the McCarthy era, it is certainly, recognizably, and directly descended from it.

Kicking and Screaming: Philosophy in the 1960s

But what about philosophy? Did what happened to American philosophy during the McCarthy era have lasting effects, not only on philosophy itself but also on broader areas of American academic culture?

Given the general absence of discussion, the answer will not be easy to find. Yet there is some prima facie evidence that it did; and the haggard figure of philosophy (or the philosopher) occasionally turns up, like a familiar character actor's face, in various scenes from the subsequent decades. We need look no farther than the Port Huron Statement, the manifesto of Students for a Democratic Society (SDS), adopted in 1962: "Making values explicit . . . is an activity that has been devalued and corrupted. The conventional moral terms of the age, the politician moralities—'free world,' 'people's democracies'—reflect realities poorly, if at all, and seem to function more as ruling myths than as descriptive principles. But neither has our experience in the universities brought us moral enlightenment. . . . The questions we might want raised—what is really important? Can we live in a different and better way? If we wanted to change society, how would we do it?—are not thought to be questions of a 'fruitful, empirical nature,' and thus are brushed aside."[22]

Saddling empiricistic philosophy professors with responsibility for student radicalism would be, to say the least, overdone. But on this testimony of the students themselves, the curt dismissal of their moral and social questions, by philosophers and others, played a role in radicalizing vast sections of the student body and in lessening their respect for faculty. So did the general fecklessness of the post-McCarthy professoriat. Consider this anecdote from Ian Tyrrell: "When I told an Australian class that included one American student that Americans had not included Marxism in the American educational dialogue, the American told me that his experience in the 1960's at a prestigious private university in the East contradicted my argument. After all, while he was studying economics, his department had given the Marxists a chance; in fact they had gone to the trouble of importing a Swedish economist to give the Marxist point of view."[23]

Not all American students (or universities) were as naive as this. When administrators at my own alma mater defended the presence of CIA recruiters on campus in 1967–68 on the grounds that recruiting was open to anyone and did not imply any kind of invitation or judgment on the part of the college, my friends in SDS knew just what to do: they called up the state Communist Party and asked if they had any summer programs for students. Indeed they did; and when they arrived on campus to recruit for those programs, they were promptly turned away. This kind of spinelessness and hypocrisy merely presaged faculty capitulation to any and all kinds of student radicals in the next few years. Having learned how to be lackeys of the Right, some professors easily turned their sorely acquired skills to the Left when it, too, started to threaten.

In *The Campus War,* his 1971 account of student radicalism at Berkeley, the philosopher John Searle makes a number of suggestions about how this capitulation was abetted by residues of the McCarthy era. Faculty who had not fought McCarthyites, Searle says, felt guilty about it and so were more sympathetic to radical students than they otherwise would have been (Searle 128). Others, who had fought more bravely, had developed such a strong sense of left-wing solidarity that they found it hard to conceive that they, and the free speech they cherished, might have enemies on the left (Searle 130).

More generally, Searle paints a picture of faculty fighting hard on behalf of academic freedom—but fighting, alas, an earlier war. Although McCarthy had some student sympathizers, the McCarthy era's threats to academic freedom tended to come from above—from boards of trustees like Reed's or administrations like Harvard's. A decade later, says Searle, faculty were wholly unable to recognize threats from below: "If the trustees try to interfere with free speech by banning a revolutionary speaker from campus, [the faculty] want the president to fight the trustees like a tiger. If the radicals interfere with free speech by refusing to allow a pro–Vietnam War speaker to speak by heckling him, jeering at him, or shouting him down, the same liberal faculty wants the president to show some understanding of the students' frustration" (Searle 138).

If philosophy had more serious troubles during the McCarthy era than other disciplines did, such sympathies and blind spots would be more pronounced among philosophers than elsewhere. Perhaps that is why Allan Bloom in *The Closing of the American Mind* (which I will discuss shortly) uses a "famous professor of philosophy" as his paradigm of faculty cravenness at Cornell (Bloom 313).

Another of Searle's points applies more directly to philosophers. He locates some of the "irresponsibility" of the faculty in a particular mind-set whose origins he does not question: "The basic actions of the faculty member, the core of his professional activity so to speak, lie in teaching students and conducting and publishing research. *In each case he seeks to impart the truth or as nearly what is the truth as he can get according to professional standards of evidence and reason. . . .* He could regard it correctly as a violation of professional ethics if he made his utterances for the purpose of achieving some practical effects rather than for the purpose of communicating the truth. Not only does he not consider the consequences of his actions when making moral utterances but he would consider it somewhat immoral to do so" (Searle 132; emphasis added).

This mentality is, of course, what I call "Allenian." True to the spirit of Raymond B. Allen, it denies the teacher and scholar any other goal than finding and communicating the truth. If someone should say that his or her purpose as a teacher is to produce educated Americans, or moral people, or a fuller appreciation of art—for Searle that person is, apparently, abandoning his or her vocation: "As scholars [the faculty] are not trained to consider the consequences of words" (Searle 134).

Who, one wonders, would have trained them to do so? Certainly not Quine, who, as I showed in chapter 2, carefully (but happily) turns away from all temporal contexts of sentence utterance as a condition for doing philosophy of language. Perhaps, then, a speech act theorist? Not one like Searle himself, who took the detailed, differentiated, and multilayered accounts of speech acts in Austin and Wittgenstein and based them all on predication, so that the heart of each and every speech act turns out to raise "the question of the truth of the predicate expression of the object referred to."[24]

If this book so far teaches anything at all, it is that the relation of philosophy to its culture and times is much more complex than many philosophers think it is. The solitary *Seinsdenken* of a Heidegger, the transcendental pretensions of a Habermas or a Rawls, and the dizzying semantic ascents of a Quine all presuppose not only that history and culture can be left behind but also that they can be left behind rather easily. The former claim, I think, is true; the latter, almost criminally naive. It is in fact very difficult for a philosopher to leave behind the determining characteristics of her own culture, many of which are invisible to her and are all the more powerful for that. Plato's timeless Republic, after all, was founded on slavery, which the *Republic* mentions fewer than ten times, always in passing.[25]

The situation is compounded when we are seeking to uncover society's relation, not to philosophy but to an absence of philosophy. What is the nature of this absence? And what is the nature of this American philosophy that never was?

The Cultivation of Language

In fact, there are or have been many kinds of philosophy, flourishing at other times and in other places, that could have various effects on various cultural and social problems. In some cases, their absence from the post-McCarthy American scene has been sufficient to prevent whole lines, and even fields, of inquiry from ever opening up. In other cases, inquiries that began in the absence of such philosophy found it, or something like it, essential to their progress.

The result, in the case of disciplines such as literary theory and cultural studies, has been a *rediscovery* of authors such as Hegel, Heidegger, and Marx. Such rediscovery, I will argue, cannot make conscious use of such philosophical approaches and insights without articulating them on a philosophical level. The philosophy of science provides examples of yet another tack: the *reinvention* of philosophical projects largely excluded from American philosophy since the McCarthy era. In reinventing central aspects of the philosophical projects of thinkers such as Hegel or Heidegger, some of America's most important philosophers of science have developed insights from those thinkers without, apparently, knowing that they were doing so. In the rest of this chapter, I will discuss examples of such rediscovery and reinvention. In the next chapter, I will offer a philosophical paradigm that can move American philosophy beyond the self-imposed, but little understood, limitations that have been carried down from the McCarthy era.

One of the tasks traditionally assigned to philosophy, but missing almost entirely from its most recent American versions, is a certain cultivation of language. The idea of this task, and of its importance, stems from the commonsense realization that language is the basis for all human cooperation. Without words with which to engage one another, we can only walk away from one another in sheer indifference—or fight.

Many philosophers, down through history, have agreed that language needs cultivation if it is to be a fertile basis for human cooperation. And they have also agreed, as against the poets, that such cultivation needs to be done rationally rather than intuitively (at least in part). But just what this all involves has been understood very differently by different philosophers. What is it about language that needs cultivating? Into what do we want to reshape and redefine language? By what standards do we measure its defects and our emendations? What *kinds* of things are those standards? What sorts of rational tools do we need and use?

At *Euthyphro* 7b–d, Socrates distinguishes what we would call "descriptive" terms from what we would call "value" terms. If a dispute arises about numbers, we can calculate and resolve it. If one arises about such empirical phenomena as size and weight, we can measure and resolve it. But disputes about value terms, such as (in Euthyphro's case) "holy," are much more intractable, for there is no accepted procedure for resolving them. Yet such resolution is all the more necessary. For these are "the things about which we differ, till, unable to arrive at a decision, we grow hostile . . . to each other, you and I and everybody else."

Over two thousand years later, with much less elegance, Kant also called for a philosophical cultivation of language:

> In philosophy, one must not imitate mathematics by starting from a definition. . . . In a word, in philosophy the definition, as involving rigorous distinctions, must conclude rather than begin the work.[26]

Even less elegantly, Hegel put it this way:

> It would go ill indeed for our cognition if we had to surrender exact conceptions of such objects as freedom, justice, morality, and even God himself, making do with vague, generalized images whose details were left

to the whim of each individual—just because those objects cannot be measured or calculated or expressed in a mathematical formula. The ruinous
practical consequences of such a theory are immediately obvious.[27]

And, finally, Heidegger:

> In the end, it is the business of philosophy to preserve the *force of the
> most elemental words,* in which Dasein expresses itself, from being leveled
> down by the common understanding into an incomprehensibility which
> operates as a source of many pseudoproblems.[28]

This task of cultivating language by providing good definitions is an
important one. Plato, in his *Cratylus,* assigns it to the *nomothetês,* the
"rarest of all artisans" (*Cratylus* 389a). When Aristotle says that freedom
is "badly defined" in democratic states, he means nothing less than that
defining freedom as the capacity of everyone to live just as she pleases
destroys the social fabric (*Politics* 1310a 25–36).

The need to cultivate language is in fact keenly felt in America,
where, as Thomas Jefferson put it, "New circumstances call for new
words, new phrases, and for the transfer of old words to new objects."[29]
The need has hardly disappeared since Jefferson's day. The drafters of the
Port Huron Statement showed they felt it when they complained, in my
earlier quotation, that "the conventional moral terms of the age . . .
reflect realities poorly, if at all." Eric Foner has usefully traced the American debates that have raged over the meaning of the word "freedom" and
that have shaped much of this country's history. He notes, tellingly, that
those debates have gone on without significant philosophical input:
"Despite their devotion to freedom, Americans have not produced many
abstract discussions of the concept. There is no equivalent in our literature to John Stuart Mill's *On Liberty* or the essay 'Two Concepts of
Liberty' by Isaiah Berlin."[30]

But America's semantic awkwardness goes far beyond the word
"freedom," of course—important though that is. Americans today, for
example, do not really have words with which to identify their sexuality:
"gay" tends to mean "joyous," or "bright and showy," and it is never
clear whether it includes lesbians. "Straight," for its part, tends to mean
not only "honest" but "dull" or even "unintelligent" (hence the proliferation of pro-gay rights posters identifying their holders as "straight
but not stupid").

Americans often cannot exactly name their racial background, either. The dominant racial group is called "white," a term that cannot be accurately applied to any European skin color. The subdominant group, for its part, has an agonized history of renaming itself, with "Negro" giving way to "colored" and thence in turn to "black," "Afro-American," and "African American." American Indians, rightly insulted to be called by a name applied in error by Columbus, started calling themselves "Native Americans," but that phrase did not solve all the problems. Its first word, coming from the Latin *nascor,* brought with it a whole European systematic of "nature" and "nation," whereas the second word is, of course, the name of a European, Amerigo Vespucci. The term "American" itself ought, strictly, to designate anyone living between Baffin Island and Tierra del Fuego. Reserving its application to the inhabitants of the United States is a synecdoche of a sinister cast. What about Canadians and Brazilians? Are they not Americans too? Or are we, as we so often behave, alone in the New World?

The cultivation of language is thus clearly as necessary in the United States as it is elsewhere, if not more so. Philosophers have approached it down through the millennia, when they have, with the view that the business of language is simply to describe and explain the world, that is, to tell us what is in the world and how its components interact with one another. The philosophical standards by which words are to be judged, therefore, traditionally concern how well they perform those functions. Do our words faithfully convey the nature of reality, or do they falsify it?

From there, answers to the question of how to cultivate language diverge, depending on how one understands the reality to which words ought to conform. For Plato, such reality is not to be found in the sensory, changing world we experience and live in, for nothing we experience *really* is anything: grass is not *really* green, snow is not *really* white, and so on. Our words, then, should conform to the eternal and unchanging domain of the Forms, the "real" world to which the *nomothetês* had to look when framing words.

For Aristotle, the reality to which words conform consisted preeminently in that aspect of our experienced world that is unchanging—an aspect that he called "substance" (*ousia*) or form (*eidos*). Jettisoning such "realistic" metaphysics, nominalists of various stripes suggested that our words should conform to concepts or to other qualities of the conceiving soul, or even that general terms were purely arbitrary *flatus vocis.*

Empiricists, finally, demanded that words be faithful to our sensory experience. David Hume, to take a famous case, argued that we have no such experience of causal power. We do not sense the fire heating the water, only that the fire is hot and that the water becomes so. We should therefore stop talking of causal power altogether; "causal power" is a bad phrase.[31] This approach was carried to its point of absurdity with our old friends, the logical positivists. A. J. Ayer, in his bombshell book of 1936, *Language, Truth, and Logic,* argued that

> [e]thical inquiry consists simply in saying that ethical concepts are pseudo-concepts and therefore unanalyzable. The further task of describing the different feelings that ethical terms are used to express, and the different reactions that they customarily provoke, is a task for the psychologist. . . . As ethical judgments are mere expressions of feeling, there can be no way of determining the validity of any ethical system, and indeed, no sense in asking whether such a system is true. All that one may legitimately inquire in this connection is, What are the moral habits of a given person or group of persons, and what causes them to have precisely those habits and feelings? And this enquiry falls wholly within the scope of the existing social sciences.[32]

From a contemporary perspective, Ayer's account of ethics seems oddly backward. Neoconservative cultural critics, as will be seen later in this chapter, tend to view science and the pursuit of truth as their allies against postmodern relativism. But Ayer enlists both science and Allenian thinking about truth in the service of a thoroughgoing moral relativism. He has, in fact, rediscovered Plato's original distinction between terms that inform us about the world and have clear meanings and value terms that are not of that sort at all. Not having the robust metaphysics of Forms that enabled Plato to determine the meaning of value terms, Ayer throws them out altogether.

The key point in Ayer's analysis is, as might be expected, the equation of ethical validity with truth. It is because the truth of ethical statements cannot be determined that the validity of ethical systems also cannot be determined. But of course most moral disputes are not about the truth or falsity of statements; they are about the rightness or wrongness of actions and customs. Whether the latter sort of debate can be reduced to the former without remainder—whether to debate that killing your mother is wrong is just the same thing as to debate the truth of the sentence "Killing your mother is wrong"—is not something I will go into here, for another kind of debate altogether is occluded by Ayer's analysis, and that is the question of the *moral,* not the cognitive, adequacy of the vocabulary within which we debate.

The Jewish moral vocabulary, for example, differs from the Christian in having a highly developed body of thought concerning idolatry. Do Christians therefore have a tendency to worship false gods? Certainly no self-respecting Jew could easily get away with the kind of public statement that one John Quincy Mitchell made in a letter to the editors of *Time* magazine, published November 16, 1998, shortly after the martyrdom of Matthew Shepard. Homosexuals, wrote Mitchell, should "come to terms with the unchangeable fact that God unequivocally disapproves of their sexual conduct, and [of] those who approve such behavior." Idolatry, of course, is the worship of images humans themselves have made rather than of the true God. But as much Jewish thought on the matter makes clear, some of the most beguiling images we construct of God are mental, like Mitchell's. The fact that the Jewish moral vocabulary has a developed body of thought on idolatry makes Jews more aware of this than Christians (or "Christians") like Mitchell.

If the Christian vocabulary is unduly sparse when it comes to idolatry, the classical Greek moral vocabulary famously has no word for "will." To Plato or Aristotle, that we could actually do something that goes against both our desires and our reason is simply unthinkable, because those are the only things in us that can lead to action at all. But Augustine found himself doing just such a thing. When he became a Christian, he committed himself to a religion that was both at war with humans' sensual nature and eager to proclaim its intellectual absurdity (*credo quia absurdum est,* in Tertullian's famous phrase—quickly amended by a thoughtful pagan to *credo quia absurdus sum*). Augustine's Christian experience thus led him to enrich the pagan moral vocabulary in extraordinarily important ways.[33]

The possibility of such enrichment is not even envisaged by Ayer, who before he begins has implicitly restricted philosophical inquiry to debates about the truth of statements. But there is a difference between debating whether a statement is true—whether, in Searle's terms, a given predicate expression is true of a given thing—and questioning whether that predicate expression itself is in some sense or other a good one. The latter sort of inquiry is ill suited to a philosophy that, like so much American philosophy after the McCarthy era, takes its cues from natural science. This point is implicit in my previous quotes from Plato, Kant, and Hegel, all of whom carefully contrasted the cultivation of language with mathematics. The reason they do so is, of course, that truth is a standard by which we can evaluate sentences, but not words—at least not directly. There is no word that has a higher truth value than any other, because any term can be truthfully asserted or denied of anything in the universe; no word enables us to state more truths than any other.

There is, however, an *indirect* sense in which words can be evaluated with respect to truth: not in trying to determine whether they are somehow truer than other words, but whether they are clear enough to permit truth values to be assigned at all. This was the main philosophical concern of the linguistic analysts, who believed that philosophy should be largely if not wholly concerned with sorting out the meanings of words. It is they who carried out recent philosophy's clearest version of the cultivation of language, and they are an important resource for future philosophy—much more important, I think, than they have recently seemed to many philosophers. However, any fruitful appropriation of their methods would have to face up to two things.

One is that the capacity to be used to make clear assignments of truth value is not the only criterion by which to judge words. On that model of the cultivation of language, the goal is to have a set of criteria for a term that will tell us, for everything in the universe, whether that term can be truthfully predicated of it or not. But some words derive their merits precisely from the fact that they *keep* us from doing this. It has been pointed out that in Britain, for example, the word "noble" has two meanings. On the one hand, it means "possessed of a superior degree of excellence, and hence worthy of special respect." On the other, it means "selected for public acclaim by politicians currently in power." This ambiguity can be very useful politically, because it enables politicians to reward their friends and helpers by conferring on them a property that the public can easily confuse with that of intrinsic excellence. Some words function socially in virtue of their ambiguity, then, and the capacity to make consistent truth claims is not the only thing by which a word should be judged.

The linguistic analysts were no fans of representational theories of language, the view that language somehow mirrors reality. But they were never able to focus on criteria for the use of words other than truth, so their cultivation of language was reduced to sorting out the various uses of words. This was perhaps allied with the other thing that must be faced if we are to rehabilitate them today: their refusal to take seriously the critical dimension of their own project. Whereas J. L. Austin used to say that "ordinary language" (by which he meant what many call "the king's English") was only the "first word" and not the final standard by which language was to be measured,[34] other linguistic analysts operated with an uncritical reading of Wittgenstein's claims that "every sentence in our language 'is in order as it is'" so that philosophy "leaves everything as it is."[35] It is as if they believed that somehow their analyses would lead them back to the speech of the shopkeepers and divines of an English town, when Wittgenstein's own analyses should have shown them that he was preparing extensive transformations in language and its relations to the world.

In America, where shopkeepers and divines rarely even try to understand one another, linguistic analysis would have had to be deeply radicalized to have a chance of addressing anything genuine—not radicalized in the sense of becoming somehow leftist but in the sense of going deeply into the roots of language in a pluralist society.

After the McCarthy era, of course, the times were hardly ripe for radicality in either sense. When in 1967 I was unhappily contemplating a military career, I spoke to the commander of the Reserve Officers Training Core (ROTC) at my local university—a Navy commander. Upon hearing that I was interested in philosophy, he mused that the United States could use more philosophers than it had. "When the Secretary of Defense was recently asked by Congress if we were winning the war in Vietnam," he said, "he answered that the Vietcong were not sending as many people back to the North as they were sending south." The commander grinned wryly and then, in a perfect parody of much ordinary language philosophy, said: "That's an odd concept of victory."

But then "Vietnam" was not really a "war" at all, was it?

Philosophy and Cultural Indifference

I have suggested that without a common vocabulary with which to discuss issues, we are left with the alternatives of mutual indifference or, as Plato points out, strife. Both of these, it is obvious, characterize much of American culture today. In particular, as I showed in earlier chapters, both have characterized American philosophy: the strife between analytical philosophers and metaphysicians has now settled into the mutual indifference of analytical and continental philosophy.

The most devastating attack on cultural boredom, on indifference to others raised to an intellectual principle, remains Allan Bloom's 1987 *The Closing of the American Mind.* Its portrait of the American university student includes discussions of racial separateness, lack of parenting, the role of divorce, and other disconnecting factors in the lives of students. The portrait culminates by invoking a thirteen-year-old boy doing his math homework while listening to his portable tape player: "And in what does progress culminate? A pubescent child whose body throbs with orgasmic rhythms; whose feelings are made articulate in hymns to the joys of onanism or the killing of parents; whose ambition is to win fame and wealth in imitating the drag-queen who makes the music. In short, life is made into a nonstop, commercially prepackaged masturbational fantasy" (Bloom 75). Most of Bloom's argument aims to show that American universities are not about to pull youths such as that out of their narcissistic loneliness.

Bloom's book generated an enormous discussion. The many condemnations of it, most of them amply justified, have tended to focus on such themes as Bloom's rage at the arrival of large numbers of African American students on campus ("when the black students at Cornell became aware that they could intimidate the university" [Bloom 95]); his attacks on feminism ("the woman's movement is not founded on nature" [100]); his hatred of newer paradigms in the humanities (deconstruction "appeals to our worst instincts and shows us where our temptations lie" [379]), and his blatant falsifications of history (McCarthyism "had no effect whatsoever on curriculum or appointments" [324]).

But such condemnations do not exhaust the import of Bloom's book, for in spite of all the furor, there was, and is, a strange silence among Bloom's critics concerning two of the book's major themes. One was his portrayal of just what has happened to the American university students he most cares about—the white male ones now orgiastically imprisoned by their compact disc players. I have heard echoes of Bloom's account of their cultural ignorance and indifference, less viciously phrased, from more than a few professors who do not share either Bloom's explanations of such phenomena or his view that the fate of that particular group of students coincides with the fate of the West. Indeed, there is a good deal of evidence that about those students Bloom's intu-itions remain largely right. Richard Flacks and Scott L. Thomas, for example, have recently documented the high degree of disengagement among white male college students: "We found that, compared to white males, African-American and Latino males were more likely to interact with faculty members outside class. Further, African-American and La-tino students of both sexes were more involved in cultural and commu-nity activities than white males were: They were more than twice as likely to report going to plays, concerts, films, or museums. They were three times as likely to say they participated in social service groups."[36] One hopes that Bloom would rejoice to see his educational ideals being thus approximated—even if by African American, female, and Hispanic stu-dents. But when it comes to the white males with whom *The Closing of the American Mind* is almost exclusively concerned, Flacks and Thomas's data—from 1996—would give him no reason to change his mind.

The other thesis, still more important and still less discussed, is that of the centrality of philosophy to culture. A large part of *The Closing of the American Mind* (pp. 243–312) is devoted to a discussion of the history of philosophy. Culminating in Bloom's thesis that "Heidegger's teachings are the most powerful intellectual force in our times" (Bloom 311–12), the discussion has much wider import than Heidegger stud-ies. What is crucial about Heidegger, says Bloom, is an issue that has gone undiscussed by Heidegger's American "popularizers," from Paul de Man to Richard Rorty. This is the question of whether Heidegger was right about Plato and Aristotle. And Heidegger's key encounter with Plato and Aristotle, for Bloom, involved asking about their relation to Socrates. Were they worthy followers of him, or did they betray his view that even if truth cannot be found, the search for it is more important than life itself (Bloom 310–11)?

There is not much beyond this in Bloom's history of philosophy, most of which is warmed over from Leo Strauss and every bit as tenden-tious as the rest of the book. There is, for example, no serious engage-ment even with the "most powerful intellectual force," Heidegger; the only Heideggerean writing discussed is the *Rektoratsrede,* Heidegger's disastrous inaugural address as rector of Freiburg University in 1933. Even that is given little more than passing mention. And Heidegger's real question concerning Plato, Aristotle, and their mentor concerned Being, not the search for truth. But there is no doubt about the validity of three of Bloom's contentions concerning philosophy: it can indeed put us into connection with the entire history of Western culture as no other field can; we need such connection if we are to live effectively today; and those two facts are unknown to most American academics, let alone their students (why else the lack of discussion of them in the wake of Bloom's book?).

Like his portrayal of white male college students, Bloom's portrayal of American philosophy still held years after his death: "[American philosophy] has a scientific component, logic, which is attached to the sciences and could easily be detached from philosophy. This is serious, practiced by competent specialists, and responds to none of the permanent philosophic questions. History of philosophy, the compendium of dead philosophies that was always most lively for the students, has been neglected, and students find it better treated in a variety of other disciplines. Positivism and ordinary language analysis have long dominated, though they are on the decline, and are evidently being replaced by nothing" (Bloom 378).

Contemporary American philosophy figures in Bloom's book as part of his general lament. He does not explain how it sank to such a state. Nor can he, given his view that the McCarthy era "had no effect whatsoever on curriculum or appointments." But the characteristics he highlights in the immediately preceding quotation—American philosophy's scientism, its divorce from history, and the absence of anything to replace classical analytical philosophy—are among those that I have argued were fostered by the McCarthy era. If we accept my diagnosis—that the collapse of American philosophy was the result not of an influx of women and African Americans into the universities but of external politics—we will have an explanation for the situation Bloom laments. We will also have, as I will argue in the next chapter, a remedy.

The Rediscovery of Philosophy
in Literary Theory and Cultural Studies

Nowhere is the absence of philosophy from the American academy more keenly exhibited than in the fields of literary theory and cultural studies. In both fields, researchers quickly discovered that they could not make much progress without undertaking a profound and exhausting encounter with the canonical tradition of Western thought. This discovery applied even when those researchers were keenly aware, from the "pretheoretical experience" of their own daily lives, of how inadequate that thought was. The situation has been aptly formulated by Henry Louis Gates Jr.: "Black writers, like critics of black literature, learn to write by reading literature, especially the canonical texts of the Western tradition. Consequently, black texts resemble other, Western texts. . . . Black literature shares much with, far more than it differs from, the Western textual tradition."[37]

The result of this, for Gates, is that even a book that attempts "to identify a theory of criticism that is inscribed within the black vernacular tradition" must use theoretical concepts derived, ultimately, from Western philosophy. Importantly, Gates seeks to use the canonical concepts of the Western tradition as analogs to the theory he is after, rather than as its foundation. Instead of prescribing limits to the theorizing of African American texts, the Western canon provides theories with points of both difference and similarity to the conception of "Signi-fyin(g)" that Gates advances.[38]

Because of considerations like these, the study of literatures and cultures inevitably pushed toward generality and abstraction, becoming what is today called "theory." Along the way, researchers in both fields encountered Hegel, Heidegger, and Marx—thinkers who, because of their attitudes toward sentential truth, are missing from most American philosophy departments.

Both literary theory and cultural studies are (in general) products of the diverse and fascinating epoch called "postmodernism," which in the wake of the 1960s has mounted intellectual challenges to the hierarchies and centers of the West by valorizing what the West in general regards as abject and marginal. In doing this, as Fredric Jameson has noted, post-modernism operates in a strictly Hegelian fashion: "As though it had studied under Hegel, . . . the postmodern lifts up, and cancels, all that junk [*Aufhebung*], including the hamburger within the diremption of its gourmet meals and Las Vegas within the rainbow-flavor landscape of its psychedelic corporate monuments."[39]

The idea that something as inconspicuous as a hamburger, or as lowly as Las Vegas, can provide important insights into anything at all is first to be found, before postmodernity, in the *Zusätze*, or supplements, to certain writings of Hegel's. There, such seemingly trivial or even uncomfortable things as animal magnetism and somnambulism, not to mention mollusks and insects, are shown to be moments in the cosmic play of Absolute Spirit (of which more in chapter 5).[40]

Hegel is not, of course, the only thinker with whom literary theory and cultural studies must reckon. Stuart Hall has spoken about "wrestling" with Marx, and especially with Louis Althusser's interpretation of Marx: "It was not just a matter of where Marx happened to be born, and of what he talked about, but of the model at the center of the most developed parts of Marxist theory, which suggested that capitalism evolved organically from within. . . . Whereas I came from a society where the profound integument of capitalist society, economy, and culture had been imposed by conquest and colonization. . . . I remember wrestling with Althusser . . . I felt, I will not give an inch to this profound misreading, this super-structuralist mistranslation, of classical Marxism . . . I warred with him, to the death."[41]

With respect to literary studies, Paul de Man has described how the close reading of texts undertaken by new criticism, coupled with that approach's larger concern for the unifying properties of form, led the new critics willy-nilly into the circular practices of hermeneutics. These, in turn, had been philosophically articulated in Heidegger's account of interpretation as a movement between the reader's *Vorhabe,* or prepossession, of intuitions concerning a work's unity and the phenomenal details that she actually encounters in the text.[42]

But drawing analogies with philosophical theories and traditions, wrestling with Marx, and practicing what Heidegger talks about do not amount to engaging with them philosophically. It may be argued that cultural studies and literary theory need some sort of engagement with philosophers, but not a *philosophical* engagement—whatever that is. In fact, though, this is not the case, as Frank Lentricchia has written: "The questions that theory raises are complicated; they have an ancient philosophical history; they cannot easily, and sometimes they cannot at all, be successfully posed and explored in the context of the usual forms of literary analysis and literary history."[43]

The foregoing three examples of concrete encounter, in very different ways, can illustrate this in more detail. First, it seems that the required encounter with all three thinkers—Hegel, Marx, and Heidegger—must be what I will call "general"; it must deal with their thought as a whole, and not just that part of it that is of immediate relevance. It may be true that what contemporary researchers find most helpful in all three thinkers is a series of individual insights concerning specific issues in various discourses (for example, views on how texts are to be interpreted). But Hegel, Heidegger, and Marx—as well as most philosophical thinkers—in fact viewed those very insights as mere corollaries of their deeper concerns and projects, that is, of their philosophies themselves. Our ultimate evaluation of their views cannot, then, be confined to issues of their usefulness to us. It must also take into account the strength of the foundations on which those useful views are formulated as resting. And those are philosophical foundations.

We see this stated very clearly in the case of Hall's "wrestle" with Marx. For how can Hall know that the Eurocentric myth of autochthonous capitalism is central to Marxist theory without having traversed the whole domain of that theory? How can he tell the difference between what is intrinsic to the whole Marxist approach and what is merely an accidental remnant of Marx's European birth? Only a general encounter with Marx's thought can teach him this. In the case of Hegel, the issue is well articulated by Rolf-Peter Horstmann: "The long sought goal of an appropriate understanding of a dialectical theory can be brought into range only via the clarification of the *foundations* and *presuppositions* of the logico-metaphysical constitution of [Hegel's] philosophy; it cannot be reached through analysis of the *results* of such a philosophy."[44] And de Man puts the same problem for Heidegger: "Heidegger's exegetical method flows directly from the premises of his philosophy; it is inseparable from it to the point that one cannot speak here of 'method' in the formal sense of the term, but rather of Heidegger's very thought in relation to the poetic."[45]

To understand and make critical use of the results of Hegel's, Heidegger's, and Marx's thought—indeed, to understand any results whatsoever as such—we must know something about how those results were obtained. In their cases, as well as in those of other philosophers, specific results always come from a much larger project that also needs to be understood and wrestled with. When Hegel talks about poetry, for example, he is locating it within a conceptual cosmos in which it is *not* philosophy, religion, the state, and so on. To understand what he does say about poetry, and about specific poems, we must see how poetry contrasts with those other domains—and this ultimately means studying Hegel's system as a whole. When Heidegger comes to talk of poetry, he too is thinking of it as not philosophy, not religion, and emphatically as not the *Gestell*, the challenging frame that modernity clamps down around everything. Hence, to understand either Hegel or Heidegger even on something as specific as a single poem, we must understand what they think poetry is—and what it is *not*, which means that we must understand their philosophies in a comprehensive way. Marxism, for its part, approaches literature via a class analysis that extends far beyond, and certainly cannot be understood or legitimated solely in terms of, the category of literature. Our encounter with those philosophies, then, should be what I call "general."

Moreover, neither Hegel nor Heidegger nor Marx can be understood without being placed in historical perspective. By this I mean not merely placing them in the history of their own times (early German industrialization for Hegel; its later form for Marx; Weimar and the Nazis for Heidegger) but understanding their place within the overall history of thought, and in particular of philosophy. Heidegger supposedly once referred to his entire philosophy as "my series of readings of Aristotle," and Hegel was defined in my presence (by the eminent Hegel scholar Emil Fackenheim) as "Aristotle plus mediation." Both descriptions are exaggerations, of course, but any honest confrontation with either thinker has to determine by how much—the same as for Kant, Leibniz, Spinoza, and the other philosophers with whom Hegel and Heidegger contended all their lives.

The reason for this is intimately connected with what theorists such as Gates seek from the Western canonical tradition. Like other researchers into previously marginalized and excluded discourses, Gates cannot use the Western tradition as a foundation—as providing basic premises for his investigation. He cannot, for example, simply take over Kantian concepts of the beautiful and the sublime and then ask whether Zora Neale Hurston's *Their Eyes Were Watching God* matches up to them. Still less would he want to abide by Kant's or Hegel's dicta in that regard (had they ever written on Hurston, which was impossible for more than one reason). Rather, he wants to remain for a while at the level of the concepts of beauty and sublimity themselves, to see what similarities and differences they have with concepts that are to be derived from the African American tradition ("Those *beautiful* vessels, robed in purest white, so delightful to the eyes of freemen, were to me so many shrouded *ghosts*").[46]

Literary theorists and students of culture such as Gates, then, take very much to heart Gilles Deleuze's observation that "[c]oncepts do not await us all made, like heavenly bodies. They have to be invented, fabricated, or rather created, and would be nothing without the signature of those who create them."⁴⁷ Because the philosophical tradition for such theorists is a source of concepts, rather than of truths, they are directly pushed to the historical dimension of philosophers such as Hegel and Heidegger, for the philosophical invention of concepts, as these two and other philosophers practice it, does not consist in simply spinning concepts out of one's head into some sort of ethereal web of beliefs. Rather, it relies for its legitimacy upon very specific diagnoses of what is inadequate in previous concepts. Hence, when Heidegger comes to write about Hölderlin, one of his main concerns is to appropriate Hölderlin's poetry for his own views, in opposition to the traditional interpretations that ally Hölderlin to his college roommates, Hegel and Schelling. And this means showing that Hegel and Schelling could not philosophically understand Hölderlin: that aesthetic concepts derived from their philosophies are inadequate to Hölderlin's poems.⁴⁸ The general projects in which Hegel and Heidegger engage—like those of other philosophers—thus do not comprise two separate facets, one in which they put forward their own doctrines and another in which they consider the doctrines of previous thinkers. Rather, the new concepts that they invent are created out of earlier conceptual repertoires to which Hegel and Heidegger respond on all levels and at all times. Hence, any encounter with Hegel and Heidegger must be not merely general but *historical* as well.

The issue of historicality comes to the fore in Fredric Jameson's discussion of Hegel in *The Political Unconscious*. Jameson writes that Althusser's account of Hegel crucially attributed to Hegel a Leibnizian view of causality as expression, so that anything and everything was to be seen as the manifestation of an inner, essential substrate.⁴⁹ In fact, as Jameson notes, this is an extraordinarily naive reading of Hegel, for whom—in opposition to Leibniz—there is no essence or substrate below the surface, and for whom reality is merely the chaining together of appearances.⁵⁰ Althusser, in other words, is not a trustworthy intermediary between ourselves and Hegel—any more than he is between ourselves, as Hall found, and Marx. We need to go back to Hegel, in short, because Althusser cannot be trusted. But can we trust Hegel? Is his critique of Leibniz justified? Are his innovations on Leibniz as warranted as he says they are? Whether we remain with Hegel, or Leibniz, or Althusser, our decision is a matter for historically informed and nuanced discussion.

De Man is similarly untrustworthy as an intermediary between our-selves and Heidegger. Anyone with a good knowledge of Heidegger will be suspicious that, in the earlier quote, de Man assigns to Heidegger's thought such things as "premises" and, indeed, that he calls it a "philoso-phy" at all. In virtue of the critique of presence that motivates Heideg-ger's entire thought, and of Heidegger's equation of presence with par-ousia, even more suspicion will be aroused a few pages later when de Man, without citing a single passage, tells us that for Heidegger "[t]he essence of poetry consists in stating the parousia, the absolute presence of Being."[51] Given that in the modern epoch, according to Heidegger, knowledge is conceived as the absolute presence of a representation of a thing in a mind,[52] such a reader will be even more troubled than is de Man when he writes that "Heidegger, in his forward to his commentaries on the poetry of Hölderlin, claims to write from the standpoint of the ideal commentator."[53] In fact, the trouble is with de Man: Heidegger, the foe of premises, presence, and parousia alike, makes no such claim.[54]

Intermediaries, in short, are dangerous. Althusser is undependable with respect to Hegel because, as Jameson notes, his attribution of expressive causality to Hegel enabled him to use "Hegel" as a polemical code word for "Stalin."[55] De Man, for his part, was presumably moti-vated by the anxiety of influence: a Heidegger who stands for absolute presence of any kind is easier to deconstruct than a Heidegger who questions it. The lesson in both cases is the same: intermediaries are dangerous.

This leads to another lesson: that history itself is dangerous, because history is nothing other than a series of intermediations. We cannot read Leibniz today without knowing about Hegel, or read Hegel without knowing about Marx. But our knowledge, like Eve's, is dangerous, be-cause all intermediaries are dangerous. Understanding the philosophical foundations of our most basic concepts thus requires a constant trade-off between history (intermediation) and directness (immediacy).

Jonathan Culler has defined theory as "an open ended corpus of writings which have an impact on domains other than those to which they ostensibly belong."[56] Such desirable passages from one domain to others cannot be made, of course, through thin air; the insights of any theorist in any domain cannot reach theorists in other domains unless there is a third domain, one of common intelligibility, to serve as a connecting term between the other two. The traditional name of that domain is "philosophy," so it is not surprising that cultural studies and literary theory find themselves compelled, even in America, to deal with philosophers such as Hegel and Heidegger.

But this third domain requires tending; it cannot be taken for granted. Hence, *any* encounter with thinkers such as these should be (1) generalized, (2) historicized, and (3) without intermediaries. The first two of these characteristics, certainly, could best be realized by having the thinkers in question taught in philosophy departments rather than in departments of comparative literature or cultural or minority studies, for the very generality of Hegel's and Heidegger's thought both makes them philosophers and ensures that the history within which they locate themselves will be the history of philosophy.

Hegel and Heidegger represent alternatives to analytical philosophy. As I will argue in the next chapter, they diverge from it at precisely the crux posed to philosophers by the McCarthy era: they do not think that the truth that philosophy seeks is a property of propositions or sentences, and hence neither sees the goal of his own discourse as in any way timeless, selfless, or scientific. It is unsurprising, then, that they are only rarely taught in American philosophy departments.

The absence of such teaching has led, in part, to a great deal of unnecessary autodidacticism. Otherwise, Americans are left with the situation Bloom describes with respect to the main words of the Western tradition: "All [that] language was produced by philosophy and was in Europe known to have been produced by philosophy, so that it paved a road to philosophy. In America its antecedents remain unknown. We took over the results without having had any of the intellectual experiences leading to them. But the ignorance of the origins and the fact that American philosophy departments do not lay claim to them—are in fact just as ignorant of them as is the general public—means that the philosophic content of our language and lives does not direct us to philosophy" (Bloom 379).

The Reinvention of Philosophy by Philosophers of Science

The flip side of this sort of indifference is the kind of antagonism manifested in the culture wars that have ravaged the land for the better part of the last decade. Originally ignited by Bloom's book, these verbal battles have scorched vast areas of the American community. They extend from the politics of presidential impeachment to arcane evaluations of scientific practice.

My discussion here will locate itself toward the latter end. It is not my intention to deal with the culture wars in any comprehensive way, for the underlying circumstance they point to is clear enough. With philosophy isolated in small, homogeneous philosophy departments and unwilling to communicate with the broader society, Americans have not articulated or sorted out their basic values, so different groups hold what seem, at least, to be incompatible sets of them. Although certain ancient Athenians once resolved such issues as the nature of the good life by question and argument, that is, by philosophy, Americans are unable to do that and get only so far as epithetic wars of words and catch phrases—even, alas, in the academy.

Thus, Gertrude Himmelfarb can—in a gesture typical of an entire genre—publish a book calling for Americans to base their society on various values that are held to be absolute, without once mounting an argument that such absolute values actually exist or, if they do, which ones they are.[57] Indeed, the proscience fighters in the science wars continually surprise critics by their lack of philosophical knowledge and acumen—even when they are philosophers themselves. Examples are Adolph Grünbaum's attack on Habermas as an advocate of hermeneutics (Habermas's criticism of it was trenchant) and Stephen Weinberg's bizarre nineteenth-century definition of "positivism" as the denial of the reality of theoretical entities.[58]

This lack of acumen is, in some ways, only to be expected. The wealth and prestige of American science are to some extent artifacts of the cold war, and, as Andrew Ross has argued, the science wars are artifacts of the cold war's end: "Seeking explanations for their loss of standing in the public eye and for the decline in funding from the public purse, conservatives in science have joined the backlash against the (new) usual suspects—pinkos, feminists, and multiculturalists of all types."[59] That science is a value-free enterprise was one of the dogmas of the 1950s, of course; another of its dogmas, as I showed in chapter 1, was that philosophy was at best trivial and at worst dangerous.[60] Those who today maintain the first attitude are, by fiat of history, prone to the second as well. They should not, therefore, be expected to have much grasp of the subtleties of philosophical thinking.

Perhaps equally surprising is the lack of philosophical acumen among the critics of science. Any critique of science that claims, for example, that reality is merely what scientists, in pursuit of their own or somebody else's wealth or power, proclaim it to be is simply silly, because it was refuted millennia ago. If we are going to use words at all, our experience has to exhibit some regularity. If the color green never recurs, for example, I cannot talk about green things. And words like "electron" and "cosine," as well as "freedom" and "rights," are out of the question altogether. In the face of this, Cratylus, the radical follower of Heracleitus, gave up language altogether and went around pointing at things, which he thought were too unique and fleeting even to be namable. But Cratylus found no followers (we can imagine that, unable to speak, he was not much of a teacher). So, in short, regularities exist, and the point of science is to capture and explain them. True, there is a long path from the kind of regularity that we call "green" to the kind that physicists call "charm," but the path is there, and it is foolish to deny it.

It is not exactly that this debate, philosophically uninformed as it is, does not get going. It is rather that, as Val Dusek has pointed out, it has a distinctly odd cast, because the opposing sides come out of a very old script—a philosophical one. The scenarist is Kant, and the script is the quarrel he set forth between dogmatism ("The science warriors have typically been naive realists and dogmatic objectivists") and skepticism ("Most of the leading sociologists and literary critics who have publicly responded to them have tended toward sophomoric skepticism").[61]

Like the rest of the culture wars, this inability to go forward leads back to a crisis of truth in which it must be decided whether absolute values exist, how we can know them if they do, and how we can replace them if they do not. Kant's own middle way, unfortunately, no longer holds. His account of the transcendental structures of the human mind was rapidly, and aptly, classed by later German philosophers not as a healing middle ground but as merely a form of dogmatism whose categorical vision is turned inward.

In the next chapter, I will advance a paradigm that I think resolves this crisis. In the meantime, I would like to fix briefly on the work of two philosophers of science who have gotten out of the Kantian dichotomy of dogmatism versus skepticism (or as we call them now, realist versus relativist) and who have therefore escaped the science wars—but whose escape required them to reinvent considerable portions of Hegel and Heidegger. The two philosophers are Arthur Fine and David Hull.

Consider, first, Fine's *The Shaky Game,* published in 1986. In it, Fine seeks to "try to take science on its own terms, and try not to read things into science" (Fine 149). This is a close counterpart to what Heidegger called "phenomenology," that is, "letting what shows itself be seen from itself," as opposed to engaging in any "free-floating constructions and accidental findings."[62] Fine, like Heidegger, believes that various kinds of theories are being read into the phenomenon of science, resulting in several competing overall accounts of what is really a multifaceted enterprise. Among those accounts are realism (Fine 113–22) and two varieties of "anti-realism," namely "behaviorism," which glosses truth as what is acceptable to a community of researchers, and "empiricism," according to which science is not committed to the view that theoretical entities actually exist but does require that they be "empirically adequate," that is, that they figure in a scientific theory that has a model in which all truths about observables are represented (Fine 139–47).

All three of the approaches criticized by Fine are theoretical impositions on science and, as Heidegger would put it, cover over its true nature. Realism, for its part, sounds very much like a theoretical version of what Heidegger calls "presence-at-hand" (*Vorhandenheit*). Like anything basic to *Being and Time*'s analysis of Dasein, presence-at-hand itself is not a strictly cognitive matter but is a mode of comportment, a way in which Dasein encounters beings. Its theoretical weight is measured out for Heidegger in assertions (*Aussagen*), in which "what is encountered as objectively present [that is, present at hand] is determined . . . in such and such a way."[63]

The two main versions of anti-realism are also conceptual impositions on experience. Behaviorism, as Fine presents it, needs to get from the ways in which people actually do accept truth claims to some ideal of how they should do so, and there is no way to do this: what distinguishes truth from untruth cannot be behavioristically grounded other than as a report of the actual behavior of a community, which leaves it floating free of justification (Fine 140–41). Thus forsaking justification in favor of consensus, or of the common denominator of the understandings of a community, Fine's behaviorism approximates what Heidegger calls "idle talk": the inauthentic speech whose goal is agreeing with other people, rather than being right about whatever we are talking about.[64] Empiricism, which has no ready analog in *Being and Time,* is another theoretical imposition of the type *Being and Time* condemns, for it draws a line between "observables," about which truth claims can be made, and "unobservables," which are (at best) empirically adequate. The distinction between what is observable and what is not, Fine argues, is "forced on us a priori by this empiricist philosophical stance" (Fine 144). None of these interpretations, then, gets us to science itself.

This, Heidegger would say, occurs because all three approaches view science itself theoretically. To view something theoretically is for Heidegger to cover over the contexts of meaningfulness in which we normally encounter it. Suppose I have a pen, but I do not actually use it to write the letter that will go in the envelope and then to the mailbox in the direction of my Aunt Bertha in Milwaukee. Suppose, in fact, that I block out all such context from my encounter with the pen. Then there is nothing to do but stare at it: I have achieved a relation to it that is what the Greeks called *theorein,* contemplation. The contexts of meaningfulness that are bracketed out in this artificial, theoretical stance are, in the normal course of things, gathered together into the dynamic structure Heidegger calls "world." "World" in the Heideggerean sense, then, is just the most extended context in which something can be meaningful for us. It includes, therefore, all the contexts in which we can be meaningful for ourselves: the horizons of meaningfulness that it gathers together permeate our existence from top to bottom. *Being and Time* is largely an account of what Heidegger calls "Being-in-the-World." Fine puts it in similar ways: "We are *in* the world, both physically and conceptually. That is, *we* are among the objects of science, and the concepts and procedures that we use to make judgments of [scientific] subject matter and correct application are themselves part of that same scientific world" (Fine 131–32). The problem with overall accounts of truth, and with the ensuing views of what science is and how it works, is for Fine that they are attempts to break loose from the environing structures of world: "[The realist] cannot (really!) stand outside of the arena, nor can he survey some area of the playing field and mark it out as what the game is about" (Fine 131).

The same holds, though Fine does not put it that way, for the behaviorist and the empiricist: they both presuppose a conception of science to define it explicitly. The behaviorist does this when she tries to move from the actual ways in which communities accept truth claims to the ways in which they should do so, and the empiricist when she attempts to apply her distinction between observable and unobservable to science viewed from the outside. Fine thus claims, and Heidegger would presumably agree, that science is too basic a phenomenon of our world for us to find an outside purchase in terms of which to define it.

Hence Fine's own viewpoint, which he calls the "natural ontological attitude," sees science not as something with a timeless essence demarcatable for eternity from nonscientific activities but as "a set of practices with a history. That history constrains our understanding of current practices and structures our evaluations of promising problems and modes of inquiry" (Fine 10). In talking about historical constraints on what problems are to be investigated and how, Fine may seem to have overshot Heidegger in the direction of Foucault. But he has not, at least not in the direction of the Foucault who, famously or supposedly, denied that people could resist power or, indeed, do anything whatever as moral agents, for truth in Fine's view requires a certain sort of agency: that involved in accepting scientific theories and the truth claims they contain. When we do this, we accord to the unobservable theoretical entities postulated by that theory (for example, in the case of nuclear physics, quarks) not mere empirical adequacy but the same general sort of reality that we accord to things in our everyday dealings with the world: "What is it to accept the evidence of one's senses and, *in the same way*, to accept confirmed scientific theories? It is to take them into one's life as being true, with all that implies concerning adjusting one's behavior, theoretical and practical, to accommodate them" (Fine 127). It is, in Heidegger's terms, to accord them an authentic place in our world, within the overall context of significance that structures our behavior.

Fine is not, to be sure, competing with Heidegger. The world he talks about is a scientific one, as my previous quote from Fine's page 131 attests, and it abides by standard rules of scientific usage. Its semantics, for example, is not Heideggerean but Davidsonian and Tarskian (Fine 130, 133–34).

But it is not clear that Heidegger would not accept Fine's move here.

Such semantics is indeed a presupposition of science itself, constitutive of much of the behavior of scientists, and any philosophical account of science would have to accept this—especially a phenomenological account such as Heidegger would seek to give. Insofar as Fine sees science as involving the commitments and relations of everyday life—as being "rooted in everyday thinking" (Fine 149)—it even seems that Fine's philosophy of science could furnish what Heidegger calls an "existential concept of science," one that goes beyond seeing science as merely "an inferential context [*Begründungszusammenhang*] of true, that is, valid sentences,"[65] to show how it is rooted in the comportment of Dasein.

I do not know whether Fine's thought actually does that, but the fact that such a question can even be asked shows that Fine has found himself in intellectual proximity to Heidegger. Given that his work never mentions Heidegger and does not make use of any distinctively Heideggerean terminology, I take him to be reinventing some of Heidegger's insights for his own purposes.

David Hull does the same. In his *Science as a Process,* Hull sets out to "provide an evolutionary account of the interrelationship between social and conceptual developments in science" (Hull 12). In the course of doing so, he sounds some strikingly Hegelian themes.

In the first place, Hull considers it essential, if we are to understand science, not to view scientists as "isolated knowing subjects confronting their experience." Any such view could not account for the way scientists build on the work of other scientists, especially from previous generations, or for how individual bias is eliminated in science (Hull 22). In Hegel's account of consciousness in the *Phenomenology of Spirit,* the great source of bias for the individual is her own body. It is, in fact, because of the ascetic individual's bias against her body in toto that she needs the intermediation of a community (Hegel 136–38). What such intermediation brings about in the *Phenomenology*'s next section is "reason" that observes nature—Hegel's term for natural science itself, which for him as for Hull is thus always a communal enterprise.

The basic principle of the scientific community for Hull is its members' drive for recognition: "The desire for recognition is very close to a cultural universal among human beings" (Hull 281). What scientists particularly want to be recognized for, according to Hull, is their discoveries. This leads, in Hull's view, to what he calls "cooperative competition": scientists, all pursuing their own individual interests, find that it is in those interests to cooperate with one another to get at the truth; the result, directly intended by none of them, is the advance of science itself (Hull 310–11).

For Hegel, recognition by others is essential to one's human status itself (Hegel 111–15). The kinds of communities humans form are at first antagonistic, but as the book moves on, the cooperative dimension increases until we have Spirit, which Hegel characterizes as "[t]he I that is We, and the We that is I"—a combination, then, of competition and cooperation (Hegel 110). This is a gloss on Hegel's own famous "cunning of reason," according to which each individual's pursuit of his or her own personal interest advances the human species as a whole.

Because for Hull scientists are thus internally related to one another in and through the scientific community to which they belong, the standard model of speech act theory, in which precedence is given to the intention of the speaker in determining what an utterance means, does not apply: "Not until scientists publish their views and discover the reactions of other scientists can they possibly appreciate what they have said. . . . What the receiver thinks the sender intended is what matters" (Hull 288–89). Similarly for Hegel: "[I]n speech and action the inner turns itself into something else, thus putting itself at the mercy of the element of change, which twists the spoken word . . . into meaning something other than [it is] in and for [itself]. . . . The results of the actions, through . . . the influence of others, lose the character of being something constant in the face of other individuals" (Hegel 187).

That Fine and Hull could, while pursuing their very different projects, reinvent so much of Hegel and Heidegger is a testament to their creativity. The Hegelian themes in Hull's work, like the Heideggerean ones in Fine's, do not result from conscious attempts by either American to trade upon either German. Nor, however, do I think they are merely coincidences. Although Fine and Hull cannot be reduced to Heidegger and Hegel, the places where they have reinvented them are important. The key is that both Fine and Hull, for all their differences with each other, take science to be anything but a timeless, selfless quest of truth. They see it as activities and processes engaged in by human communities. That is the point where the approaches of Hegel and Heidegger become indispensable to thinkers today—and ripe for reinvention by analytical philosophers.

Conclusions

The political pressures of the McCarthy era, aided by the demographics of the profession, helped philosophy come to see itself as just the sort of timeless, selfless quest of truth that people like Fine and Hull have discredited for science. Like other aspects of the McCarthy era, such as its attack on Hollywood and its codification of police repression, this has had indirect, but lasting, effects on American culture in general.

Among those effects, I have argued, has been the absence of what I call the critical cultivation of language. Nothing is as important to a society as the words its members use to communicate with one another. At the most general (and basic) level, the cultivation of those words has for the last two thousand years been a task for philosophers, along with poets. When philosophy abandoned it for a quasi-scientific quest to prove propositions (or argue for sentences), it allowed our verbal infrastructure to decay. The results can only be indifference and strife, a few mild instances of which I have documented here.

What is needed, and what I will undertake to sketch in the next chapter, is a philosophical approach to language that does not view it merely in terms of timeless and selfless notions such as truth and reference, but that seeks to articulate and evaluate the ways in which the words *now* available in *our* language guide our thought and action. Such a project would amount to the linguistic side of the "tremendous work" that D. W. Gottshalk set forth for philosophy in the APA presidential address I quoted in chapter 1: "Nothing more, yet nothing less, than revealing our [language] in its true light, of depicting its elemental actualities, and its inherent and imperative possibilities. It is the task of *critical, reflective* [linguistic] *self-understanding*" (*APA* 24:30; emphasis added).

Other effects of the absence of philosophy from American culture include the fact that people in a variety of other disciplines have found that authors generally excluded from American philosophy since the McCarthy era are in fact vital for their work. This has led to rediscoveries and reinventions of those thinkers. Workers in literary theory and cultural studies, for example, have rediscovered thinkers such as Hegel, Heidegger, and Marx. In the process, they have also discovered—sometimes to their horror—that any genuine encounter with these thinkers, and others like them, must itself be philosophical in nature: general, historical, and without intermediaries. Meanwhile, some of the most subtle and fruitful work in the philosophy of science has involved itself in reinventing central aspects of thinkers such as Hegel and Heidegger. In all these cases, I suggest, literary theorists, students of culture, and philosophers of science find themselves shouldering ongoing and unnecessary burdens left by the McCarthy era. It is not, of course, that such theorists do not do good work; but they would do their best work more easily, I suspect, if they had been exposed to those thinkers, and others, in a way that was general, historical, and immediate.

5

Philosophy out of the Ditch

A Post-McCarthy Paradigm

American philosophy, if I am right so far, is in no danger of stagnation. Stagnation, in fact, might be a welcome reprieve from such things as the repeated emigration of prominent figures to other fields and the numerical decline in departments and individual philosophers, which I noted in chapter 3. These problems, serious as they are, might in fact be suspected of awakening the specter of something well beyond stagnation: complete extinction. But that is also unlikely. Philosophy's ancient prestige guarantees that some universities will always feel obliged to have philosophy departments (though, as a frustrated Ivy League dean is said to have told a philosophy job candidate in the early 1990s, that may be the *only* reason).

What philosophy may well arrive at in this country, however, is the status of an anachronistic laughingstock. The supposedly scientific view of philosophy as a timeless, selfless quest of truth, long discredited for science itself, continues in practice to hold sway among American phi-

losophers, who seem unable to visualize any goal for their inquiries
except the truth of sentences. They pursue that goal, to be sure, with
exemplary rigor. But it is now getting clear, I hope, that their rigor has
very carefully set limits. An exclusive focus on the truth of sentences
rigorously *suppresses* philosophical discussion of philosophy itself, and
especially of its recent disciplinary history. Without such discussion,
philosophy's intellectual history also remains opaque. The opacity, of
course, may be useful. But only to a few.

Where might American philosophy, intelligently informed about
its origins and prospects, go from here?

Beyond Rorty

Twenty years ago, Richard Rorty published his electrifying *Philosophy
and the Mirror of Nature.*[1] In it, he attacked philosophy's claim to be the
foundation for other parts of culture. Philosophers made that (extraordinary) claim for themselves, Rorty argued, in the name of their supposed possession of a rationally grounded theory of representation—of
what it is for the mind to "mirror" reality accurately (Rorty 3–4).
Because the most up-to-date vehicle of such mirroring is the true sentence (as opposed to such embarrassing antiquities as ideas and propositions), Rorty's criticism of analytical philosophy was kin, though not
actually ancestral, to the criticism of the status of sentential truth as
philosophy's only goal, which was discussed in chapter 2. (The main
difference would seem to be that Rorty's critique is developed without
any mention of political influences.)[2]

Rorty's acute critique of analytical philosophy and his always fascinating contributions to American culture generally qualify him as the
first American philosopher of the post-McCarthy era. He is the kind of
philosopher America would have produced more of, had the McCarthy
era never happened. His *Philosophy and the Mirror of Nature* remains
today the most important sustained attempt to understand the inner
conceptual workings of analytical philosophy and to find a way out of its
problems.

But there is a serious problem with the book, and indeed with
Rorty's subsequent thought, for having put paid to the old paradigm—
actually, to several of them—Rorty refused to supply a new one: his way
out of analytical philosophy was to abandon philosophy altogether. At

the end of his book, he conceded that philosophy may indeed have a future as a distinct discipline—either through some revival of foundationalism or through a new version of systematic philosophy "which has nothing whatever to do with epistemology" (Rorty 393–94). But as far as Rorty himself was concerned, philosophy should abandon its distinctiveness and become merely an edifying voice in the cultural conversation. Just what this would mean, however, cannot be spelled out, for "edification" consists merely in "finding new, better, more interesting, more fruitful ways of speaking" (Rorty 360)—and general rules can hardly be given for that. Even those philosophers for whom Rorty's vision of an edifying philosophy was attractive—probably a small group to begin with—would be unable to find their way to it, for it consists of nothing more than an intellectual version of the biblical injunction "Be fruitful and multiply."

I suggest that Rorty's inability to provide a new philosophical paradigm—indeed, his refusal even to seek one—is rooted in the fact that, in spite of his rebellion, he remains in crucial respects an analytical philosopher, bound to some of the McCarthy era's most crippling presuppositions. Consider, as a first example, the relation of philosophy to its history. To be sure, the history of philosophy is not for Rorty, as it was for Reichenbach, a mere compendium of errors. But neither is it what I, in the spirit of Hegel's *Phenomenology,* would call a "history"—a record of certain problems solved and a documentation of various dead ends. The history of philosophy for Rorty is merely a series of "accidentally produced" metaphors that "stretches backward and forward through past and future time" (*CIS* 20, 41, 61). The dismissal is more respectful than Reichenbach's, but just as definitive, for a series of accidental metaphors can have no reasonable hold over us today: we are not its results in any rational sense but merely what has tumbled out of it.[3]

Viewing ourselves as rational results of the past means seeing ourselves as growing out of, and carrying on, a specific tradition of innovation and problem solving. It does not mean that we should always emulate our past. The history of the Western world includes, among other defects and many glories, the kind of basic immorality that produced incessant wars, pogroms, slavery, and the Holocaust. Past philosophy has not been unaffected by this. It includes Aristotle on slavery, Aquinas on women, and the complicity of empiricism in racism and the slave trade.[4] These are all things that can be learned from, if only so that philosophers today do not repeat them—or any more basic errors from which they arose. Moreover, today's philosophers would hardly be the first to try to learn the lessons of the past. The whole history of philosophy has been a sustained, if largely unsuccessful, effort at precisely that. That is why the history of philosophy is far from being a mere compendium of metaphors. And it is why the results of that history—including, of course, analytical philosophy—have a rational hold on us today. Contemporary philosophy, in all its forms, has resulted from a process of critique and innovation that is as old as Western civilization itself. (Exactly as old, in fact.)

But Rorty does not see the past this way, so instead of replacing or supplementing analytical philosophy with any sort of historically alive critical approach, he invents the "ironist," a thinker who is (somehow) free to invent new vocabularies de novo, that is, without any heed to what has gone before.[5] The ironist is not motivated by specific problems or things that she sees as having somehow gone wrong but, much more abstractly, by Harold Bloom's "anxiety of influence." She wants to show that she is not a "copy or a replica" of other people but personally unique (*CIS* 23–24). The result of this is a view of the past as something to be avoided altogether.

Taken on Rorty's abstract and global level, the only way to be unique is to have a unique vocabulary—and the only way to get that is to create it oneself, rather than spend one's life "shoving around already coined pieces" (*CIS* 23–24). In undertaking such creation, the ironist not only ceases to be determined by the vocabulary she has inherited but actually creates a new one, thus achieving what Rorty calls "autonomy" (*CIS* 23–24, 27, 43, 97; also compare 20, 80). But achieving autonomy, for Rorty as for Kant, has nothing to do with solving problems or with learning from the past in any way. Its aim is instead to "create a style so distinctive as to make one's books incommensurable with those of one's precursors" (*CIS* 126).

This appeal to incommensurability means, in turn, that the aim of the ironist is precisely *not* to be able to learn from the past. All her hopes ride on the future, to which her relationship is for Rorty a matter of luck: "[W]ith luck . . . her [new] language will strike the next generation as inevitable. *Their* behavings will bear [her] impress" (*CIS* 29). Rorty's ironist therefore shuns equally the high points of philosophy's history— Aristotle's account of moral deliberation or Hume's criticism of causality, for example—and its low points, like the ones mentioned three paragraphs ago. Such equal nontreatment of highs and lows, of course, is manifestly unfair to the highs and strangely unconcerned about the lows. Should a German version of Rorty's ironist, for example, feel free to forget about the Holocaust?

In another unrecognized perpetuation of certain strands of analytical philosophy, Rorty holds that freedom is not a social phenomenon (as it is for such continental philosophers as Hegel, Marx, and Heidegger) but—like ironic autonomy—a characteristic of the isolated human mind.[6] The inside of that mind, moreover, is construed along analytical lines as basically a basket of beliefs, that is, of events or attitudes that claim to be true or false (*CIS* 88). Though the beliefs are webbed together and supplemented by desires (the basket shakes, in other words), there is no hint that the mind could contain anything like actions, or impulses to action—to say nothing of Husserlian essences, Heideggerean *Verständnis,* or Hegelian negativity.

Again, Rorty sees the "canonical sequence" of philosophers—Plato to Kant—as founding vocabularies based on the "appearance-reality distinction" (*CIS* 76). Where Heidegger sees philosophy as the forgetting of Being and Derrida as the project of presence, Rorty, like Quine and Reichenbach, still sees it as the pursuit of truth (*CIS* 28–29 [but also 68], 88, 76). Which, to close the circle, is why the history of philosophy is just a succession of metaphors: there is, apparently, nothing else for philosophy to be other than "attempts to capture the true shape of the world" (*CIS* 60). Since it cannot do so truthfully, it can only do so in metaphors.

With regard to truth itself, Rorty is only halfway out of analytical philosophy. We hear early in *Contingency, Irony, and Solidarity* that where there are no sentences there is no truth; indeed, it is because only sentences can be true that truth for Rorty is something we make rather than find (*CIS* 5, 9–10). Truth is thus for Rorty, as Bruce Wilshire has argued, a property of assertions, in which view Rorty agrees fully with analytical philosophy.[7] He differs from it because, as we have seen, he does not want true sentences to be the goal of inquiry. Rather, the goal of edifying philosophy, if it has to have one, would be new ways of talking.

But to become edifying, philosophy must abandon one of its most basic, and praiseworthy, traditional features. Philosophy has always been a sort of inquiry that examines itself (a point to which I shall return shortly). This means, in part, that philosophy traditionally places itself under standards of excellence that it itself undertakes to state and justify. But if all edifying philosophy can do is come up with happy accidents that reshape our language, no standards are possible, for accidents, though they may be serendipitous, are not standardly so.[8] A philosophy that operates by accident is thus no philosophy—as Plato argues in the *Ion,* it is poetry. The upshot is that Rorty, again like many analytical philosophers, cannot conceive of any alternative way of doing *philosophy.*

Finally, the kind of global rejection of the past supposedly exemplified by Rorty's ironist is either impossible or close to it. There is a story that the French philosopher Étienne Gilson, in his youth, undertook to write a book showing the thoroughness and profundity with which Descartes had carried out his claim to have escaped the restrictions of medieval philosophy.[9] Upon investigation, he discovered that Descartes had escaped those restrictions so little that his thought was actually a continuation of scholasticism rather than its overthrow—and Gilson himself became a Thomist. Rorty's case, I am afraid, teaches the same lesson. In spite of his repeated claims that the ironist can escape her inherited vocabulary, he has himself shown no ability to do so—and this is unsurprising, for those claims themselves are wildly overblown. The idea that a human being could ever create anything at all de novo is suspect on its face, if only because it so nonchalantly applies to us a characteristic that was in earlier days assigned to God alone: radical creativity. The most we mortals have ever been seen to do precisely is shuffle around the precarved pieces of our vocabulary, while occasionally whittling some of them into slightly different shapes. There is, moreover, no need to do more, for as the previous chapter hinted, the philosophical tradition contains resources that permit both a more radical critique of analytical philosophy than Rorty's *and its reinstatement* in a new (or very old) alternative paradigm.

Truth, Sentences, and Essential Temporality

I will begin to introduce this paradigm by summing up one of the basic lessons of this book in a single question: what would a philosophical approach be like that would *enrage* Raymond B. Allen? What sort of philosophy, in other words, would the leading academic Red hunter and nemesis of the APA least like to see going on in the United States?

It is important to notice, I think, that the worst news here is the good news. It is that the doctrine that Raymond B. Allen and his like wielded as a club against philosophy so long ago—the doctrine that philosophy should be a timeless, selfless quest of truth—was a *philosophical* doctrine whose validity should be debated by philosophers themselves. Nuclear physicists professionally presuppose that their aim is objective truth about subatomic particles. Chemists do not question the goal of providing true sentences about molecules. But philosophers, from *Republic* 7 (523c–e) on, have been different: philosophy has been the discipline that decides its own nature. (My claim earlier in this chapter that philosophy articulates and justifies its own standards was a reformulation of that ancient idea.)

In this context, Quine's cold war "naturalization" of philosophy into something differing from science only in degree meant two things.[10] First, philosophy would pursue the same goal as the natural sciences. Second, and more radically, it would pursue that goal in the same way the sciences do: by according it the status of a presupposition.[11] There is nothing wrong with such departures from tradition when they are recognized and argued for, but, as I showed in chapter 2, they have not been: Quine presents his gesture as a commonplace regarding truth and does not even relate it to the (more defensible) positions of his analytical forerunners Frege and Tarski.

Allen's injunction thus engaged the very nature of philosophy in ways that did not apply to other disciplines: it imposed a philosophical doctrine on philosophers. This bad news is good news, because it means that we philosophers can overcome that imposition with the very techniques we are so good at: clarifying and criticizing people's presuppositions, in this case our own.

"Philosophy is a timeless, selfless pursuit of truth" has only to be asserted openly to look dubious. How *could* it be argued for? Who, to begin with, is qualified to say what "philosophy" is? Why should philosophy be defined without regard to its temporal and social dimensions? What, furthermore, can the sentence mean? What is it for philosophy, or anything human, or even truth itself, to be "timeless and selfless"? How can something timeless be a "pursuit"? Or something selfless?

Given that we are all in time in rather important ways—we are born, die, and act in time—to be timeless is, in rather important ways, to be selfless as well. So let us look first at what it means to be timeless.

Taken at its extreme, the timeless, selfless quest of truth seeks truth that is itself timeless, and I will begin by discussing the possible timelessness of philosophy's goal. There are different ways for truth to be timeless, and one of them is for it never to change: any sentence is timeless if it is either always true or always false. There is, of course, an old and honorable metaphysical notion that there really is a domain for which this holds—call it God, the Forms, or logical space. Some philosophers, like Parmenides, have even seen fit to claim that this is the only domain there is. Though most philosophers have not been so extreme, it is a fact that philosophy has been trading off notions like this for millennia. It is perhaps only fitting that the passage of time, which these views despise, has done nothing to solve the problems with them.

Those problems are enormous. Right at the beginning, Parmenides had to face the fact that even if true Being never changes, our knowledge of it does: in addition to the timeless "way of truth," he said, there is a "way of seeming" on which mortals "wander two-minded" (that is, they are not wholly right about things but not wholly wrong either).[12] From the perspective of that path, even the Pythagorean theorem is temporal in that it has a history—the history of our encounters with it. The Pythagorean theorem itself may somehow be independent of that history, but our knowledge of it clearly is not: what we now know about the Pythagorean theorem is what we have learned at some point in the past. To want to know the theorem independently of the history of those past encounters is to want to know it independently of any relation it has to us: to know what it was like before any human had ever thought of it and what it will be like when no human thinks of it any longer.

And that, as Kant argued, is impossible, for we can never know anything whatsoever without bringing it into some sort of relation to ourselves: the categories in terms of which we know anything are in part supplied not by the thing but by our minds.[13] We need not accept Kant's whole transcendental account of our cognitive apparatus to see that from this point of view, the real, timeless nature of the Pythagorean theorem, the nature that it had before there were any human beings and will (perhaps) have after there are no more, cannot even be stated. Consider the normal way the theorem is written today: $a^2 + b^2 = c^2$. This formulation is known, of course, to most high-school students, but it is also conditioned by history, which gave us our alphabet and superscripts. The Greeks wrote it differently. The ancient Egyptians, as far as we know, could hardly have written it at all, for hieroglyphics does not easily tolerate the arbitrariness of variables. And future cultures may find our way of stating the relationship of the lengths of the sides of a right triangle to be, if not wrong, seriously misleading. So $a^2 + b^2 = c^2$ is in part a cultural product, legitimated by the fact that it is the product of the history of our encounters with what it expresses. It follows that the "real" Pythagorean theorem, the one that existed before the big bang (if it did), cannot be expressed as $a^2 + b^2 = c^2$, or indeed in any human notation, without subjecting it to the thought patterns of those who are doing the expressing. It cannot be expressed as it "really" is. How, then, can it be conceived?

This, I take it, is one more case of the ontological mischief that timeless truth, and the timeless propositions in which it is (somehow) tenselessly expressed, have made for philosophy from its earliest years on down. There is certainly more. Where, for example, does the timeless Pythagorean theorem reside when no one is thinking about it? In some sort of timeless mathematical space? Is that a different space from the one it resided in before there were any right triangles? What about before there was space at all? Did the Pythagorean theorem come into being with the big bang? Or was it somehow there even before, as an unanswered possibility? There is no need to repeat here either all this ontological bombast itself or the gradual story of its exposure and condemnation by thinkers as disparate as Nietzsche and Quine.[14] Let us turn, rather, to time-bound sentences: those that are true (or false) not eternally but at some time (or time span) t. Are they "timely"?

If they are, then for a sentence to be in time is to possess truth at some times and not to possess it at other times. But this leaves some important things open, in particular the question of whether such changeability in truth value is taken to be an essential characteristic of the sentences whose values change or accidental to them. This is important because, in the latter case, our philosophy has not really become timely at all. If change in truth value is accidental to sentences, then it drops out when we consider the true, or basic, nature of sentences as such, just as eye color drops out when we consider the basic nature of human beings. It can safely be ignored in philosophical accounts (which, after all, concern the essences, or basic natures, of things), and we are back at timeless propositions or something murkily akin to them. In other words, we have advanced from eternal truths only to temporal ones from which the temporality has been abstracted: from what Spinoza would call *aeternitas* to the domain of what he would call *sub specie aeternitatis*.[15]

Consider, in this regard, Donald Davidson's view that to understand the meaning of a sentence is to understand the conditions under which it would be true.[16] Although Davidson does not deny that truth values for sentences can change ("Truth . . . is not a property of sentences; it is a relation between sentences, speakers, and dates"), his suggestion is advanced as holding for all sentences, irrespective of whether their truth value changes or not.[17] And this means that their timeliness is, in the classical Davidson, mentioned but never really broached.[18] There is good reason for this, because such timeliness is a mere accidental modification to an atemporality that belongs to the sentence as such—and to which philosophical investigation, always seeking the more general, ineluctably turns. Accidentally time-bound truth thus equates, in Davidson's practice if not in his theory, to a sort of de facto timeless truth.

So, with Raymond B. Allen at our heels, let us commend ourselves to what I will call "essentially time-bound" truth, by which I mean truth *sub specie temporis:* truth that is understood in terms of how it comes into being, changes, and passes away.[19] Many philosophers of science (among them Arthur Fine and David Hull, whom I discussed in chapter 4) can tell us why such understanding is important. Alasdair MacIntyre, extending their sort of view from philosophy of science to moral theory, tells us as well. Because his project contains informative similarities to and differences from the one I have in mind, discussing it will enable me to specify the domain of the kind of philosophical inquiry I am proposing: what sorts of things we are to inquire about.

MacIntyre argues that the truth or falsity of any moral view can only rarely be determined (I, of course, would echo Carnap and say "never"). What we really are after as a matter of moral guidance is the moral theory that is "rationally superior" to its rivals, and deciding this is a complex matter that must take into account "the social and historical contexts of activity and enquiry in which [arguments] are or were at home and from which they characteristically derive their peculiar import" (MacIntyre 266–68).

One of MacIntyre's most basic lessons is thus the degree to which what I call "intellectual history" determines the contemporary shape of an academic discipline such as philosophy. One way to view such history is as a history of arguments, and MacIntyre has some sympathy for this approach: "As in the case of natural science there are no general timeless standards. It is in the ability of one particular [moral philosophy] to identify and to transcend the limitations of its rival or rivals . . . that the rational superiority of that particular moral philosophy and that particular morality emerges" (MacIntyre 268–69).

The nature of rational superiority is thus determined by the circumstances of the time. Hence, part of deciding that one moral philosophy is rationally superior to another is deciding what "rational superiority" itself is. As far as moral theory in MacIntyre's sense is concerned, both issues will be decided by argument (otherwise the superiority in question would not be rational), so the history of moral philosophy will for the most part be a history of arguments. The job of the moral philosopher is to look to historical debates to see which moral views can be established as rationally superior to the others.

One important point implicit in this (but not made clear by MacIntyre) is that we cannot in this historical effort confine our attention to the arguments actually being made around us here and now. The rivals of a particular philosophical point of view may well include possibilities that, for any of a variety of reasons, are not currently being mentioned. Valuable arguments and insights that have been forgotten, or even suppressed, may lurk anywhere in the history of philosophy. Heidegger, for example, has famously argued that metaphysics took a major wrong turn with Plato.[20] So also might there be important insights that have been passed over since Heracleitus, or Empedocles, or even Thales. Hence, MacIntyre's project, as he recognizes (270), is incompletable: valuable insights will always be lurking in history's unexplored corners.

The domain of moral arguments thus stretches further than MacIntyre explicitly acknowledges (though his philosophical practice, which importantly involves resurrecting the moral theory of Aristotle, suggests that he is aware that current debates often exclude or suppress possible arguments: compare MacIntyre 1–3). But I am going to go further yet and suggest that our historical attention, in this effort, should not turn exclusively or even primarily to arguments. Arguments, like sentences, have both structure and content, and argumentative structure tends to change much more slowly than argumentative content, if it changes at all.[21] Just as syntax changes more slowly than the meanings of the words that it connects, so rules of inference change more slowly than the sentences they connect. The first figure of the classical syllogism, Barbara, is as valid today as when Aristotle first codified it, but he could not have constructed any syllogisms at all using terms for "hard drive" and "random access memory." Neither could Carnap.

The temporal record of an argument or even an individual thesis includes how it came from what preceded it, how it gave way to what followed it, and how it changed in the meantime. This record concerns much more than merely whether previous or subsequent philosophers accepted or rejected that thesis. It is largely a matter of how advancing that thesis at a particular time changed the field of debate, permitted certain things to be thought and said and done, and foreclosed the thinking and saying and doing of other things. These aspects of the temporal record of a thesis or argument are usually deposited less in its syntactic or logical form than in the individual words it contains. It is to those words, then, that we should turn *first* in investigating the essential temporality of theses and arguments. There is little use, for example, in sorting through the logical structure of the *Phaedo*'s arguments for the immortality of the soul unless we know something about what Plato meant by *athanatos* and *psychē*.

MacIntyre turns to history, then, but only partway. Like Davidson with sentences, MacIntyre tends to view moral theories as what I would call only accidentally temporal, so that the past and future of moral views drop out of the analysis. Sometimes, to be sure, the rational superiority of one moral view to some other such view will at least be indicated by the fact that it came from that other view—as when Catholicism modified "Thou shalt not kill" into "Thou shalt not kill except in cases of legal execution, just war, and so forth." In such cases, the temporal origins of a moral view are important to understanding its rational superiority over the views it modifies. But for one view to be rationally superior to another, it is by no means necessary that it be a modification of it. The Catholic view might have been derived from earlier understandings of the biblical commandments without being in any way superior to them, and it might be superior to them while coming from somewhere else altogether.

To recur to my previous quote from MacIntyre: one moral philosophy may be able "to identify and to transcend the limitations" of its rivals without being in any way descended from them. And rational superiority is what MacIntyre wants us to look for, not accounts of how moral views come to be and pass away. The latter issue is sometimes relevant, but not essential, to the former. It is possible, though MacIntyre would of course deny that it actually happens, that *no* moral philosophy ever developed from any other.

To clarify what is at stake here, let me go back to the idea of a wrong turn in the history of philosophy. One way to construe that sort of thing is as a disagreement about the truth of one or more sentences: $\phi\ x$ or $\sim \phi\ x?$ If we make the wrong choice, we take a wrong turn. In either case, the debate is about the truth of a sentence, and so is the kind of debate with which analytical philosophers will be familiar. It is easy to turn it into a debate about the rational superiority of one of the two sentences (provided we have a currently workable definition of *rational superiority!*).

But sometimes debates take the form of whether ϕ itself has been adequately defined, and there issues of truth are often uninformative. Is it true or false, for example, that adultery includes sexual relations between a married man and his brother's childless widow? Though some robust essentialists—following Plato—have tried to turn this sort of thing into a debate about truth, doing so is difficult in today's philosophical world, for it requires us to establish that there is such a thing as adultery, a thing that has a nature to which our definitions must correspond. And even if we were convinced of that, it would not really help decide the practical issue.

Suppose it is true, for example, that adultery does not cover such an act. It would still be possible for people to feel very strongly, and even to argue, that it should, that is, that adultery just is not what it should be. They may have excellent reasons for their view and lament the unfortunate fact that adultery is what it is. They may have such acts judged by the same authorities that judge adultery, using the same standards and subjecting them to the same penalties—all without actually calling them adulterous—in which case, alas, their arguments will have degenerated into just the kind of semantic fiddling that moral realists despise. In the face of this, it seems more promising to view the issue, from the start, not as a debate about what adultery really is but as a matter of which acts we want to permit in our society and which not. It is, as Searle might say, the *consequences* of definitions that matter, not their truth.[22]

The distinction between debates about truth and debates about consequences is hardly absolute, and I do not mean that philosophers should abjure *all* attention to arguments—but, equally, argument is not all there is to philosophy. Some of the important consequences of a definition, to be sure, are inferential ones, and philosophers—like other thinkers—often decide how to define a concept by drawing inferences from it. Thus, it is sometimes hard to distinguish one kind of dispute from the other. When, for example, Aristotle argued that forms were in things instead of being separate from them, as Plato had thought, was he establishing a truth about forms or redefining the Greek term *eidos?* His argumentation, in *Metaphysics* 1.9 and elsewhere, suggests the former, but the virtual entirety of his philosophy explores the *consequences* of the redefinition: the fact that it enables him to show, for example, why humans always beget humans rather than other sorts of things, or to account for the fact that sometimes we knowingly do what is wrong. Pursuing the *essential* temporality of sentences thus leads us eventually, I suggest, to turn our primary philosophical attention from sentences (and arguments and beliefs) altogether, and to words and concepts.

Attention to the words in which philosophical theses are couched is useful in another way: it helps delimit the subject matter of our investigation. If we cannot understand the truth of an essentially temporal sentence without understanding how it came to be true, we must in the course of that understand how it came to be at all. A sentence comes to be in being uttered. But where do utterances come from? What precedes their utterance?

The answer is many things, far too many for philosophers. MacIntyre puts it—perhaps more problematically than he realizes—as follows: "The subject matters of moral philosophy at least—the evaluative and normative concepts, maxims, arguments, and judgments about which the moral philosopher enquires—are nowhere to be found except as embodied in the historical lives of particular social groups and so possessing . . . expression in institutionalized practice as well as in discourse, interaction and interrelationship with a variety of forms of activity" (MacIntyre 265).

This risks losing all specificity to the inquiry. As Wittgenstein and

Austin show in many detailed investigations, any utterance presupposes a social background—what Wittgenstein called a "form of life"—that is intertwined with other social contexts, often to an undecidable extent. To describe the social background of the use of any word, it seems, means describing a fair amount of the lives of those who use it. Moral philosophy (in MacIntyre's case) thus comes close to swallowing all of history: what can humans do that *cannot* be written about from MacIntyre's point of view?

To get a grip on all this, consider the following. Among the many, many things that precede the utterance of any sentence whatever are the words in which it is couched. They, too, are essentially temporal: words come to be, change, and die away, and that is no accidental fact about them. What precedes a word? Usually, some earlier version of itself, with a somewhat different sound or meaning. Thus, if we are going to understand any sentence as intrinsically temporal, we need to understand not only the social circumstances presupposed by its utterance, and so forth, but also the way the words in it came to be (their past) and how their availability contributes to our present situation (their future).

With this, we get a separate, moderately sized domain for philosophical history: it is *the history of the words* in which philosophical sentences and arguments are couched. Words like "beauty," "cause," "form," "individual," "justice," "measure," "other," "self," "truth," and "unity" are in several senses philosophical words. First, although everybody thinks *with* them, history teaches that it is primarily philosophers who have thought *about* them. Moreover, philosophy is, among many other things, a set of attempts at the most general and basic knowledge we can get. Words that are common to discourses in many different domains—what the Medievals called the *notiones communes*—are then part of philosophy's concern. Those same words are basic in the sense that other words may be defined in terms of them (legal responsibility, for example, is a species of causation; racial difference is a form of otherness). Philosophers have traditionally thought about such words, then, because they are the most general and basic ones we have.

The philosophical approach I am sketching here takes for its domain not a set of beliefs, theses, or arguments—still less a set of truths—but a set of words: our most general and basic ones. It tries to see those words as essentially temporal: as devices that connect us with the past and open up our futures.

Connecting with the Past: Narrative

Questions remain, among them:

- In what sense is such philosophy *not* aimed at establishing truths about the words it investigates, truths that are quite traditionally stated in sentences?
- How does that philosophy work? How does it do justice to temporality in ways that other approaches do not?
- Does it share with other philosophical approaches the characteristic of being somehow normative?
- How does it differ from neighboring paradigms, such as history of language, or more traditional versions of linguistic analysis?

Those questions bring us under the tutelage of one of philosophy's greatest and most cryptic masters: Hegel. It passes for a truism in some parts of the Hegel world that Hegel's philosophy has not, in general, been understood by English-speaking philosophers. But that is inaccurate, because among the things I do not understand are those I have never encountered, and most philosophers, today, have encountered Hegel. The encounter is usually fleeting and tends to come very early in one's philosophical education, but it is almost always there. At a minimum, a few of Hegel's many unfathomable pages are examined and he is dismissed, either as an abstruse mystery to think about later or as just what we do not want philosophy to be.

I have argued elsewhere that Hegel is many things, but neither of those.[23] As I will consider him here, Hegel is also not a pompous metaphysician, historical kibitzer, or a crypto-theologian. He is, rather, a rigorous conceptual historian who takes other people's truths, as well as his own, and forges connections between them—and with us. In so doing, he teaches us how to connect with the past without just saying true things about it.

There is a major difference between merely stating truths about the past and actually connecting such truths to the present. Suppose a planet is discovered orbiting Aldebaran, and the configurations of various interstellar fields allow for one, and only one, visit to that planet by earthlings. During their visit, the members of an earth expedition find the planet to be civilized. The planet's inhabitants have never traveled to the stars themselves, but they are superior historians. They have in fact a book of their own history, which contains only true sentences about their past. The visitors bring the book back with them to earth, translate it, and publish it. But the stargate has closed: earthling and Aldebaranian (to name the planet's inhabitants after the local star) will never meet again.

The published account of the Aldebaranian past would of course be true. Some of it might even have been verified by the space travelers, so that their fellow earthlings would know that it contained truth. But however true it might be, it would not be a history that earthlings could connect with. Not only would Aldebaranian history not be our history, but it could never join with our history. The Aldebaranians and the earthlings would remain in two different cultures, incapable of affecting one another except during their single encounter.

It is possible to attempt a history of philosophy that is like the Aldebaranian history book: one that truly states the doctrines of past philosophers but does not relate them to us today. Such a history could be read equally well (or poorly) by people from any historical period, as long as they knew the language in which it was written: it would reflect a "timeless, selfless quest of truth." But such a *merely true* account of the history of philosophy—one that accurately reflects the historical way philosophy actually unfolded but ignores the position of the historian— is just not on the Hegelian table. The history of philosophy is not, for Hegel, a set of neutral facts that could simply be reported in a timeless, selfless way. Among its results are ourselves—including many of our most important words (if not, anymore, our most basic beliefs). And from *our* standpoint, the history of philosophy presents not merely a set of historical developments but a series of gains and losses. Each such gain or loss, when identified as such, develops a connection between ourselves and our past, for it shows us *how* the past resulted, among other things, in us.

Consider a more down-to-earth example. Abraham Lincoln won the election of 1860. To see that fact as a gain for us is to place ourselves into an ongoing narrative of liberation, justice, and civil rights. It is to connect ourselves, as Americans, with that election in ways that an Aldebaranian, or even a Parisian, would not be connected—even though they could (other conditions being met) verify the *fact* of Lincoln's victory and its connections with the start of the Civil War and other subsequent developments. Liberation, justice, and civil rights are ongoing processes that connect contemporary Americans, in a positive way, with Lincoln's victory. Those same ideas link us in a negative way with the Dred Scott decision; to see that as a positive development would mean that we no longer valued liberation, justice, and civil rights, and would force us to see ourselves in very different ways indeed—morally repugnant ones. It would force us to become different people.

In sum, when we recount a historical development not from a timeless, selfless standpoint but guided by the knowledge that we ourselves are among its results, we see it not as a set of ethically neutral events but as a set of gains and losses. The standard with reference to which we identify a historical development as either a gain or a loss for us is what I call a "narrative link."

Historians create such links at least as much as they find them, and not only in ethics. As an example of the kind of invention I have in mind I will consider a discourse that is thought to make a radical break with what has gone before: that of Michel Foucault. Can narrative links be established between it and previous discourses?

Of course. Take Sartrean freedom. (As France's leading philosopher from the 1940s to the 1970s, Sartre is presumably an important figure in Foucault's intellectual past.) Such freedom may be defined as the radical capacity of an individual to make his or her own possibilities. Plug that into the philosophical problematic after it has been transformed by what Merleau-Ponty calls the "acquisition of language."[24] After that acquisition, freedom can no longer be innocently located in the individual, for, as Heidegger and Wittgenstein show, we are all subservient to the languages we speak. But Sartrean freedom can be relocated in language itself: discourse can be seen to remake its own possibilities in the most existentially radical ways. That capacity, more or less, is what Foucault calls "power."

We now have, and surprisingly easily, a narrative that flows from Sartre to Foucault. Let us now give the theme of this story a name: the capacity to re-create oneself will be "anagenesis." When that re-creation occurs via a passage from the subject to language, it will be "situating anagenesis." We thus produce a new middle term that historically connects Foucault to Sartre. It is a story that begins with freedom as a property of the individual consciousness and transforms it into a power of language. "Situating anagenesis," the name of this story, is what I call a narrative link: it denotes the story of one concept, that of Sartrean freedom, turning into something else, that of Foucauldian power.

Suppose now we undertake to produce narrative links among Peripatetic economics, the novels of Jane Austen, and contemporary quantum physics. No such links exist, of course, but we invent some. Such inventions are clearly not true to anything, for there is nothing in the historical facts of the case to which they correspond. They do not show (or explain) how Jane Austen emerged from Peripatetic economics, because in fact she did not. The conceptual links that connect our present situation to the past in this case do not preexist our investigation but are forged by it. And this is quite generally true: there was no such thing as situating anagenesis until I began spinning my tale of how Sartre's thought turned into Foucault's. There is also no narrative of American liberation unless Americans today identify Lincoln's 1860 victory as a gain. The criterion for evaluating these links is not truth: situating anagenesis and American liberation do not correspond to antecedently existing realities.

Unlike traditional narratives, which can in Kantian terms be called "determining narratives" and against which Lyotard and Derrida famously inveigh, this sort of narrative link does not preexist the narrative itself.[25] Each link is simply the result of one particular effort at narrative construction, carried out on a particular set of discourses as analyzed in particular ways. It is not present at the origin and confirmed in its power by the events narrated but formed out of those events, as, for Kant, a concept is formed via reflective judgment.[26] Thus, the construction of narrative in new investigation results not in a set of true propositions or sentences that report on something else but merely in a set of connecting words.

Any more detailed discussion of procedures and methods for such creation would be out of place here; it is to some extent, like all thinking, a contextualized matter of serendipitous invention. But we are not, I claim, in quite the unphilosophical situation where Rorty leaves us, for there are standards by which to judge the narrative links that result from such invention. What are those standards? Why would a philosophical narrative that bounced from Peripatetic economics to Jane Austen to quantum physics be loonier, though not false, than one that moved from Sartre to Foucault?

The question is important, because I earlier characterized philosophy as a discourse that places itself under standards of success and failure that it itself states and justifies. And Hegel can give us the answer, for his philosophical system, as I have argued elsewhere, is a giant rationalization of cultural memory. It makes no standard truth claim at all. What it does claim is twofold: it claims to be comprehensive, and it claims to be ordered. Those together—what I call, though somewhat unhappily, "Nobility"—constitute the excellence of narrative linkage. What they say is that a narrative, philosophical or otherwise, is better if it links together more material, and links it with enhanced rational transparency. Narrative links are validated by the fact that they can order a diversity of material into comprehensible narratives. In some cases, of which the history of philosophy is one, that material includes ourselves.

Each side of Nobility can be specified further. The material linked in philosophical narrative as I am sketching it here is philosophical words at different stages of their meanings. These stages, for Hegel, can be either historical or conceptual. In his *Science of Logic,* he presents what could be called "conceptual narratives." He traces causality, for example, from its emptiest possible meaning—one in which the cause is not distinct from the effect (like the "dormitive power" of opium)—through the increasing differentiation of cause from effect and to their final reassimilation in "reciprocity," a relation in which the cause is just as much the effect as the cause and vice versa.[27]

In a historical narrative of the notion of cause, by contrast, later thinkers on the meaning of the term would be reconstructed as revising and extending the views of earlier ones. Such a narrative is presented, though not as linguistic, by Aristotle in *Metaphysics* 1. There, Aristotle reconstructs the development of earlier thought on causality from the material through the moving, formal, and final causes. Again, Aristotle's account is not to be judged wholly by its conformity to antecedently existing reality. He crafts it with some degree of creativity, opposing Heracleitus as the philosopher of change a bit too neatly to Parmenides as the philosopher of eternity. (Because we lack independent sources for most of the material Aristotle covers, we will never know just how creative he really was.)

My interest here is in historical narrative. Its various stages must, of course, be truthfully reported. If Thales, Anaximander, and the other pre-Socratics did not say at all what Aristotle has them say—if they really wrote about swine husbandry, for example—then his narrative is untrue. The forging of narrative links in philosophy thus does not allow us to abandon attempts to uncover the truth about the past. We still try to describe it accurately, to get the facts right, but we do not *stop* there. We go on to place our descriptions into a narrative to make clear that we—now, today—are among what has followed from the past. Hence, the past—at least the philosophical past I am talking about—is not something *accidentally* temporal on which we report but something *intrinsically* temporal with which we connect.

A philosophical narrative may include only true statements but fail to be comprehensive because there are not a lot of facts available for it to comprehend. This is true for the Peripatetic–Austen–quantum-theory narrative I mentioned earlier: there is a lot of room between its stages, and there is just no way to fill it in. None of the historical developments between, say, Theophrastus and Austen helps us to construct a narrative that connects the two. Hence, the narrative is not false—its various stages are truthfully reported—but, so to speak, "spacey."

Other times, and often more seriously, facts are available that should be connected by a given narrative, but they are left out of it. In that case, though not stating or relying on any untruths, the narrative is less Noble than it would otherwise be. If, for example, there was an eighth sage of Miletus who maintained that "cause" denoted nothing other than a constant conjunction of sensory impressions, it would make Aristotle's narrative in *Metaphysics* 1 quite untidy indeed. But he would be wrong to leave that person out altogether; he would, rather, have to reconceptualize his narrative links to allow for the missing sage. More tellingly, it was not, strictly speaking, false for historians of the American West to focus on characters who were not African Americans; they may have described their selected historical objects accurately enough. Such behavior was deeply ignoble, however, for the resulting narrative failed comprehensiveness in morally repugnant ways.

Turning to the other side of Nobility, rational transparency, we find that Hegel has an account of it as well. What I am calling rational transparency is commonly viewed as a function of simplicity: a single explanation for many things is more rationally transparent than many different explanations. Hegel's view of it is even less reified and is contained in his view of what he calls "determinate negation." "To negate" for Hegel means, very generally, to move on from a thing.[28] In determinate negation, just one feature of a thing is moved on at a time (hence, I prefer to call it "minimal negation").[29] For a historical development to be "transparent" is just for it to be reconstructible as a series of minimal negations—the fewer, of course, the better. Such negations are not explanatory factors (and dialectics does not explain anything). They are merely a certain way of organizing data.

A minimal change is not necessarily a trivial one. It changes only a single aspect of the situation, but that aspect might be central to it. If we look at the criticisms of Plato's theory of forms in the ninth chapter of the first book of Aristotle's *Metaphysics,* for example, we find that they are all directed to just one of its assertions: that forms are separate from the things of which they are the forms. This single, minimal negation of Plato's philosophy, however, was central enough, as I noted earlier, to produce a massive transformation in philosophy itself.

When the transparency is "rational," as I use that term, each such change can be seen to solve a problem in the preceding stage (typically, for Hegel, a contradiction). Noble narrative is thus a way of reconstructing the past as a cumulative series of solutions, rather than as a compendium of error (Reichenbach) or of accidents (Rorty). Such accumulated solutions are important. They underlie our present lives and societies as the skeletons of dead coral underlie tropical islands. Like islanders, we live on them and off them. But because problems arise more quickly than reefs grow, we must be aware of the deeper trajectories those solutions are taking, of the direction and speed with which our cultural reef is growing, for those are the directions and distances in which we, and our descendants too, may grow.

To accept a narrative as Noble, then, is to accept it as reconstructing our history as a series of solutions to problems. Since solutions are better than problems, this means legitimating the past. But only in a sense—only as what I am calling "rational." Legitimating the past as rational is not (pace Hegel) the same as accepting it as good. The development of the great colonial empires, for example, was highly rational: problems arose one after another and were often brilliantly solved. But imperialism was nonetheless evil. To accept a narrative as having rationally resulted in one's own situation does not mean accepting it as one that should not be negated—minimally, but perhaps at its very core.

Hegel is commonly viewed as having attempted something truly magnificent and as having failed preposterously to achieve it. But when we view his systematic thought as philosophical narrative, it turns out to be quite achievable (though still not exactly modest in its pretensions). It is achievable because Nobility is not an absolute concept, the way truth is for logicians: it is not a matter of all or nothing. Nobility has degrees, and failure to get things exactly right does not mean that we have to start over. Rather, it means that we have to remodel our narrative to take account of new truths and (perhaps) eliminate what turn out to have been falsehoods. The play of what Hegel calls "Absolute Spirit," to which I referred in chapter 4, is merely the activity of such remodeling.

Given that this sort of inventive narrative is possible, and that there is a standard by which it can be judged, why should philosophers, and others, bother with it? What is the value of this sort of connection to the past? A full discussion of this question must await my explanation of the other side of the paradigm I am advancing, the side of what I call "demarcation," but several general reasons can be given now. Some of them hold for philosophical history in general; others hold specifically for the kind of narrative I am sketching here.

First, a broadly Hegelian argument suggests that narrative in general is inherent in the way we experience time. The repetition of a past event often changes the present more than the event itself. It is the repeated passage of water that wears grooves in rock. Living things exploit this: skin that is repeatedly exposed to cold becomes hardened, and ears repeatedly exposed to loud noises become deaf. It is thus natural for all living things to respond, not merely to events but to the repetition of events. And nature, for Hegel, is preeminently a realm of repetition: no matter how many times the earth goes around the sun, it will continue to do so in the same way.

It is humans, by contrast—and humans, admittedly, of a certain cultural background—who view endless repetition as something to be avoided and assert, with Santayana, that "those who cannot remember the past are *condemned* to repeat it."[30] It is at this point, then, that narrative sets in: when people become afraid that unless they understand the past, they will repeat it in the present. Philosophical narrative, linking us to the past by way of negation, shows us in detail how the past is different from the present, and so shows us how not to repeat it. It is a way of recognizing the distinction between unique events, such as the big bang, and those that get repeated, such as the coming of spring, without restricting the latter to *mere* repetition.

A second set of reasons for historical narrative in general is ethical in nature. In general, philosophers—like other human beings—ought not to obliterate their past. Those who created it were people like ourselves;

it is not fair to forget them and the contribution they have made to our being. Indeed, if we take the Golden Rule seriously, we are forbidden to do so, for who would want, having forgotten her predecessors, to be forgotten in turn? Even Rorty's ironist, we saw, wants future generations to build on her work. But then the ironist must admit that she is building on the work, and the sacrifices, of previous generations.

Third, if philosophy is merely a matter of seeking true sentences, then its history is of only accidental relevance, for as I have pointed out, to know whether a sentence is true is not to know where it came from. But if an important part of philosophy is, as I suggest, a matter of procuring good (or Noble) words, then things are different. The history of philosophy is important to philosophers, first, because it is a truism that we often cannot understand where we are without understanding how we got there. If the current rate of unemployment is 6 percent, for example, it is very important to know if the rate three months ago was 3 percent or 9 percent. The same kind of thing holds for the words we all use and philosophers think about. The final stage of a philosophical narrative is the standpoint of our current philosophical vocabulary. If we can see that vocabulary as having emerged from others—if we can understand it in its essential temporality with regard to the past—then we can understand much of what is really under way and at stake in our language.

It is wholly naive to think that the basic philosophical constituents of our current lives—the words we use to understand and articulate ourselves and our situations—are finished tools that stand passively and permanently at our disposition. Rather, like the unemployment rate, they have trajectories and momenta of their own. They are characters in a history that is far older than any of us is, and that we must understand if we want to influence it. Thus, it is well worth knowing that the reference class of the word "freedom" in America has been gradually enlarging through the centuries to accommodate more and more kinds of people, and that the defining characteristics we associate with being free—the criteria of freedom—have often (but not always) followed this drive rather than pushed it.[31]

Finally, there is another, more revealing kind of ethical import to the specific kind of historical narrative I am sketching here—narrative that claims Nobility rather than truth. Philosophers are often asked, usually by nonphilosophers, to provide a reason for living. This is not a task easily discharged, but traditional philosophers sought to do so. Plato, for example, composed the *Phaedo* partly as a grand argument against suicide. His overall argument rests on the view that we are put on this earth to be tested and that to walk away from life is to fail the test. Many other philosophers have made other versions of this argument, but it fell apart in modernity, when philosophers generally abandoned recourse to divine assignments and the like. Kant undertook a rearguard action, here as in so much of his philosophy, seeking to derive an injunction against suicide by appealing to the nature of the human mind rather than to outside authority.[32] Today, of course, philosophers no longer see it as their business to seek arguments against suicide at all.[33]

Noble narrative, if I can call it that, provides an argument against suicide, for as long as I am implicated in an unfinished narrative, I have reason not to commit suicide. One good reason to go on living is that one has certain tasks left undone, and Noble narrative, just because it is not true, is a task never completed.

The incompleteness revealed by this form of ethical import is of two kinds. First, suppose that the American narrative of freedom, which I mentioned earlier, claimed to be true. This would mean not just that one's descriptions of the various events and testimonies concerning the meaning of freedom down through American history were true but that their linkage into a single story was true as well. This would in turn commit us to the idea that there was a single entity, Freedom itself, developing through the centuries until it reached America and, eventually, us.[34] The result of this would inevitably be some degree of quietism. The only issue open for us, who stand at the end of the narrative, is whether we want to help Freedom in its further unfolding. For a few of us—the grand historical actors of our time—that decision may have some meaning, but for the rest of us, it is mere foolishness to think so. Freedom will do quite well, or not so well, without our help. The narrative is basically complete without our efforts.

That grand truth claim itself is patently *un*true, however. There are numerous ways to connect the various facts and testimonies. There are plenty of people who would claim, for example, that they are to be linked together as part of a tale of American hypocrisy, rather than American freedom. Given the fact that freedom has always been to some degree, certainly in America, an exclusionary concept—we who are free thereby differ from, and are better than, those others who are not free—such a narrative might well include the established facts as easily as does our competing narrative of freedom.

And so before the narrative can include us as its final stage, we must *do* something: we must *accept* it. There is no narrative of freedom—indeed, no freedom—until we make that narrative ours. Freedom is nothing over and above us and our actions, and to the extent that we value it—accept its narrative as ours—we engage ourselves to keep it moving along. We undertake to act as if the narrative of freedom, rather than its competitor, has resulted in us—for the moment. If freedom's narrative depends on my commitments, it is incomplete without my participation, and if I am making such commitments and participating in such stories, I am not killing myself.

This does not exhaust the essential incompleteness of philosophical narrative, for if it is not true that there is a thing called Freedom that is somehow bringing itself to realization all around me, then it is not (strictly) true that my present situation is already structured by that thing. To accept the narrative, e.g., of freedom, then, is actually to change my situation. In such acceptance, I come to understand my standpoint as a stage in a story of freedom (small f), and a standpoint understood, usually at least, is a standpoint transformed (think of a person who comes to realize that she has, for a long time, been in love with someone). So for me to accept a philosophical narrative is to put myself into a new situation in which I understand what is now my previous situation as having been the outcome of a narrative of freedom. And I must once again decide whether to accept that narrative as applying to my new situation, and so on. I am thus part of—I make myself part of—a narrative that will never end. As long as I accept such a narrative, I cannot ever, reasonably, kill myself.

The same holds if I reject the narrative of freedom at any stage. If I come to understand that my previous understanding of my situation was false—because, perhaps, what I thought was freedom was really only hypocrisy—my own story continues, but it metamorphoses into the narrative of something else, not freedom: a new narrative link must be forged.

For these arguments to work, a narrative, philosophical or other, has to be accepted in a special sense: as one whose final stage (so far) is ourselves. Why, in any particular case, should we do that? The Hegelian answer is that we should accept such a narrative, in such a way, because it is Noble. This means, on the one hand, that we think it is complete up to now: all the relevant established facts are to be found among its various stages. And it is rationally transparent: each phase arises as a minimal change that solves problems in the preceding one. The narrative itself is held together not by a single overarching, developing thing (such as the infamous World Spirit) but merely by a succession of solutions—of minimal negations.

Our situation is a state of affairs that (1) contains us and (2) is in some way temporary. All of the reasons I have given for engaging in philosophical narrative—that it shows the historical trajectories of our basic words, keeps us from abandoning reality altogether, and provides ways to recognize our surroundings as neither wholly unique nor exactly replicable—point toward our situatedness. Philosophical narrative is thus one way of clarifying and establishing—of codifying—our situation. It does so by reconstructing the development of our most basic and general words, which constitute the philosophical core of that situation, in a Noble way.

My proposal that narrative, even of a certain rarefied sort, be included in the basic philosophical tool kit would (I hope) have appalled Raymond B. Allen, but it will also scandalize many others, even today. This is partly because such narrative has long had a suspect status within philosophy. Plato, in the *Phaedo,* calls acceptance of his example of it there a "noble risk" (*kalos kindunos,* 114d6). Human situatedness itself, indeed, is an ancient bugbear of philosophy. Philosophers have traditionally been oriented toward states of affairs that are *not* temporary, that is, that are either truly timeless in that they never change at all (like Platonic Forms) or that are de facto timeless in that change is merely accidental to them (like Aristotelian essences). But science has taught us that more and more of what we thought were permanent states of affairs really are temporary and is now pointing us to the possibility that *everything* is temporary—that even the laws of nature change.[35] However unpalatable it may be to philosophical traditionalists, the basic ontological category is no longer form, essence, substance, and so forth—all versions of permanence—but situation. This means that philosophical narrative must be removed from the suspect status to which Plato originally relegated it and accorded full status in the philosophical tool kit.

Contemporary suspicions of narrative are not all grounded in ancient tradition or in the recent politics of truth; they have a variety of sources. Two broad lines of criticism come from within continental philosophy. Before going onto the other, demarcative side of the paradigm I am sketching, I will briefly suggest how they can be answered.

First, thinkers such as Jacques Derrida, Michel Foucault, and Thomas Kuhn, as well as Richard Rorty, have certainly shown that the kind of continuity that philosophical narrative seeks is not the only way things happen. Rupture, in other words, is a historical fact. Gaston Bachelard was perhaps the first to argue this when he claimed against Emil Meyerson that the movement from Newtonian to relativistic physics cannot responsibly be reconstructed as the kind of step-by-step improvement that philosophical narrative, at least of my (Hegelian) kind, trades in. Rather, the theory of relativity transformed, all at once, our concepts of space, time, velocity, simultaneity, algebra, rationalism, realism, humanity, and causality.[36] What Einstein achieved was not a gradual displacement of Newtonian physics but the simultaneous transmutation of a number of its fundamental concepts into radically new ones. For seeing this, Bachelard is credited by Georges Canguilhem with introducing the idea of epistemic break, so crucial to postmodern thought.[37]

But rupture, while real enough, is not a condition of all history, partly because history has no universal conditions. Uncovering rupture is not the sovereign aim of inquiry, partly because inquiry has no single sovereign aim. In particular, the kind of inquiry I am proposing here does not have the sovereign aim of corresponding to the facts, on which the above thinkers—and particularly Foucault—covertly trade.[38] That Einstein's theory did not in fact come about as a step-by-step series of minimal negations has no bearing on the question of whether or not it can be reconstructed that way. In analytical geometry we learn that *any* set of points on a coordinate plane can be connected by a line whose formula can be given in an equation. Similarly, I suggest, for vocabularies and discourses. No matter how disparate and even incommensurable two of them might seem, we can take it as a regulative ideal that there is some set of mediating or narrative words in terms of which both can be understood. Or rather (and this is the whole point), there *will be* such a set if we are sufficiently industrious and imaginative to invent it. For the reason that Kuhn, Foucault, Derrida, and Rorty do not discover such middle terms is *precisely that they are looking for them.* If they wanted them (which of course they do not), they could rather easily invent them.[39]

The other criticism of narrative is Habermasian in inspiration and goes like this. Philosophy is supposed to attain universal truth, but any narrative begins with a particular set of initial conditions and develops (or is construed to develop) out of them by a particular set of negations. Therefore, no narrative can gain universality, or be called philosophical.

This argument, seeking to vindicate universality, relies oddly on two very particularized concepts. One is its notion of philosophy as necessarily seeking universal truths. What would Aristotle, whose standard definition of a universal (*kath' holou*) is that it can be in more than one place at once (*Metaphysics* 7.13.1038b10–12) make of the view traded upon by this argument that what is universal is somehow *everywhere* at once? Although seeking universal truth in this sense is hardly an unphilosophical thing to do, resting an argument of any kind on such a restricted meaning for philosophy is a dangerous move. More seriously still, this line of argument presupposes a particular concept of universality: a static and absolute one in which the universal is opposed to the particular.

Narrative as I have described it in fact achieves universality, but of a different and more dynamic kind, for it is intrinsic to a philosophical narrative link to get *more* universal as time goes on. A philosophical narrative link that covers five different stages in a reconstructed development will, in a sense akin to Aristotle's, be more universal than any one of those stages. If it then comes to cover six stages, it will become more universal still. As I argued earlier, philosophical narratives are never finished because their final stage is our situation—a situation that is changed simply by being narratively comprehended. As time passes, our philosophical narrative will, unavoidably, come to cover six stages, and then seven, and so on. . . . The inevitable enrichment of narrative material as time passes will thus, when brought together by narrative links, raise those links to higher and higher levels of universality.

This concept of universality as something that needs to be painstakingly constructed by process of addition, rather than attained all at once by some argument or act of quantification, is of ancient date. Julian the Apostate championed it, for example, in his expansion of the Roman pantheon to include ever-newer gods, and opposed it to the monotheistic universalism of the Christians, whose god—once accepted—reigned always and everywhere.[40]

True, such narrative universality will never get to the absolute, monotheistic universality called for by thinkers in, for example, Habermas's version of the Kantian tradition: a universality that claims that its structures, like the commandments of a single god, can never be violated (or never without fault). To see why, we must turn from the essential past of philosophy to its essential future, and from what I call "narrative" to what I call "demarcation."

Opening Up the Future: Demarcation

Hegel has this to say about the future: "The past is the preservation of the present as reality, but the future is the opposite of this, the becoming of the present as possibility, and thus as formless (*gestaltlos*). From out of this formlessness the universal first comes into form in the present; and hence in the future no form can be perceived."[41] True to what might be called the "essential imperfect" in Aristotle's formula for essence, *to ti ên einai,* Hegel is saying here that something becomes real (*wirklich*) only when it survives the inevitable transition from present to past. Something is real for us, in this sense, only when it is retained and remembered; something that exists just for a moment and leaves no trace on us is unreal. We cannot remember something if we do not know what it was, and so such memorializing of the past requires determinate knowledge of it. This in turn requires determinacy on the side of the object memorialized: we cannot know what it is if it has (or had) no specifiable properties.

The future, as opposed to this, has no form, but is the source of form. It is that out of which the universal comes to us: that is, as I argued above, it is that which guarantees the increasing universality of our thought. It is somewhat surprising, then, that Hegel should conclude elsewhere that the future can be philosophically ignored. Commenting on—and in the final sentence endorsing—Epicurus, he writes: "Mere privation, which is what death is, is not to be confounded with the feeling of being alive, which is positive; and there is no reason for worrying oneself about it. It is no concern of ours whether [the future] is or is not; we are to have no uneasiness on that account. This is the correct way to think about the future."[42] In spite of the fact that the future is the source of form, it is for Hegel something of no concern to us as humans—or as philosophers, who think about things in the correct way. Hegel's justification for this, however, is merely an ancient bromide about fearing death. His appeal to this bromide, to be sure, enables him to avoid an important problem: as the source of *form,* the future is indeed formless and is something that philosophy, which even for Hegel aims at clarity, cannot speak about.[43] However, as the *source* of form, it is also something with which we must deal, to which we are not only open but toward which we are ineluctably under way.

It is a truism that the future cannot be described, for we can only describe what is or has been before us, and the future does not even exist yet. The standard view, then, is that the future can only be inferred from the present—but such inference, as Hume taught us, is at bottom a scandal.[44] The view that the future will *in any way* resemble the past rests upon nothing more than a habit, instilled in us by the fact that it always has so far. However, habit proves nothing, and it is Humeanly possible that tomorrow the sun will not rise, pigs will fly, and two plus two will equal five. As long as we take what Heidegger calls an "inauthentic" view of the future, this feature of it can be dismissed as something merely accidental to our experience of the present. We cannot, of course, be sure that anything we know or love will exist tomorrow; but the possibility that it will not is usually small enough that it hardly matters.

What we need to realize is that this small scandal, the radical unknowability of the future, is not accidental, but essential to the present moment in which we live. The key argument that this is the case was made by Heidegger, who takes the fear of death much more seriously than do Hegel and Epicurus. In *Being and Time,* death is the "possibility of no more possibilities." It is wholly unknown what death is and when it will come.[45] But each of us knows *that* it is coming, sometime, whatever it is. Death, in short, is the final shapelessness (*Gestaltlosigkeit*) of our future.

As such it determines, in its current absence and impending presence, the shape and scope of our lives right now, for our lives are shaped by the commitments we make, and it is the fact that we are going to die, at some unknown time, that requires us to make those commitments. If I were going to live forever, for example, I would not have to choose a life partner. I could marry every other member of the human race and live a hundred years with each. Nor would I have to commit myself to a career, or to a community: I could be a Philadelphia lawyer for sixty or seventy years, then move into medicine in Houston or boxing in Marseilles for a couple of centuries, and then take up subsistence farming on the slopes of Mount Everest. It is because we are mortal that the major decisions we make require us to let some possibilities go past definitively.

Our unknown but impending future thus structures our present to its very core, and this is the fact missed by Hegel and Epicurus. Each of us, always, is feeling along the edge of something radically unknown but impending, and the necessity of that *tâtonner* is essentially what it is to have a future. The future on this view is not something we describe or connect with, for there is nothing in it to be described or connected with. It is a gap that we *open up*.

Heidegger thus agrees with Hegel about the essential opacity of the future, and about the fact that it is, so to speak, coming at us. He does not agree that the future can therefore be left to itself. True, it is not coming at us with a determinate and cognizable form: the future is not something we know. Rather, it shows up in our present experience as an emptiness. This emptiness, however, this place in our experience where there is nothing to be known, is not a gap in the usual sense. It is not what the ancients would have called a *kenon,* a void, for it is a gap into which we are constantly being pulled, a dynamic gap that shapes our lives. It is what I call a *diakenon*—an emptiness that, like our death, gathers a being or beings around itself.[46]

That a set of beings, or of aspects of one being, is diakenically gathered is evident when

1. none of them is adequately understood apart from the others;
2. none grounds or explains the others;
3. no yet more basic phenomenon can ground, or explain, all of them together.

I suggest that for anything to have what I call an "essential future" is for it exhibit this sort of structure. The activity of aiding this sort of exhibition is what I call "demarcation," and it constitutes the other half of what I call "situating reason": the half that opens philosophical thought up to the future.

Because we will never know anything fully, our encounters with things are always incomplete and under way toward further encounters; they always have an essential future, and everything we experience has diakenic aspects. The various techniques and gestures of demarcation, like those of narrative, can thus apply to anything whatsoever. From the present point of view, they apply most particularly to the dialectical continuities established in philosophical narrative. Once such a narrative is constructed, we may "demarcate" it in two general ways. One is to disaggregate its own constituents, as Bachelard did to Meyerson's dialectical reconstruction of the theory of relativity. The other is to show such a narrative to stand in a diakenic relationship to various things external to it. Among the latter, most important will be the historical situations from which its own truths are drawn and other narratives connecting those same situations with each other. In the former case, we undermine our narrative by showing that in fact it does not quite fit the facts it claims to connect. In the latter, we show that another narrative is possible, perhaps even more than one. In both cases (and in contrast to the kind of demarcation which merely disaggregates the stages of a narrative from each other), demarcation leads to a proliferation of narratives and to further invention of possibly useful narrative links.

Like dialectical continuity, diakenicity is not so much a matter of what is in things as of how we take them. To claim that a thing or group of things exhibits diakenic gathering does *not* mean, in particular, that more traditional kinds of unity are not to be found in it. A claim of diakenic gathering means that we have not yet discovered all of the possible unifying factors and that there is a definite space within the thing as we have experienced it so far where such factors may come to be. The diakena in a thing, then, are just those parts at which it is open to its own, and our, futures.

Diakena thus do not (exactly) preexist the demarcative activity that exhibits them, any more than do narrative links. A philosophical demarcation is no more "true" or "false" than a philosophical narrative is. But, like narrative, demarcation has standards of its own. If on the one hand no relationship between two things is discernible, so that they simply fall apart into mutual indifference, then they do not exhibit what I call "diakenic gathering." If on the other hand their relationship can be made conceptually clear, in which case either one of them grounds the other or some third thing with a nature of its own grounds both, then they also do not exhibit diakenic gathering.

How could we show this? How could we, as demarcative philosophers, open up unpredictable futures for philosophical utterances? For an utterance, as for anything else, to have a future is for it to be essentially conditioned by something unknown but impending. And since the business of an utterance, philosophical or otherwise, is to say something, this something that it says—its meaning—must also be so conditioned. The utterance's future thus includes the ways it will be understood by those who hear it, and those ways must therefore be unpredictable. An essential, "scandalous" unpredictability must be built into the sentence right now, because the future of a thing is essential to it.

We show this essential unpredictability by showing how very slippery utterances are, here and now—how easy it is for them to slip the bonds of clarity, truth, and what traditionally stands behind both: speaker's intention. Derrida's critique of the role of speaker's intention in speech act theory is a model of this.[47] But behind Derrida, and more important for present purposes, looms the difficult figure of his (and our) obscure mentor, Heidegger. Not the Heidegger who listens for Being to tell him that Hitler is smart enough to follow his orders, but the Heidegger who resolutely declares that Being is not a being and therefore does not *say* anything, but echoes silently from the looseness in our words.

In the case of an utterance, the beings gathered by this silent center are the words it contains, which are necessary to each other but do not quite fit together. We show the gathering that operates in a philosophical utterance by considering its individual words, each in turn. We try to see how each sets up the next and helps it, in turn, set up the word that will follow it, in ways that cannot be conceptually clarified. I will discuss this type of thing in even less detail than I did Hegelian dialectics, for it is much easier and, I think, more informative to show it being done in a specific case than to try to state, in a few pages, how it is to be done in general.[48]

I use as a paradigm of this approach Heidegger's discussion of Parmenides in the second part of his *What Is Called Thinking?* (*WD* 113–245). Heidegger here takes a saying (*Spruch*) of Parmenides that, in Greek, is *chrê to legein te noein t' eon emmenai*. This is usually translated as "it is necessary to say and think that being is." Heidegger, working toward a translation of his own, first separates the saying's different parts with semicolons and writes them on separate lines, as follows:

chrê;
to legein te noein t';
eon;
emmenai

Was Heisst Denken? (182)

He then translates each line in turn, showing that a more literal translation of the saying is much more disconnected than the standard English or German one: "Needful; the saying also thinking too; being; to be." Even when translated in such a disconnected (or, as Heidegger calls it, "paratactic") way, the utterance appears to have unity of some sort. Heidegger traces out that unity by going through each stage (phrase) of the utterance in turn, showing how each can have meanings other than those traditional translators have given it.

As might be expected, Heidegger does not produce a new and finished translation of the saying. The last version he gives, in the next-to-last lecture of the book, is: "Useful is the letting-lie-before-us, so (the) taking-to-heart, too: beings in being" (*WD* 228). In the final lecture, Heidegger criticizes the final three words of this version but does not insert any new version of them into his translation. The ultimate sense of the saying that he is working toward thus remains unstated: "Every primal and proper identification states something unspoken, and states it so that it remains unspoken" (*WD* 196). Every primal and proper identification, in other words, leaves a future open.

Heidegger's procedure here shows clearly how a temporalized approach such as his own differs from the consideration of a sentence with respect to its truth value, in which the sequence of the words is a matter of indifference. It also shows how demarcative thinking can open new horizons, new futures, even for an utterance that scholars have long "comprehended" so well that they have reduced it to an "obvious platitude" (*WD* 172).

Part of this undertaking is phenomenological: Heidegger must simply *show* that the words in a sentence stand as stages in the emergence of something that does not unite them in any conceptually clear way. Part of it is also negative: he must show that certain unifying factors commonly appealed to—explanations and commonalities—are not tenable. The chief enemy of such diakenic gathering in the case of utterances is the grammatical structure usually attributed to them. In terms of such structure, the various parts of the sentence are brought together by an act that, on its most basic level, is an act of predication. Heidegger destabilizes that sort of nondiakenic gathering by separating the various parts of the sentence from each other and turning attention to the individual words in it, and to their surpluses of meaning. For predication, unlike diakenic gathering, can tolerate only one meaning for each word it unites.

That is why, throughout his interpretations of poets and thinkers, Heidegger never presumes that any word is being used in its standard meaning. As in the case of Parmenides, he is willing to go to the very back of the dictionary entry for a word, and even beyond, to come up with new possibilities. In this approach, ambiguity is a *positive* resource of language. The different meanings of a word, themselves standing in diakenic interplay, can open up a future for an utterance. As Heidegger puts it in *The Question of Being:* "[Every authentic Saying] always traverses the essential ambiguity of the word and its uses. The ambiguity of Saying in no way consists in a mere collection of meanings which turn up arbitrarily. It rests in a play which, the more richly it unfolds itself, remains the more rigorously bound by a concealed rule. . . . Therefore, Saying remains bound by the highest law. It always goes through the essential ambiguity of words and their applications."[49]

When we see that the way to relate to our future is not to describe (or predict) it but to open it up by demarcating the present, we understand the future as much more tractable and promising than when we view it simply as a set of not-yet-facts. And to see our situation as tractable and promising is, of course, to *make* it tractable and promising.

Like narrative, as I discussed it earlier, demarcation thus does not aim to state truths about its object. Rather, it changes that object, as Heidegger's discussion of Parmenides' saying actually changes that saying, because the unsuspected depths that Heidegger claims to reveal in the saying are not there, certainly not for us, until he reveals them. The normal, grammatical way of understanding the saying is not destroyed by Heidegger's procedures; it is simply deprived of its status as the only way to understand it. Another way to put this is to say that the saying itself is transformed by being placed into a different language game from the one in which we thought it functioned.

This does not mean that Heidegger rejects or dispenses with true sentences and true beliefs, as Habermas claims.[50] If it were false, for example, that any Greek had ever uttered the words of Parmenides' saying—if, like the works of Ossian, the saying was a modern forgery—Heidegger's treatment of it would be falsified. On every page of his texts, in fact, Heidegger makes traditional truth claims, and he often argues for them. But such truth is not the main goal of his thought. Like the equally traditional truths with which Hegel begins, truth claims for Heidegger are a medium, not the goal, of his discourse.

Heideggerean interpretation thus transforms what it interprets. Insofar as we are situated by what it interprets—as we are by the basic philosophical words we use to express and understand ourselves—such interpretation changes our situation, and changes us. Like the kind of truth given us by Hegelian thinking, Heideggerean truth, what he seeks in his discourse, is not only temporal but "selfing." It gives us richer selves. Philosophy that is inspired by the narrative thinking of Hegel and the demarcative thinking of Heidegger is the very opposite, then, of the timeless, selfless quest of truth enjoined upon American philosophy by Raymond B. Allen and his henchmen during the McCarthy era.

The practices of Heideggerean *Destruktion,* Derridean *déconstruction,* and the like are a rich and anarchic panoply, as befits a type of thought that seeks to restore to philosophical words their multiple unknowns impending, or essential futures. Whether it will ever be reduced to the kind of reflective systematicity exhibited by Hegel's ways of reconstructing the past, to say nothing of the tidy rules of inference to be found on the jackets of logic books, is doubtful to say the least; for the future is opaque, and our openness to it is a mystery even to ourselves. Thought that opens up a future—that is, demarcation—is more an art than a science, and the more rigorous for that.

Conclusion

The view that philosophy must, in order to be rigorous, be *restricted* to investigating the truth of sentences or propositions is a hidden protocol, inflicted on it during the McCarthy era and never openly debated since. Once that view is exposed for what it is, many new perspectives open up. I have sketched one of them here: a paradigm that would relate philosophical thought to the past and future just as rigorously as analytical philosophy relates it to the present. It is not a paradigm that abandons the discipline of truth that analytical philosophy has so diligently followed but one that supplements it with ways of relating thoughtfully to the past and to the future. Those ways cannot be reduced to truth-based discourse, but they presuppose it in important ways. The techniques, and many of the issues, of analytical philosophy can thus find their place within the paradigm I am advocating, but when they do, they will be treated in ways that explicitly connect them to their past and open them up to their future. Those treatments will come under standards that philosophy itself can formulate and try to justify—as I have done here.

I call this paradigm "situating reason" to draw attention to an odd fact about us human beings: that although we are, as individuals and groups, always parts of larger but temporary states of affairs, we vary between awareness and forgetfulness of that fact. We may need to be reminded both that we are situated and of what the salient constituents of our current situation are.

This has been a primary function of philosophy since Plato. The Platonic dialogues are much more, philosophically speaking, than a collection of arguments. They present a group of people getting progressively clearer on their situatedness in general by contrasting it with the world of Forms, which never changes and so is not a situation. They also get clearer on some of the basic ingredients of their current situation—on the earthly values represented by individual Forms such as Beauty, Holiness, and Justice. Situating reason can be viewed as a continuation of this Platonic project by Hegelian and Heideggerean means—means that, unlike Platonic thought, do not make even a contrastive appeal to the timelessness of anything.

Philosophy has not been alone in the task of clarifying our situation. Art, religion, moral deliberation, and humanistic scholarship in general perform various versions of it in various ways, but philosophy has pursued it in a distinctive fashion. For one thing, it has aimed to develop and clarify the most general elements of our current situation. Those elements, being general, are not like physical objects. They are more akin to what philosophers have traditionally thought of as concepts, which are accessible through the words we use to talk and think about them. And hence philosophy gets one of its most important and productive tasks: to care for the growth and development of words, especially philosophical ones, for unless we want to continue to give posthumous victories to

Raymond B. Allen and his like, we have to take seriously the fact that concepts, or words, have histories that need not only to be *described* but *connected* with so that their unpredictable future—and ours—can be *opened up.*

This task is, for sure, an important one. For as I suggested above, the words that are specifically philosophical are precisely those that are most central to our language and culture: philosophers think *about* the words other people think *with,* words such as "cause," "freedom," "God," "mind," "subject," "predicate." We all know these words, everybody uses them, other discourses trade upon them. As Hegel put it:

> [Such basic words] further the viewpoints and principles which have validity in the sciences and constitute the ultimate touchstone (*Halt*) for the rest of their material, are for all that not peculiar to [those sciences], but are common to the culture of a time and people. . . . Our consciousness contains these representations, it allows them validity as final determinations, it moves forward on them as its guiding, connecting concepts. But it does not know them, does not make them themselves into the objects and interests of its examination.
>
> To give an abstract example, every consciousness has and uses the wholly abstract determination, "Being." "The sun *is* in the sky," "the grapes *are* ripe," and so on forever. In higher culture there are questions of cause and effect, force and expression, etc. All [our] knowing and representing is interwoven with such metaphysics, and governed by it; it is the net in which is caught all the concrete material that occupies us in our ways and doings. But for our ordinary consciousness, this web and its knots are sunken in multilayered material. It is the latter which contains the interests and objects which we know, which we have before us. Those universal threads are not set off and made objects of our reflection.[51]

It is thus philosophy's job to care—and to care *critically*—for the central conceptual switchyard in which the rails of our thoughts, languages, and communities come together. And who *doesn't* need philosophy so conceived? Certainly every American does, and urgently—for as I suggested in chapter 4, even American academics live in a culture whose store of common concepts and mutual understanding is, to say the least, in need of repair.

Philosophy has traditionally done its work not in the name of aesthetic pleasure or religious faith but in that of reason. This has made of it, in the modern world, a uniquely precarious enterprise, for the development and prestige of science have made it easy, as well as politically convenient, to restrict rationality itself to what science does best of all: to the pursuit of true sentences. That pursuit is not situating, however, for it only accidentally informs us about ourselves. It is formally irrelevant to science as conventionally understood whether a state of affairs described or predicted by a scientific theory is the one in which we find ourselves, and the changing truth value of scientific sentences is merely accidental to them. Science is not geared toward informing us about ourselves as essentially temporal beings and should not be twisted around to do so.

Nowhere is that fact more obvious than in the case of American philosophy. Its attempt to be rigorously scientific, foisted on it during the McCarthy era, resulted in a situation in which virtually all American philosophers were sadly ignorant of the real condition of their own profession and of the political events and forces that had shaped it. A greater turn from the Delphic maxim *gnôthe seauton,* "know thyself," could hardly be imagined.

The work of Hegel and Heidegger, and of their followers, has begun to remedy this situation. It expands the repertoire of rationality beyond the truth-based model of thesis and argument, in which analytical philosophy specializes, to encompass the techniques of narrative and demarcation. With this we have the tools to clarify the general features of our situation, which means connecting it to the past and opening up its essential future.

To think of the future of philosophy along such lines is to think of an almost unimaginable amount of work. If we are going to connect philosophy's words to their past, for example, the main philosophical languages must be learned, along with the standard techniques of logic. Analytical and continental philosophy must, in this, definitively come back together, because continental philosophy, in its Hegelian and Heideggerean dispensations, respectively, responds to the past and the future—and the past and future cannot be connected except through the present, that is, through the truth-oriented techniques of analytical philosophy.

Learning the basics of languages and logic is only the beginning. The fundamental and general ingredients of our situation—what I have here called "philosophical words" and elsewhere have called "parameters"—must be identified (or reidentified), dialectically connected with what went before, and diakenically opened up to what may come after.[52] The nature of situatedness itself, which as I remarked is, in the age of the Internet, taking over from identity (substance, essence, form, and so forth) as the most basic ontological concept, needs to be clarified, and the implications of all this for such fields as ethics and the theory of knowledge need to be examined.

Will American philosophy find thinkers to match those challenges? Pulling oneself up by the bootstraps out of a disciplinary ditch in which one has lain, unknowing, for half a century is no easy task. My own adventures as a philosopher suggest, sadly, that American philosophy will not be able to accomplish this and is doomed to further shrinkage and irrelevance while the important jobs we need it to do go undone. But stranger things have happened. In the meantime, I am afraid one question remains: What really happened to American philosophy during and after the McCarthy era?

We do not have even a rough idea. My efforts in chapters 1 and 2, for example, were largely confined to the currently available *written* record. A final historical judgment must await supplementation (or, if warranted, correction) of the unpleasant information assembled there, and that can come only when philosophers who lived through the McCarthy era break their strange silence on the subject. Such discussion, whatever its result, can be argued to be absolutely necessary if American philosophers, analytical and continental, are to understand the strengths and weaknesses of their own traditions.

As Thales learned when he fell in the ditch, philosophers must watch their feet as well as the stars.

Notes

Introduction

1. The story is told by Diogenes Laertius in his *Lives of Eminent Philosophers,* trans. R. D. Hicks, Loeb Classical Library (Cambridge, Mass.: Harvard University Press, 1972), 1:35, sec. 1.34.

2. Biographical information on these thinkers is available in Paul Edwards, ed. in chief, *The Encyclopedia of Philosophy,* 8 vols. (New York: Macmillan, 1967). See the articles on Aristotle, 1:152; Heidegger, 3:459; Kant, 4:305; Locke, 4:488; Plato, 5:315–16; Socrates, 7:481. For Hegel, see Clark Butler and Christiane Seiler, ed. and trans., *Hegel: The Letters* (Bloomington: Indiana University Press, 1984), 641–45.

3. Lewis White Beck, "Neo-Kantianism," in Edwards, *The Encyclopedia of Philosophy,* 5:428. For the Young Hegelians, see the introduction to Lawrence S. Stepelevich, ed., *The Young Hegelians* (Cambridge: Cambridge University Press, 1983), 1–15.

4. Giovanna Borradori, *The American Philosopher,* trans. Rosanna Crocitto (Chicago: University of Chicago Press, 1994), 7; Richard J. Bernstein, "Pragmatism, Pluralism and the Healing of Wounds," *APA* 63, no. 3 (1989): 11; Richard Rorty, "Philosophy in America Today," in *Consequences of Pragmatism* (Minneapolis: University of Minnesota Press, 1982), 214.

5. See Reiner Schürmann, "De la philosophie aux États-Unis," *Le temps de la réflexion* 6 (1985): 303–21.

6. See Abraham Edel, "The Fact-Value Dichotomy as a Chapter in Social-Intellectual History," in *Exploring Fact and Value,* vol. 2 of *Science, Ideology and Value* (New Brunswick, N.J.: Transaction Books, 1980), 339–63. Edel is operating on a more general level than I am here, investigating American intellectual life as a whole.

7. The locus classicus for this way of defending Heidegger is Hannah Arendt, "Martin Heidegger at Eighty," trans. Albert Hofstadter, in *Heidegger and Modern Philosophy,* ed. Michael Murray (New Haven, Conn.: Yale University Press, 1980), 293–303.

8. George R. Stewart, *The Year of the Oath* (Garden City, N.Y.: Doubleday, 1950), 11.

9. Aristotle, *Nicomachean Ethics* 1.2.1094a28–b1.

10. This fact was conveyed to me by Judith Butler. Nancy Fraser is now again affiliated with a philosophy department, at the Graduate Faculty of the New School University; her primary appointment, however, remains in political science.

11. The results of hiring decisions are evident from the *Directory of American Philosophers;* the profiles of most major departments have not changed, in this regard, in the last thirty years.

12. Randall Collins, *The Sociology of Philosophies* (Cambridge, Mass.: Harvard University Press, 1998), 751.

13. See the symposium on the authorship of the "new" theory in *Synthese* 104 (1995): 178–283, including papers by Jaako Hintikka, Gabriel Sandu, Quentin Smith, and Scott Soames. In James Baillie's anthology *Contemporary Analytical Philosophy* (New York: Simon and Schuster, 1997), the most recent essay was from 1973, a strange stretching of the word "contemporary."

14. Schürmann, "De la philosophie aux États-Unis," 321.

1

1. See, for example, the remarks by Carl Hempel at the beginning of his introductory book in the philosophy of science, *Philosophy of Natural Science* (Englewood Cliffs, N.J.: Prentice-Hall, 1966), 2: "Many branches of empirical science have come to provide a basis for associated technologies,

which put the results of scientific inquiry to practical use and which in turn furnish pure or basic research with new data, new problems, and new tools for investigation. . . . But apart from aiding man in his search for control over his environment, science answers another, disinterested, but no less deep and persistent urge: namely, his desire to gain ever wider knowledge and ever deeper understanding of the world in which he finds himself. In the chapters that follow, we will consider how these principal objectives of scientific inquiry are achieved." Needless to say, "these objectives" do not include the practical effects of science, to which Hempel cannot bring himself here to devote a full sentence and to which the book never returns.

2. Arthur Fine, "The Viewpoint of No-One in Particular"; Philip Kitcher, "Truth or Consequences?" and Robert Nozick, "Invariance and Objectivity," in *APA* 72, no. 2 (1998): 9–63. The defensiveness about truth and objectivity suggested by these convergent choices of topic is, as Fine recognizes, quite in order.

3. For the history of logical positivism, see the essays in A. J. Ayer, ed., *Logical Positivism* (New York: Free Press, 1959).

4. C. L. Stevenson, *Ethics and Language* (New Haven, Conn.: Yale University Press, 1944).

5. A. I. Melden, *Rights in Moral Lives* (Berkeley: University of California Press, 1988).

6. This figure is taken from Nicholas Rescher, "American Philosophy Today," *Review of Metaphysics* 46 (1993): 741.

7. See the report of Ruth Barcan Marcus, chair of the APA Committee on Placement, to Eastern Division's business meeting of December 28, 1968. She notes ominously that the ratio of job seekers to jobs has doubled since the previous year (*APA* 42 [1969]: 136). I will discuss the philosophy job market in chapter 3.

8. Giovanna Borradori, *The American Philosopher*, trans. Rosanna Crocitto (Chicago: University of Chicago Press, 1994), 7; Richard J. Bernstein, "Pragmatism, Pluralism and the Healing of Wounds," *APA* 63, no. 3 (1989): 11; Richard Rorty, "Philosophy in America Today," in *Consequences of Pragmatism* (Minneapolis: University of Minnesota Press, 1982), 214.

9. A. J. Ayer et al., *The Revolution in Philosophy* (New York: St. Martin's Press, 1965).

10. Richard Boyd, Philip Gasper, and J. D. Trout, eds., *The Philosophy of Science* (Cambridge, Mass.: MIT Press, 1991).

11. Quine's response is available as W. V. O. Quine, "A Letter to Mr. Oster-
    mann," in *The Owl of Minerva: Philosophers on Philosophy,* by Charles J.
    Bontempo and S. Jack Odell (New York: McGraw-Hill, 1975), 227–30;
    the passage quoted is on 228.

12. The only real exception to this is Nicholas Rescher's "American Philoso-
    phy Today," published in the *Review of Metaphysics* in 1992 (see note 6
    above). The *Philosophical Review,* in its centennial issue, published four
    articles on various fields within philosophy, such as philosophy of mind
    and language and history of philosophy (*Philosophical Review* 101, no. 1
    [January 1992]), but this was a very special issue, beginning the journal's
    second century of operation. Moreover, the articles it contained were on
    various fields *within* philosophy, not on philosophy itself. Although they
    discussed the relationship of their respective subfields to philosophy as a
    whole, they did not go so far as to discuss that common genus in its own
    right. The same urge to specialize holds in general for the summaries of
    recent research in various fields that are published at intervals in *American
    Philosophical Quarterly. APA* occasionally covers such material, but see
    chapter 3 for its limitations.

13. It is also telling that the two American philosophers who do engage most
    prominently in such discussion—Bernstein and Rorty—do not identify
    themselves as analytical philosophers, though, as I will argue in chapter 5,
    Rorty continues to maintain some of analytical philosophy's characteristic
    dogmas.

14. Richard Rorty, "Philosophy as Science, Metaphor, Politics," in *Essays on
    Heidegger and Others* (Cambridge: Cambridge University Press, 1991), 21.

15. Jürgen Habermas, *Knowledge and Human Interests,* trans. Jeremy J.
    Shapiro (Boston: Beacon Press, 1971), vii; emphasis in original.

16. For an excellent introduction to the paradoxes of self-reference, see W. V.
    Quine, "The Ways of Paradox," in *The Ways of Paradox and Other Essays,*
    2d ed. rev. (Cambridge, Mass.: Harvard University Press, 1976), 1–18.

17. Michael Dummett, *The Origins of Analytical Philosophy* (Cambridge,
    Mass.: Harvard University Press, 1993); Michael Friedman, "Overcom-
    ing Metaphysics: Carnap and Heidegger," in *Origins of Logical Empiri-
    cism,* ed. Ronald Giere and Alan W. Richardson (Minneapolis: University
    of Minnesota Press, 1996), 45–79; Peter Hylton, *Russell, Idealism and the
    Emergence of Analytic Philosophy* (Oxford: Clarendon, 1990).

18. Hylton, *Russell, Idealism and the Emergence of Analytic Philosophy,* vii.

19. Richard Rorty, *Philosophy and the Mirror of Nature* (Princeton, N.J.:
    Princeton University Press, 1979).

20. Rorty, "Philosophy as Science, Metaphor, Politics," 21.

21. For Cavell's views, see Borradori, *The American Philosopher,* 118–36.

22. Richard Hofstadter, *Anti-Intellectualism in American Life* (New York: Vintage, 1963).

23. On this synthesis, see Garry Wills, *Inventing America: Jefferson's Declaration of Independence* (New York: Random House, 1978).

24. Hofstadter, *Anti-Intellectualism in American Life,* 47–51, 55–136; for the Puritans, see 60–64.

25. Paul Edwards, ed. in chief, *The Encyclopedia of Philosophy,* 8 vols. (New York: Macmillan, 1967), 8:235, 238; also see Paul Edwards's appendix to Bertrand Russell, *Why I Am Not a Christian* (New York: Simon and Schuster, 1957), 207–59.

26. Brand Blanshard et al., *Philosophy in American Education* (New York: Harper Brothers, 1945), 8.

27. William F. Buckley Jr. and L. Brent Bozell, *McCarthy and His Enemies* (Washington, D.C.: Regnery Publishing, 1954; reprinted 1995), 336. Buckley has hardly repudiated this book. Passages from it, in fact, were reprinted verbatim in Buckley's 1999 novel *The Redhunter* (New York: Little, Brown, 1999); see George Stade, "Books of the Times" (review of *The Redhunter*), *New York Times,* June 7, 1999, B6.

28. Alistair Cooke, *A Generation on Trial* (Baltimore: Penguin, 1968), vi. Cooke is explaining why his book, originally published in 1950, had the title that it did.

29. "The Committee Speaks Out," *Los Angeles Times,* December 12, 1998, A28.

30. See the essays in Andre Schiffrin, ed., *The Cold War and the University* (New York: New Press, 1997), and Christopher Simpson, ed., *Universities and Empire* (New York: New Press, 1998), for pioneering efforts at this, as well as the bibliographical essay in Ellen Schrecker, *No Ivory Tower* (New York: Oxford University Press, 1986), 343–56.

31. Nathan M. Pusey, *American Higher Education: A Personal Report* (Cambridge, Mass.: Harvard University Press, 1978), 133–34.

32. Henry Rosovsky, *The University: An Owner's Manual* (New York: Norton, 1990), 181.

33. Sidney Hook, *Heresy, Yes—Conspiracy, No* (New York: John Day, 1953). Also see James Rorty and Moshe Decter, *McCarthy and the Communists* (Boston: Beacon Press, 1954), 142–43.

34. See "Rethinking McCarthyism, If Not McCarthy," *New York Times,* Week in Review section, October 18, 1998, 1.

35. See "Would Groucho Have Joined a Party That Would Have Him as a Member?" *New York Times,* September 14, 1998, A19.

36. "The Non-Communist Party of the First Part Was an Upstart," *New York Times,* Week in Review section, September 20, 1998, 7.

37. John Greenway, *Down among the Wild Men* (Boston: Little, Brown, 1972), 116.

38. The story is told in Jamie Sayer, *Einstein in America* (New York: Crown, 1985), 249–66; the quotes are from 256.

39. Gary Nash et al., eds., *The American People,* 2d ed. (New York: Harper and Row, 1990), 917.

40. " 'Public Affairs' Reporting Draws McCarthy Parallels," *Los Angeles Times,* September 27, 1998, 1; Alan Dershowitz, *Sexual McCarthyism: Clinton, Starr, and the Emerging Constitutional Crisis* (New York: Basic Books, 1999).

41. Robert Bellah, "Veritas at Harvard: An Exchange," *New York Review of Books* 24, no. 12 (July 14, 1977): 38.

42. Nash et al., *The American People,* 917.

43. On Cohn, see Sidney Zion, *The Autobiography of Roy Cohn* (Secaucus, N.J.: Lyle Stuart, 1988). On Cohn's outing as a homosexual, see Michael Cadden, "Strange Angel: The Pinklisting of Roy Cohn," in *Secret Agents: The Rosenberg Case, McCarthyism and Fifties America,* ed. Marjorie Garber and Rebecca L. Walkowitz (London: Routledge, 1995), 93–105.

44. Willis Moore, "Causal Factors in the Current Attack on Education," *AAUP* 41 (1955): 623–64. Also see Paul Lazarsfeld and Wagner Thielens Jr., *The Academic Mind* (Glencoe, Ill.: Free Press, 1958), 55–58.

45. Sigmund Diamond, *Compromised Campus* (Oxford: Oxford University Press, 1992), 3–4.

46. Richard Hofstadter and Walter P. Metzger, *The Development of Academic Freedom in the United States* (New York: Columbia University Press, 1955), 18.

47. Hofstadter, *Anti-Intellectualism in American Life,* 41–42.

48. Hague's comment has been immortalized in Leland H. Gregory III, ed., *Great Government Goofs* (New York: Dell, 1997), 131.

49. Lazarsfeld and Thielens, *The Academic Mind,* 166.

50. Seymour Martin Lipset and David Riesman, *Education and Politics at Harvard* (New York: McGraw-Hill, 1975), 195.

51. For Barrett's activities, see Richard Pells, *The Liberal Mind in a Conservative Age* (New York: Harper and Row, 1985), 123–24, 126–28; for Hook and Lovejoy, see Schrecker, *No Ivory Tower,* 105–9.

52. Lazarsfeld and Thielens, *The Academic Mind,* 40–41, 48, 163, 331–36; also see Hofstadter, *Anti-Intellectualism in American Life,* 13.

53. Lionel Lewis, *Cold War on Campus* (New Brunswick, N.J.: Transaction Press, 1988), 226; also see 33.

2

1. Actually, the Wiggins case was not the subject of a resolution by Western Division, which had previously adopted policies impeding voting on matters of social importance (*APA* 27 [1954]: 99). Something resembling a resolution was read at the division's business meeting, and it was suggested that a resolution might be voted on the following year (*APA* 32 [1959]: 181). None was. See Ellen Schrecker, *No Ivory Tower* (New York: Oxford University Press, 1986), 387 n. 47.

2. This is the way George R. Stewart suggests things were often done: Stewart, *The Year of the Oath* (Garden City, N.Y.: Doubleday, 1950), 83.

3. Sigmund Diamond, "Veritas at Harvard," *New York Review of Books* 24, no. 7 (April 28, 1977): 13–17.

4. Ludwig Wittgenstein, *Philosophical Investigations,* trans. G. E. M. Anscombe, 3d ed. (New York: Macmillan, 1958), 49, ¶124.

5. John Rawls, *A Theory of Justice* (Cambridge, Mass.: Harvard University Press, 1971), 137.

6. Roger Scruton, *Modern Philosophy* (Allen Lane: Penguin, 1994), 5.

7. The passage is from Allen's report to the regents of the university concerning the academic freedom cases of Joseph Butterworth and Herbert Phillips: *Communism and Academic Freedom: The Record of the Tenure Cases at the University of Washington* (Seattle: University of Washington Press, 1949), 90, 93.

8. Ibid., 40.

9. William F. Buckley Jr. and L. Brent Bozell, *McCarthy and His Enemies* (Washington, D.C.: Regnery Publishing, 1954; reprinted 1995), 336.

10. Richard Hofstadter, *Anti-Intellectualism in American Life* (New York: Vintage, 1963), 30; emphasis added.

11. See Aristotle, *Metaphysics* 9.10, and John McCumber, *The Company of Words* (Evanston, Ill.: Northwestern University Press, 1993), 98–100.

12. St. Augustine, *Soliloquien,* ed. Hanspeter Müller (Bern: Benteli, 1954), 177; St. Anselm, *De Veritate,* in *Truth, Freedom and Evil,* ed. Jasper Hopkins and Herbert Richardson (New York: Harper Torchbooks, 1967), 91–120; also see the editors' introduction, 12–25.

13. See Proclus, *In Timaeo* 2.287, 3–5: *kai dia touto kai alêtheia einai hê pros to gignoskomenon epharmogê tou gignoskontos;* cited in Werner Beierwaltes, *Proklos: Grundzüge seiner Metaphysik* (Frankfurt: Klostermann, 1965), 129; but see also 337–38.

14. See Evanghelos A. Moutsopoulos, "The Idea of False in Proclus," in *The Structure of Being: A Neoplatonic Approach,* ed. R. Baine Harris (Albany: SUNY Press, 1982), 137–39.

15. St. Thomas Aquinas, *The Disputed Questions on Truth,* trans. R. W. Mulligan, S.J., 3 vols. (Chicago: Regnery, 1956), 1:11.

16. St. Thomas Aquinas, *Summa Theologica,* part 1, question 16, article 2, cited from Anton C. Pegis, ed., *Basic Writings of St. Thomas Aquinas,* 2 vols. (New York: Random House, 1945), 1:170–71.

17. Benedict de Spinoza, *Ethics,* in *The Collected Works of Spinoza,* ed. and trans. Edwin Curley (Princeton, N.J.: Princeton University Press, 1985), 410, 472–73.

18. Immanuel Kant, *Kritik der Reinen Vernunft,* B 82–83; see Gerold Prauss, "Zum Wahrheitsproblem bei Kant," *Kant-Studien* 60 (1969): 167–68.

19. See G. W. F. Hegel, *Hegel's Logic,* trans. William Wallace (Oxford: Clarendon, 1975), 41. For a discussion, see McCumber, *The Company of Words,* 33–118.

20. Martin Heidegger, "On the Essence of Truth," in *Basic Writings,* ed. David Farrell Krell (San Francisco: Harper and Row, 1977), 113–41.

21. Bruce Wilshire, "Pragmatism, Neopragmatism, and Phenomenology: The Richard Rorty Phenomenon," *Human Studies* 26 (1997): 95–108; quote is on 103–4.

22. Hilary Putnam, "Two Conceptions of Rationality," in *Reason, Truth and History* (Cambridge: Cambridge University Press, 1981), 105–6.

23. As is shown by Gertrude Ezorsky's article "Pragmatic Theory of Truth," in

The Encyclopedia of Philosophy, ed. in chief Paul Edwards, 8 vols. (New York: Macmillan, 1967), 6:429–30. My point is not that Ezorsky had understood Carnap correctly—Thomas Ryckman has convinced me that she did not. But her misunderstanding, repeated without contradiction in so public a place, was presumably a widespread one.

24. See David P. Gardner, *The California Oath Controversy* (Berkeley: University of California Press, 1967), 229.

25. See W. V. O. Quine, "Two Dogmas of Empiricism," in *From a Logical Point of View* (New York: Harper Torchbooks, 1953), 20–46. For an example of what Quine is attacking, see the preface to Alfred Jules Ayer, *Language, Truth, and Logic* (New York: Dover, n.d.), 31–32.

26. Steve Fuller, "A Tale of Two Cultures and Other Higher Superstitions," *Democratic Culture* 3 (fall 1994): 35.

27. For a more detailed account of the hardening of analytical philosophy's views on truth as the single goal of inquiry, see McCumber, *The Company of Words,* 70–90. Also see McCumber, "Reconnecting Rorty: The Situation of Discourse in Richard Rorty's *Contingency, Irony, and Solidarity,*" *diacritics* 20 (1990): 2–19.

28. W. V. Quine, *Methods of Logic,* 2d ed. (Cambridge, Mass.: Harvard University Press, 1959), xi. In some later editions, this is on 1. The overall changes in some of those editions were major (for which see the preface to the fourth edition [Cambridge: Harvard University Press, 1982, vii–viii]), but the sentence I have quoted remains throughout. For a more recent affirmation of this dogma by Quine, see 77 of his *Pursuit of Truth* (Cambridge, Mass.: Harvard University Press, 1990) in conjunction with, of course, the book's title.

29. Quine, *Methods of Logic,* xi.

30. Ibid., xvi.

31. Gottlob Frege, "Der Gedanke," in Frege, *Kleine Schriften,* ed. Ignacio Angelleli (Hildesheim: Georg Olms Verlag, 1967), 343. An English translation, varying from my own here, is given in Gottlob Frege, *Logical Investigations,* ed. Peter Geach and R. H. Stoothoff (New Haven, Conn.: Yale University Press, 1977), 2.

32. Alfred Tarski, "The Semantic Conception of Truth," *Philosophy and Phenomenological Research* 4 (1943–44): 342–67; quote on 355–56.

33. Gerold Prauss, "Zum Wahrheitsproblem bei Kant," *Kant-Studien* 60 (1969): 171 n. 28.

34. Such conflation is evident in the phrase "of meaning and of truth and falsity" in the foregoing quote from Quine. For a critical account of it in Donald Davidson, see McCumber, *The Company of Words,* 250–77.

35. For an informed, and rare, discussion of the historical complicity between empiricism and racism, see H. M. Bracken, "Essence, Accident, and Race," *Hermathena* 116 (1973): 81–96. Complicity with racism does not, of course, immediately and totally disqualify empiricism as a philosophical approach. Much can be salvaged from it, but, I suggest, such complicity teaches us something *philosophically* important about it.

36. Hans Reichenbach, *The Rise of Scientific Philosophy,* 2d ed. (Berkeley: University of California Press, 1951), 325.

37. Ibid.

38. The treatment of Hegel in Reichenbach's book is a case in point. All the hoariest clichés are openly displayed: that Hegel believed history moved in a three-step cycle of thesis-antithesis-synthesis; that he wanted to use dialectics to predict; and so on. Ibid., 67–71.

39. David Hull, *Science as a Process* (Chicago: University of Chicago Press, 1988), 27.

40. Hilary Putnam, interview with Giovanna Borradori, in Borradori, *The American Philosopher,* trans. Rosanna Crocitto (Chicago: University of Chicago Press, 1994), 57.

41. My source is interviews with Charles Sherover and Bruce Wilshire, and Wilshire's 1985 manuscript "The Pluralist Rebellion in the American Philosophical Association: Eastern Division, 1978–1985" (hereafter Wilshire).

42. Quoted in Michael Kettle, *Salome's Last Veil: The Libel Case of the Century* (London: Granada, 1977), 6. British paranoia about homosexual influence did not die out after World War I. In 1998 the *New York Times* accused the *Sun,* a London newspaper owned by the Australian magnate Rupert Murdoch, of "raising the McCarthyite specter of cadres of secret, high-placed homosexuals foisting their own agendas on the country." Sarah Lyall, "For Blair's Cabinet, Three Outings Are Not Picnics," *New York Times,* November 11, 1998, A14.

43. K. G. Robertson, *Public Secrets: A Study in the Development of Government Secrecy* (New York: St. Martin's Press, 1982), 70–71.

44. G. W. F. Hegel, *The Phenomenology of Mind,* trans. J. B. Baillie (London: Sonnenschein, 1910). That Baillie did not check his translation with a German speaker was conveyed to me by Emil Fackenheim.

45. See Hofstadter, *Anti-Intellectualism in American Life,* 388–90.

46. Ramona Cormier and Richard H. Lineback, eds., *International Directory of Philosophy and Philosophers 1997–98* (Bowling Green, Ohio: Philosophy Documentation Center, 1997).

47. Kathleen Tweney, ed., *Directory of American Philosophers 1998–99* (Bowling Green, Ohio: Philosophy Documentation Center, 1998).

3

1. Seyla Benhabib and Drucilla Cornell, eds., *Feminism as Critique* (Minneapolis: University of Minnesota Press, 1987).

2. Judith Butler conveyed this fact to me. As I noted in the introduction, Nancy Fraser now has a second appointment in philosophy at the New School University's Graduate Faculty.

3. Evidence for the influence of the view this expresses goes well beyond the anecdotal: as I noted in chapter 1, the United States, a country that has many fine centers for the history and philosophy of science—and can even afford one for the study of the Belgian endive (at the University of Massachusetts, Amherst)—remains without a single one for the history of philosophy.

4. I e-mailed it to the divisional secretary separately from the body of the paper.

5. See "Peer Review," *Chronicle of Higher Education,* January 8, 1999, A62.

6. At http://www.udel.edu/apa/.

7. Denise K. Wagner, "Master's Degrees Are the Hot Topic at Meeting on Doctoral Education," *Chronicle of Higher Education,* April 30, 1999, A16.

8. David Hume, *A Treatise of Human Nature,* ed. L. A. Selby-Bigge (Oxford: Clarendon, 1888), 166; John Stuart Mill, *A System of Logic* (London: Longman, 1970), 147–48.

9. Alasdair MacIntyre, *After Virtue,* 2d ed. (Notre Dame, Ind.: University of Notre Dame Press, 1984), 266. See also Peter Hylton, *Russell, Idealism, and the Emergence of Analytical Philosophy* (Oxford: Clarendon, 1990), 9, 331–33; and Stuart Barnett, ed., introduction to *Hegel after Derrida* (London: Routledge, 1998), 7–9, 295 n. 18.

10. For which see W. V. O. Quine, "Necessary Truth," in *The Ways of Paradox and Other Essays,* rev. and enl. ed. (Cambridge, Mass.: Harvard University Press, 1976), 68–76.

11. Simon Evnine, *Donald Davidson* (Stanford, Calif.: Stanford University Press, 1991), 153–54.

12. See A. J. Ayer et al., *The Revolution in Philosophy* (New York: St. Martin's Press, 1965).

13. The discussion is in René Descartes, *Principles of Philosophy,* in *The Philosophical Works of Descartes,* ed. E. Haldane and G. R. T. Ross, 2 vols. (Cambridge: Cambridge University Press, 1911), 1:249–52.

14. For the evil demon, see Descartes, *Principles of Philosophy,* 220.

15. John Locke, *An Essay concerning Human Understanding,* ed. Alexander Campbell Fraser, 2 vols. (New York: Dover, 1959), 2:105.

16. Ibid., 2:148–64.

17. George Berkeley, *The Principles of Human Knowledge,* in *Berkeley's Philosophical Writings,* ed. David M. Armstrong (New York: Collier, 1965), 59–60.

18. Ludwig Wittgenstein, *Philosophical Investigations,* trans. G. E. M. Anscombe, 3d ed. (New York: Macmillan, 1958), 109.

19. Gilead Bar-Elli, "Analysis without Elimination: On the Philosophical Significance of Russell's 'On Denoting,' " in *The Story of Analytic Philosophy: Plots and Heroes,* ed. Anat Biletzki and Anat Matar (London: Routledge, 1998), 167.

20. Martin Heidegger, "Language," in *Poetry, Language, Thought,* trans. Albert Hofstadter (New York: Harper and Row, 1971), 190, 192.

21. Bar-Elli, "Analysis without Elimination," 167–68.

22. For an adumbration of some of those issues, see John McCumber, *Poetic Interaction* (Chicago: University of Chicago Press, 1989).

23. At the 1998 meeting of the board of officers of the APA, John Lachs "suggested that conversation about 'the good of the profession' be a permanent part of Board meeting agendas. . . . It was decided that the Administrative Committee should look into some *uncontroversial* projects for which we can solicit funds" (*APA* 72, no. 5 [1999]: 56; emphasis added).

24. Jorge J. E. Gracia, "Philosophy in American Life: *De Facto* and *de Jure,*" *APA* 72, no. 5 (1999): 154.

25. G. W. F. Hegel, *Science of Logic,* trans. A. V. Miller (New York: Humanities Press, 1976), 393–99.

26. Rudolf Carnap, "The Elimination of Metaphysics through Logical Analysis of Language," in *Logical Positivism,* ed. A. J. Ayer (New York: Free Press, 1959), 60–81.

27. Ibid., 69.

28. My translations will be taken, with some modifications, from Martin Heidegger, "What Is Metaphysics?" in Heidegger, *Basic Writings,* trans. David Farrell Krell (San Francisco: Harper and Row, 1977), 95–112. The earlier version is "What Is Metaphysics?" in *Existence and Being,* trans. R. F. C. Hull and Alan Crick (Chicago: Regnery, 1949), 325–61.

29. Martin Heidegger, *Being and Time,* trans. John MacQuarrie and Edward Robinson (New York: Harper and Row, 1962), ¶40, 184–91 (pagination is from the German edition and is given in the margin of the English rendition).

30. Martin Heidegger, *Die Lehre vom Urteil im Psychologismus. Ein kritisch-positiver Beitrag zur Logik* (Leipzig: J. A. Barth, 1914).

31. See Michael Friedman, "Overcoming Metaphysics: Carnap and Heidegger," in *Origins of Logical Empiricism,* ed. Ronald Giere and Alan W. Richardson (Minneapolis: University of Minnesota Press, 1996), 45–79.

32. On the early Heidegger and Aristotle, see Theodore Kisiel, *The Genesis of Heidegger's* Being and Time (Berkeley: University of California Press, 1993), 227–308.

33. Reiner Schürmann, "De la philosophie aux États-Unis," *Le temps de la réflexion* 6 (1985): 303–21.

34. For a French introduction to analytical philosophy, see Pascal Engel, *La dispute: une introduction à la philosophie analytique* (Paris: Minuit, 1997).

35. Richard Rorty, *Philosophy and the Mirror of Nature* (Princeton, N.J.: Princeton University Press, 1979).

36. A summary of the survey, which was conducted by Merold Westphal, was supplied me by Arthur Fine.

37. Hilary Putnam, interview with Giovanna Borradori, in Borradori, *The American Philosopher,* trans. Rosanna Crocitto (Chicago: University of Chicago Press, 1994), 57.

38. Schürmann, "De la philosophie aux États-Unis," 321.

39. Randall Collins, *The Sociology of Philosophies* (Cambridge, Mass.: Harvard University Press, 1998), 751.

40. A prejudice ratified in the very term "McCarthy era." A manuscript of mine was once derided by a famous analytical philosopher as "too Catholic-centric," as if that were an uncontroversial insult and as if I had not left the Catholic church some thirty-five years before.

41. I discussed the Official Secrets Act briefly in chapter 2. For the situation in Vienna, see Allan Janik and Stephen Toulmin, *Wittgenstein's Vienna* (New York: Simon and Schuster, 1973).

42. I will discuss linguistic analysis further in chapter 5.

4

1. Harvey Cox, "The Market as God," *Atlantic Monthly,* March 1999, 18–23; the quote is on 18–19.

2. Alfie Kohn, "In Pursuit of Affluence, at a High Price," *New York Times,* Science Times section, February 2, 1999, 7.

3. Aristotle, *Nicomachean Ethics* 1.5.1095b23–26.

4. Ibid., 1.5.1096a5–10.

5. Ibid., 1.5.1096a10.

6. Michael Hill, "U.S. Pays Little Heed to Philosophy," *Baltimore Sun,* January 12, 1999, 2A.

7. Jorge J. E. Gracia, "Philosophy in American Life: *De Facto* and *de Jure,*" *APA* 72, no. 5 (1999): 150–51.

8. Robert Audi, "Philosophy in American Life: The Profession, the Public, and the American Philosophical Association," *APA* 72, no. 5 (1999): 140–1.

9. Nicholas Rescher, "American Philosophy Today," *Review of Metaphysics* 46 (1993): 717–45; quote on 731.

10. David Caute, *The Great Fear* (New York: Simon and Schuster, 1978), 505. For the often-told story of the Hollywood blacklist, see 487–522.

11. For an example of such tracking of an absence, see Ian Tyrrell, *The Absent Marx: Class Analysis and Liberal History in Twentieth-Century America* (New York: Greenwood Press, 1986), esp. 71–89.

12. Sarah Kerr, "The Novel as Indictment," *New York Times Magazine,* October 11, 1998, 53.

13. America's own Arthur Miller, of course, suffered terribly during the McCarthy years. Caute, *The Great Fear,* 536–37.

14. Robert Bellah, "Veritas at Harvard: Another Exchange," *New York Review of Books* 24, no. 12 (July 14, 1977): 38.

15. See Andrew Morton, *Monica's Story* (New York: St. Martin's Press, 1999), esp. chapter 11 ("Terror in Room 1012"), 175–91; and Alan Dershowitz, *Sexual McCarthyism: Clinton, Starr, and the Emerging Constitutional Crisis* (New York: Basic Books, 1999).

16. Robert Hughes, "Pulling the Plug on Culture," *Time,* August 7, 1995, 62.

17. Josh Getlin, " 'Public Affairs' Reporting Draws McCarthy Parallels," *Los Angeles Times,* September 27, 1998, A1.

18. Edward A. Shils, *The Torment of Secrecy: The Background and Consequences of American Security Policies* (Glencoe, Ill.: Free Press, 1956), 9.

19. Edward Shils, "Do We Still Need Academic Freedom?" *American Scholar* 62, no. 2 (spring 1993): 209.

20. Lynn Cheney, *Telling the Truth* (Washington, D.C.: National Endowment for the Humanities, 1992), 19–20.

21. Jeffrey N. Wasserstrom, "Are You Now or Have You Ever Been . . . Postmodern?" *Chronicle of Higher Education,* September 11, 1998, B4.

22. "The Port Huron Statement," in *Freedom: Its History, Nature, and Varieties,* by Robert E. Dewey and James A. Gould (London: Collier-MacMillan, 1970), 370.

23. Tyrrell, *The Absent Marx,* 83.

24. John Searle, *Speech Acts* (Cambridge: Cambridge University Press, 1969), 124–25.

25. Plato, *Republic* 563b, 549a and e, 578d–e, 777d, 865c, 872c, and 868b.

26. Immanuel Kant, *Critique of Pure Reason,* trans. Norman Kemp Smith (New York: St. Martin's Press, 1965), B 758–59 (pagination is to the Berlin Academy edition, given in the margins in this translation).

27. G. W. F. Hegel, *Hegel's Logic,* trans. William Wallace (Oxford: Oxford University Press, 1975), §99 *Zusätze,* 147.

28. Martin Heidegger, *Being and Time,* trans. John MacQuarrie and Edward Robinson (New York: Harper and Row, 1962), ¶38, 220 (pagination is to the German edition and is given in the margins in the English rendition).

29. Quoted in Cynthia S. Jordan, " 'Old Words' in 'New Circumstances': Language and Leadership in Post-Revolutionary America," *American Quarterly* 40 (December 1988): 491. As Thomas Paine put it, "We see

with other eyes; we hear with other ears and think with other thoughts, than we formerly used"; Paine, "Letter to the Abbé Raynal," in *The Complete Writings of Thomas Paine,* ed. Philip S. Foner, 2 vols. (New York: Citadel Press, 1945), 2:243.

30. Eric S. Foner, *The Story of American Freedom* (New York: Norton, 1998), xiv.

31. David Hume, *Enquiry Concerning Human Understanding,* in *Enquiries,* ed. L. A. Selby-Bigge (Oxford: Clarendon, 1894), 73–78.

32. Alfred Jules Ayer, *Language, Truth and Logic* (New York: Dover, n.d.), 112.

33. Just what those enrichments are is a disputed issue. See A. Dühle, *The Theory of the Will in Classical Antiquity* (Berkeley: University of California Press, 1982), for an introduction to the discussion. Whether Augustine "invented" the will or not, he certainly made it the central ethical concept that it is today.

34. J. L. Austin, "A Plea for Excuses," in *Philosophical Papers* (Oxford: Clarendon, 1961), 133.

35. Ludwig Wittgenstein, *Philosophical Investigations,* trans. G. E. M. Anscombe, 3d ed. (New York: Macmillan, 1958), ¶¶98, 124, pp. 45, 49. For a trenchant attack on this aspect of linguistic philosophy, see Ernest Gellner, *Words and Things* (Harmondsworth: Pelican, 1968), 40–43, 58–62, 167–74. My criticism differs from Gellner's in that I think the things he criticizes are not intrinsic to linguistic philosophy per se; Hegel, in particular, had a version of linguistic philosophy that was free of such things. See John McCumber, *The Company of Words: Hegel, Language, and Systematic Philosophy* (Evanston, Ill.: Northwestern University Press, 1993).

36. Richard Flacks and Scott L. Thomas, "Among Affluent Students, a Culture of Disengagement," *Chronicle of Higher Education* 45, no. 14 (November 27, 1998): A48.

37. Henry Louis Gates Jr., *The Signifying Monkey* (Oxford: Oxford University Press, 1988), xxii.

38. Ibid., xix, xxiv.

39. Fredric Jameson, *Postmodernism: The Cultural Logic of Late Capitalism* (Durham, N.C.: Duke University Press, 1991), 97.

40. G. W. F. Hegel, *Philosophy of Nature,* ed. and trans. M. J. Petry, 3 vols. (London: Allen and Unwin, 1970), 3:187–88; *Philosophy of Subjective Spirit,* ed. and trans. M. J. Petry, 3 vols. (The Hague: Reidel, 1979), 2:243–323.

41. Stuart Hall, "Cultural Studies and Its Theoretical Legacies," in *Cultural Studies,* by Lawrence Grossberg et al. (London: Routledge, 1992), 279–80.

42. Paul de Man, "Form and Intent in the American New Criticism," in *Blindness and Insight* (Minneapolis: University of Minnesota Press, 1983), 27–29.

43. Frank Lentricchia, "On Behalf of Theory," in *Criticism in the University,* ed. Gerald Graff and Reginald Gibbons (Evanston, Ill.: Northwestern University Press, 1985), 106.

44. Rolf-Peter Horstmann, ed., "Schwierigkietin und Voraussetzungen der Philosophie Hegels," in *Dialektik in der Philosophie Hegels* (Frankfurt: Suhrkamp, 1978), 25–26; my translation.

45. Paul de Man, "Heidegger's Exegeses of Hölderlin," in *Blindness and Insight,* 246–66; quote on 246–47.

46. Frederick Douglass, *Autobiography* (1845); quoted in the epigraph to chapter 5 of Gates, *The Signifying Monkey,* 170; emphasis added.

47. Gilles Deleuze, *Qu'est-ce que la philosophie?* (Paris: Minuit, 1991), 11; my translation.

48. The essays in which Heidegger makes this case have not, unfortunately, been translated: see Martin Heidegger, *Erläuterungen zu Hölderlins Dichtung* (Frankfurt: Klostermann, 1951).

49. Fredric Jameson, *The Political Unconscious: Narrative as a Socially Symbolic Act* (Ithaca, N.Y.: Cornell University Press, 1981), 24, 32, 40, 91.

50. Ibid., 41, 51–52. For Hegel on Leibniz, see G. W. F. Hegel, *Lectures on the History of Philosophy,* trans. E. S. Haldane and Catherine Simson, 3 vols. (London: Routledge and Kegan Paul, 1896), 3:325–48.

51. De Man, "Heidegger's Exegeses of Hölderlin," 250. For Heidegger's critique of presence, and his conflation of it with parousia, see John McCumber, *Metaphysics and Oppression* (Bloomington: Indiana University Press, 1999).

52. See Martin Heidegger, "The Age of the World Picture," in *The Question Concerning Technology and Other Essays,* trans. William Lovitt (New York: Harper and Row, 1977), 115–54.

53. De Man, "Form and Intent in the American New Criticism," 30.

54. See Martin Heidegger, *Erläuterungen zu Hölderlins Dichtung,* 2d ed. (Frankfurt: Klostermann, 1971), 7–8.

55. Jameson, *The Political Unconscious,* 37.

56. Jonathan Culler, introduction to Mieke Bal and Inge E. Boer, eds., *The Point of Theory* (New York: Continuum, 1994), 13–17; quote on 16.

57. See Gertrude Himmelfarb, *Looking into the Abyss: Untimely Thoughts on Culture and Society* (New York: Alfred A. Knopf, 1994).

58. Adolf Grünbaum, *The Foundations of Psychoanalysis: A Philosophical Critique* (Berkeley: University of California Press, 1984), 7–43; Jürgen Habermas, "A Review of Gadamer's *Truth and Method,*" in *Understanding and Social Inquiry,* ed. Fred R. Dallmeyer and Thomas A. McCarthy (Notre Dame, Ind.: University of Notre Dame Press, 1977), 335–63; Stephen Weinberg, *Dreams of a Final Theory* (New York: Pantheon, 1992), 175–82. On the philosophical naïveté of the pro-science side, see Val Dusek, "Where Learned Armies Clash by Night," *Continental Philosophy Review* 31 (1998): 95–106; Roger Hart, "The Flight from Reason," in *Science Wars,* ed. Andrew Ross (Durham, N.C.: Duke University Press, 1996), 272; and Michael Lynch, "Detoxifying the 'Poison Pen Effect,'" in *Science Wars,* 242–58.

59. Andrew Ross, ed., introduction to *Science Wars,* 7.

60. See on this Robert Proctor, *Value-Free Science: Purity and Power in Modern Knowledge* (Cambridge, Mass.: Harvard University Press, 1991).

61. Dusek, "Where Learned Armies Clash by Night," 99.

62. Heidegger, *Being and Time,* ¶7, pp. 27–28, 34.

63. Ibid., ¶¶33, 44, pp. 157–58, 225.

64. Ibid., ¶35, pp. 167–70.

65. Ibid., ¶69, p. 357; my translation.

5

1. Richard Rorty, *Philosophy and the Mirror of Nature* (Princeton, N.J.: Princeton University Press, 1979).

2. My critique is not, in fact, derived from Rorty's. Its basis can be found in my dissertation: John McCumber, "The Communication of Philosophical Truth in Hegel and Heidegger" (Ph.D. diss., University of Toronto, 1978).

3. In its uninstructed rejection of history and its claim that what makes one philosopher better than another is simply having more "interesting" and

"fruitful" things to say, Rorty's thought reveals that, as with earlier versions of pragmatism, its true roots lie as much in evangelical Protestantism as in the history of philosophy. See Richard Hofstadter, *Anti-Intellectualism in American Life* (New York: Vintage, 1963), 388–89.

4. For a rare, but informed, account of this complicity, see H. M. Bracken, "Essence, Accident, and Race," *Hermathena* 116 (1973): 81–96.

5. Richard Rorty, "Philosophy in America Today," in *Consequences of Pragmatism* (Minneapolis: University of Minnesota Press, 1982), 218.

6. Thomas McCarthy has shown this for Rorty: "Private Irony, Public Decency: Richard Rorty's New Pragmatism," *Critical Inquiry* 16 (1990): 355–70.

7. Bruce Wilshire, "Pragmatism, Neopragmatism, and Phenomenology: The Richard Rorty Phenomenon," *Human Studies* 26 (1997): 103–4.

8. For further on this, see chapters 3 and 4 of John McCumber, *Philosophy and Freedom* (Bloomington: Indiana University Press, 2000).

9. The story is largely apocryphal, but see Lawrence K. Shook, *Étienne Gilson, 1884–1978* (Toronto: Pontifical Institute of Medieval Studies, 1984), 55–56. As the fourth of seven theses summing up his major dissertation, Gilson wrote, "Descartes' thought was opposed to, but sometimes conditioned by, the structure of medieval thought" (Shook 64).

10. See W. V. O. Quine, "Two Dogmas of Empiricism," in *From a Logical Point of View* (New York: Harper Torchbooks, 1953), 20–46. For an example of what Quine is attacking, see the preface to Alfred Jules Ayer, *Language, Truth, and Logic* (New York: Dover, n.d.), 31–32.

11. For a more detailed account of the hardening of analytical philosophy's views on truth as the single goal of inquiry (in Frege and Tarski a mere stipulation) into what later philosophers took as dogma, see John McCumber, *The Company of Words* (Evanston, Ill.: Northwestern University Press, 1993), 70–90. Also see John McCumber, "Reconnecting Rorty: The Situation of Discourse in Richard Rorty's *Contingency, Irony, and Solidarity*," *diacritics* 20 (1990): 2–19.

12. For this part of Parmenides' poem, see G. S. Kirk and J. E. Raven, *The Presocratic Philosophers* (Cambridge: Cambridge University Press, 1960), 270–71.

13. True, natural science seeks to do precisely this: natural scientists want to know what our experience, which is of course dependent on our minds, implies about the nature of things that are not. They want to know, in

short, what the universe is like when we are not watching it. That goal is impossible to realize, however worthwhile it is, which is why natural science has such a difficult and expensive time approximating it.

14. For a recent statement by a mathematician of the kind of view that lies behind my remarks here, see Reuben Hersh, *What Is Mathematics, Really?* (Oxford: Oxford University Press, 1997).

15. See Benedict de Spinoza, *Ethics,* in *The Collected Works of Spinoza,* ed. and trans. E. M. Curley (Princeton, N.J.: Princeton University Press, 1985), 581.

16. For which see Donald Davidson, *Inquiries into Truth and Interpretation* (Oxford: Clarendon, 1984).

17. Davidson, "True to the Facts," in *Inquiries into Truth and Interpretation,* 43.

18. By "the classical Davidson" I mean to exclude "A Nice Derangement of Epitaphs," which does open up this essential temporality of language; see Donald Davidson, "A Nice Derangement of Epitaphs," in *Truth and Interpretation: Perspectives on the Philosophy of Donald Davidson,* ed. Ernest LePore (Oxford: Blackwell, 1986), 433–46, and McCumber, *The Company of Words,* 269.

19. This concept, by the way, is enough to rehabilitate Hegelian dialectic. For if ϕx is essentially time bound, then "ϕx at time t" allows us to infer "$\sim (\phi x)$ at $(t \pm y)$." And this, when it is conceded that no minimum value of y can be specified, yields all the delights of Hegel's texts.

20. See Martin Heidegger, *Platons Lehre von der Wahrheit,* in *Wegmarken* (Frankfurt: Klostermann, 1967), 109–44.

21. We need not buy into wholly atemporal versions of logical or syntactic form to admit this. The view that linguistic categories such as noun and verb are radial structures, for example, suggests that even those categories can change historically as what is central to a given radius is displaced in favor of elements formerly peripheral. What counts as "nouniness" can thus change over time. See George Lakoff, *Women, Fire, and Dangerous Things* (Chicago: University of Chicago Press, 1987), 63–64, 289–97.

22. John Searle, *The Campus War: A Sympathetic Look at the University in Agony* (New York: World, 1971), 132–34; see my discussion of Searle in chapter 4.

23. For further on this reading of Hegel, see McCumber, *The Company of Words.*

24. See Maurice Merleau-Ponty, *Consciousness and the Acquisition of Language,* trans. Hugh J. Silverman (Evanston, Ill.: Northwestern University Press, 1973).

25. Jean-François Lyotard, *The Postmodern Condition* (Minneapolis: University of Minnesota Press, 1984). Derrida's critique is most easily found in his critique of the Hegelian *Aufhebung* in "From Restricted to General Economy," in *Writing and Difference* (Chicago: University of Chicago Press, 1978), 251–77. The narrative side of the overall project I am advocating here is of Hegelian inspiration.

26. Actually, Kant does not get a theory of concept formation out of his account of reflective judgment, but it can be done: see John McCumber, *Poetic Interaction* (Chicago: University of Chicago Press, 1989), 259–69, 279–81.

27. G. W. F. Hegel, *Science of Logic,* trans. A. V. Miller (New York: Humanities Press, 1976), 558–71.

28. A good deal of mischief has been done by reading contemporary, atemporal versions of logical negation back into Hegel. For a highly pitched example, see Karl Popper, "What Is Dialectic?" in *Conjectures and Refutations* (New York: Basic Books, 1965), 312–35.

29. See McCumber, *The Company of Words,* 143–48.

30. George Santayana, *The Life of Reason,* 5 vols. (New York: Scribner's, 1905–6), 1:12; emphasis added. See also G. W. F. Hegel, *The Philosophy of Nature,* ed. M. J. Petry, 3 vols. (London: Allen and Unwin, 1970), 1:212–15, §249.

31. See Eric Foner, *The Story of American Freedom* (New York: Norton, 1998).

32. "Destroying the subject of morality in one's own person amounts to . . . destroying morality itself, to the extent that it is in oneself"; Immanuel Kant, *Grundlegung der Metaphysik der Sitten,* in *Werke,* 12 vols. (Frankfurt: Suhrkamp, 1968), 8:554; my translation.

33. Indeed, my own efforts here are motivated not so much by a desire to keep people from killing themselves, a desire that is unlikely to be served by these few pages, as by the fact that attention to the issue of suicide enables me to show the essential incompleteness of the kind of narrative I am advocating here.

34. It is noteworthy that most English-language readings of Hegel take him to be making this sort of truth claim. For a paradigm of the genre, see Charles Taylor, *Hegel* (Cambridge: Cambridge University Press, 1975).

35. See Lee Smolin, *The Life of the Cosmos* (Oxford: Oxford University Press, 1997), for an effort to make this plausible. On the sort of view advanced by Nancy Cartwright, laws of nature that "lie" could presumably also change; see Nancy Cartwright, *How the Laws of Physics Lie* (Oxford: Clarendon, 1983).

36. This list is from Gaston Bachelard, "La Dialectique philosophique et les notions de la relativité," in *L'Engagement rationaliste* (Paris: Presses Universitaires de France, 1972), 120–36.

37. Georges Canguilhem, "L'Histoire des sciences dans l'œuvre de Gaston Bachelard," in *Études d'histoire et de la philosophie des sciences* (Paris: Jean Vrin, 1983), 185.

38. For a discussion of Foucault's self-styled positivism, see McCumber, *Philosophy and Freedom,* chapters 7 and 8.

39. That Rorty thinks narrative links are to be found rather than created follows from his distinction between the Proustian, "contingent" association of texts, which like *Contingency, Irony, and Solidarity* itself has no narrative links, and the Nietzschean "dialectical" (found) association (100). The kind of narrative I am proposing undercuts Rorty's rather too absolute opposition between "contingent" and "necessary."

40. See Garth Fowder, *Empire to Commonwealth: Consequences of Monotheism in Late Antiquity* (Princeton, N.J.: Princeton University Press, 1993), 52.

41. G. W. F. Hegel, *Lectures on the History of Philosophy,* trans. E. S. Haldane and Frances Simson, 3 vols. (New York: Humanities Press, 1974), 1:434.

42. Hegel, *Lectures on the History of Philosophy,* 2:307; translation altered.

43. "[Philosophy's] foremost requirement is that every thought shall be grasped in its full precision, and nothing allowed to remain vague and indefinite"; Hegel, *Hegel's Logic* (William Wallace, trans.) (Oxford: Clarendon, 1975), §80 *Zusätz,* 115.

44. David Hume, *A Treatise of Human Nature,* ed. L. A. Selby-Bigge (Oxford: Clarendon, 1888), 69–176.

45. Martin Heidegger, *Being and Time,* trans. John MacQuarrie and Edward Robinson (New York: Harper and Row, 1962), ¶52, pp. 257–58 (pagination is to the German edition and is given in the margins in the English rendition).

46. See John McCumber, *Metaphysics and Oppression: Heidegger's Challenge to Western Philosophy* (Bloomington: Indiana University Press, 1999), 15–16, for a discussion of this.

47. Jacques Derrida, "Signature Event Context," *Glyph* 1 (1977): 172–97.

48. I have, in fact, done that for Heidegger elsewhere, and I presuppose those discussions here. See John McCumber, *Poetic Interaction* (Chicago: University of Chicago Press, 1989), and McCumber, *Metaphysics and Oppression.*

49. Martin Heidegger, *The Question of Being,* trans. William Kluback and Jean T. Wilde, German text with English facing (New Haven, Conn.: Yale University Press, 1958), 104. The translation is my own. Perhaps fearful of the tyranny of logical positivism, then at its height, Kluback and Wilde have translated the German *merhdeutig* not as "ambiguous" but as "meaningful." This is typical of the intellectual terrorism of that period.

50. Jürgen Habermas, "Work and Weltanschauung: The Heidegger Controversy from a German Perspective," *Critical Inquiry* 15 (1989): 431–56. For a critical account of Habermas's reading of Heidegger, see the introduction to McCumber, *Metaphysics and Oppression,* 1–18.

51. Hegel, *Lectures on the History of Philosophy,* 1:57.

52. See the general introduction to McCumber, *Poetic Interaction,* 1–25.

Bibliography

Anselm, St. *De Veritate.* In Anselm, *Truth, Freedom and Evil,* edited by Jasper Hopkins and Herbert Richardson. New York: Harper Torchbooks, 1967.

Aquinas, St. Thomas. *The Disputed Questions on Truth.* Translated by R. W. Mulligan, S.J., 3 vols. Chicago: Regnery, 1956.

——. *Summa Theologica.* In *Basic Writings of St. Thomas Aquinas.* Edited by Anton C. Pegis. 2 vols. New York: Random House, 1945.

Audi, Robert. "Philosophy in American Life: The Profession, the Public, and the American Philosophical Association." *APA* 72, no. 5 (1999): 139–48.

Augustine, St. *Soliloquien.* Edited by Hanspeter Müller. Bern: Benteli, 1954.

Austin, J. L. *Philosophical Papers.* Oxford: Clarendon, 1961.

——. "A Plea for Excuses." In *Philosophical Papers,* 133. Oxford: Clarendon, 1961.

Ayer, A. J., ed. *Logical Positivism.* New York: Free Press, 1959.

Ayer, A. J., et al., eds. *The Revolution in Philosophy.* New York: St. Martin's Press, 1965.

Bachelard, Gaston. "La Dialectique philosophique et les notions de la relativité." In *L'Engagement rationaliste,* 120–36. Paris: Presses Universitaires de France, 1972.

——. *L'Engagement rationaliste.* Paris: Presses Universitaires de France, 1972.

Bal, Mieke, and Inge E. Boer, eds. *The Point of Theory.* New York: Continuum, 1994.

Bar-Elli, Gilead. "Analysis without Elimination: On the Philosophical Significance of Russell's 'On Denoting.'" In *The Story of Analytic Philosophy: Plots and Heroes,* edited by Anat Biletzki and Anat Matar, 167–81. London: Routledge, 1998.

Barnett, Stuart, ed. *Hegel after Derrida.* London: Routledge, 1998.

Beierwaltes, Werner. *Proklos: Grundzüge seiner Metaphysik.* Frankfurt: Klostermann, 1965.

Bellah, Robert. "Veritas at Harvard: An Exchange." *New York Review of Books* 24, no. 12 (July 14, 1977): 38.

Benhabib, Seyla, and Drucilla Cornell, eds. *Feminism as Critique.* Minneapolis: University of Minnesota Press, 1987.

Berkeley, George. *Berkeley's Philosophical Writings.* Edited by David M. Armstrong. New York: Collier, 1965.

Bernstein, Richard J. "Pragmatism, Pluralism and the Healing of Wounds." *APA* 63, no. 3 (1989): 11.

Biletzki, Anat, and Anat Matar, eds. *The Story of Analytic Philosophy: Plots and Heroes.* London: Routledge, 1998.

Blanshard, Brand, et al. *Philosophy in American Education.* New York: Harper Brothers, 1945.

Bloom, Allan. *The Closing of the American Mind.* New York: Simon and Schuster, 1987.

Bontempo, Charles J., and S. Jack Odell. *The Owl of Minerva: Philosophers on Philosophy.* New York: McGraw-Hill, 1975.

Borradori, Giovanna. *The American Philosopher.* Translated by Rosanna Crocitto. Chicago: University of Chicago Press, 1994.

Boyd, Richard, et al., eds. *The Philosophy of Science.* Cambridge, Mass.: MIT Press, 1991.

Bracken, H. M. "Essence, Accident, and Race." *Hermathena* 116 (1973): 81–96.

Buckley, William F., Jr., and L. Brent Bozell. *McCarthy and His Enemies.* Washington, D.C.: Regnery Publishing, 1954 (reprinted Regnery, 1995).

Cadden, Michael. "Strange Angel: The Pinklisting of Roy Cohn." In *Secret Agents: The Rosenberg Case, McCarthyism and Fifties America,* edited by Marjorie Garber and Rebecca L. Walkowitz, 93–105. London: Routledge, 1995.

Canguilhem, Georges. *Études d'histoire et de la philosophie des sciences.* Paris: Jean Vrin, l983.

——. "L'Histoire des sciences dans l'œuvre de Gaston Bachelard." In *Études d'histoire et de la philosophie des sciences,* 173–86. Paris: Jean Vrin, l983.

Carnap, Rudolf. "The Elimination of Metaphysics through Logical Analysis of Language." In *Logical Positivism,* edited by A. J. Ayer, 60–81. New York: Free Press, 1959.

——. "Truth and Confirmation." In *Readings in Philosophical Analysis,* edited by Herbert Feigl and Wilfrid Sellars, 119–27. New York: Appleton-Century-Crofts, 1949.

Cartwright, Nancy. *How the Laws of Physics Lie.* Oxford: Clarendon, 1983.

Caute, David. *The Great Fear.* New York: Simon and Schuster, 1978.

Cheney, Lynn. *Telling the Truth.* Washington, D.C.: National Endowment for the Humanities, 1992.

Collins, Randall. *The Sociology of Philosophies.* Cambridge, Mass.: Harvard University Press, 1998.

Communism and Academic Freedom: The Record of the Tenure Cases at the University of Washington. Seattle: University of Washington Press, 1949.

Cooke, Alistair. *A Generation on Trial.* Baltimore: Penguin, 1968.

Cox, Harvey. "The Market as God." *Atlantic Monthly,* March 1999, 18–23.

Culler, Jonathan. Introduction to *The Point of Theory,* edited by Mieke Bal and Inge E. Boer, 13–17. New York: Continuum, 1994.

Dallmeyer, Fred R., and Thomas A. McCarthy, eds. *Understanding and Social Inquiry.* Notre Dame, Ind.: University of Notre Dame Press, 1977.

Davidson, Donald. *Inquiries into Truth and Interpretation.* Oxford: Clarendon, 1984.

——. "A Nice Derangement of Epitaphs." In *Truth and Interpretation: Perspectives on the Philosophy of Donald Davidson,* edited by Ernest LePore, 433–46. Oxford: Blackwell, 1986.

———. "True to the Facts." In *Inquiries into Truth and Interpretation,* 37–54. Oxford: Clarendon, 1984.

Deleuze, Gilles. *Qu'est-ce que la philosophie?* Paris: Minuit, 1991.

De Man, Paul. *Blindness and Insight.* Minneapolis: University of Minnesota Press, 1983.

———. "Form and Intent in the American New Criticism." In *Blindness and Insight,* 20–35. Minneapolis: University of Minnesota Press, 1983.

———. "Heidegger's Exegeses of Hölderlin." In *Blindness and Insight,* 246–66. Minneapolis: University of Minnesota Press, 1983.

Derrida, Jacques. "From Restricted to General Economy." In *Writing and Differance,* 251–77. Chicago: University of Chicago Press, 1978.

———. "Signature Event Context." *Glyph* 1 (1977): 172–97.

———. *Writing and Differance.* Chicago: University of Chicago Press, 1978.

Dershowitz, Alan. *Sexual McCarthyism: Clinton, Starr, and the Emerging Constitutional Crisis.* New York: Basic Books, 1999.

Descartes, René. *The Philosophical Works of Descartes.* Edited by E. Haldane and G. R. T. Ross. 2 vols. Cambridge: Cambridge University Press, 1911.

Dewey, Robert E., and James A. Gould, eds. *Freedom: Its History, Nature, and Varieties.* London: Collier-MacMillan, 1970.

Diamond, Sigmund. *Compromised Campus: The Collaboration of Universities with the Intelligence Community, 1945–1955.* Oxford: Oxford University Press, 1992.

———. "Veritas at Harvard." *New York Review of Books* 24, no. 7 (April 28, 1977): 13–17.

Dummett, Michael. *The Origins of Analytical Philosophy.* Cambridge, Mass.: Harvard University Press, 1993.

Dusek, Val. "Where Learned Armies Clash by Night." *Continental Philosophy Review* 31 (1998): 95–106.

Edwards, Paul, editor in chief. *The Encyclopedia of Philosophy.* 8 vols. New York: Macmillan, 1967.

Engel, Pascal. *La dispute: une introduction à la philosophie analytique.* Paris: Minuit, 1997.

Evnine, Simon. *Donald Davidson.* Stanford, Calif.: Stanford University Press, 1991.

Fine, Arthur. *The Shaky Game.* Chicago: University of Chicago Press, 1986.

Flacks, Richard, and Scott L. Thomas. "Among Affluent Students, a Culture of Disengagement." *Chronicle of Higher Education* 45, no. 14 (November 27, 1998): A48.

Foner, Eric S. *The Story of American Freedom.* New York: Norton, 1998.

Frege, Gottlob. *Logical Investigations.* Edited by Peter Geach and R. H. Stoothoff. New Haven, Conn.: Yale University Press, 1977.

Friedman, Michael. "Overcoming Metaphysics: Carnap and Heidegger." In *Origins of Logical Empiricism,* edited by Ronald Giere and Alan W. Richardson, 45–79. Minneapolis: University of Minnesota Press, 1996.

Fuller, Steve. "A Tale of Two Cultures and Other Higher Superstitions." *Democratic Culture* 3 (fall 1994): 35.

Garber, Marjorie, and Rebecca L. Walkowitz, eds. *Secret Agents: The Rosenberg Case, McCarthyism and Fifties America.* London: Routledge, 1995.

Gardner, David P. *The California Oath Controversy.* Berkeley: University of California Press, 1967.

Gates, Henry Louis, Jr. *The Signifying Monkey.* Oxford: Oxford University Press, 1988.

Gellner, Ernest. *Words and Things.* Harmondsworth: Pelican, 1968.

Getlin, Josh. " 'Public Affairs' Reporting Draws McCarthy Parallels." *Los Angeles Times,* September 27, 1998, A1.

Giere, Ronald, and Alan W. Richardson, eds. *Origins of Logical Empiricism.* Minneapolis: University of Minnesota Press, 1996.

Gracia, Jorge J. E. "Philosophy in American Life: *De Facto* and *de Jure.*" *APA* 72, no. 5: 149–58.

Graff, Gerald, and Reginald Gibbons, eds. *Criticism in the University.* Evanston, Ill.: Northwestern University Press, 1985.

Greenway, John. *Down among the Wild Men.* Boston: Little, Brown, 1972.

Grossberg, Lawrence, et al. *Cultural Studies.* London: Routledge, 1992.

Grünbaum, Adolf. *The Foundations of Psychoanalysis: A Philosophical Critique.* Berkeley: University of California Press, 1984.

Habermas, Jürgen. *Knowledge and Human Interests.* Translated by Jeremy J. Shapiro. Boston: Beacon Press, 1971.

———. "A Review of Gadamer's *Truth and Method.*" In *Understanding and Social Inquiry,* edited by Fred R. Dallmeyer and Thomas A. McCarthy, 335–63. Notre Dame, Ind.: University of Notre Dame Press, 1977.

———. "Work and Weltanschauung: The Heidegger Controversy from a German Perspective." *Critical Inquiry* 15 (1989): 431–56.

Hall, Stuart. "Cultural Studies and Its Theoretical Legacies." In *Cultural Studies,* by Lawrence Grossberg et al., 275–94. London: Routledge, 1992.

Harris, R. Baine, ed. *The Structure of Being: A Neoplatonic Approach.* Albany: SUNY Press, 1982.

Hart, Roger. "The Flight from Reason." In *Science Wars,* edited by Andrew Ross, 259–92. Durham, N.C.: Duke University Press, 1996.

Hegel, G. W. F. *Hegel's Logic.* Translated by William Wallace. Oxford: Clarendon, 1975.

———. *Lectures on the History of Philosophy.* Translated by E. S. Haldane and Frances Simson. 3 vols. New York: Humanities Press, 1974.

———. *Phenomenology of Spirit.* Translated by A. V. Miller. Oxford: Oxford University Press, 1979.

———. *Philosophy of Nature.* Edited and translated by M. J. Petry. 3 vols. London: Allen and Unwin, 1970.

———. *Philosophy of Subjective Spirit.* Edited and translated by M. J. Petry. 3 vols. The Hague: Reidel, 1979.

———. *Science of Logic.* Translated by A. V. Miller. New York: Humanities Press, 1976.

Heidegger, Martin. "The Age of the World Picture." In *The Question Concerning Technology and Other Essays,* translated by William Lovitt, 115–54. New York: Harper and Row, 1977.

———. *Basic Writings.* Translated by David Farrell Krell. San Francisco: Harper and Row, 1977.

———. *Being and Time.* Translated by John MacQuarrie and Edward Robinson. New York: Harper and Row, 1962.

———. *Erläuterungen zu Hölderlins Dichtung.* Frankfurt: Klostermann, 1951.

———. "From a Dialogue on Language." In *On the Way to Language,* translated by Albert Hofstadter, 1–54. New York: Harper and Row, 1971.

———. "Language." In *Poetry, Language, Thought,* translated by Albert Hofstadter, 189–210. New York: Harper and Row, 1971.

——. *Die Lehre vom Urteil im Psychologismus. Ein kritisch-positiver Beitrag zur Logik*. Leipzig: J. A. Barth, 1914.

——. "On the Essence of Truth." In *Basic Writings,* translated by David Farrell Krell. 113–41. San Francisco: Harper and Row, 1977.

——. *On the Way to Language*. Translated by Albert Hofstadter. New York: Harper and Row, 1971.

——. "Platons Lehre von der Wahrheit." In *Wegmarken,* 109–44. Frankfurt: Klostermann, 1967.

——. *Poetry, Language, Thought*. Translated by Albert Hofstadter. New York: Harper and Row, 1971.

——. *The Question Concerning Technology and Other Essays*. Translated by William Lovitt. New York: Harper and Row, 1977.

——. *The Question of Being*. Translated by William Kluback and Jean T. Wilde. German text with English facing. New Haven, Conn.: Yale University Press, 1958.

——. *Was Heisst Denken?* Tübingen: Niemeyer, 1971.

——. *Wegmarken*. Frankfurt: Klostermann, 1967.

——. *What Is Called Thinking?* Translated by Fred D. Wieck and J. Glenn Gray. New York: Harper and Row, 1968.

——. "What Is Metaphysics?" In *Basic Writings,* translated by David Farrell Krell, 95–112. San Francisco: Harper and Row, 1977.

Hempel, Carl G. *Philosophy of Natural Science*. Englewood Cliffs, N.J.: Prentice-Hall, 1966.

Hill, Michael. "U.S. Pays Little Heed to Philosophy," *Baltimore Sun,* January 12, 1999, 2A.

Himmelfarb, Gertrude. *Looking into the Abyss: Untimely Thoughts on Culture and Society*. New York: Alfred A. Knopf, 1994.

Hofstadter, Richard. *Anti-Intellectualism in American Life*. New York: Vintage, 1963.

Hofstadter, Richard, and Walter P. Metzger. *The Development of Academic Freedom in the United States*. New York: Columbia University Press, 1955.

Hook, Sidney. *Heresy, Yes—Conspiracy, No*. New York: John Day, 1953.

Horstmann, Rolf-Peter, ed. *Dialektik in der Philosophie Hegels*. Frankfurt: Suhrkamp, 1978.

———. "Schwierigkeiten und Voraussetzungen der Philosophie Hegels." In *Dialektik in der Philosophie Hegels,* 9–30. Frankfurt: Suhrkamp, 1978.

Hughes, Robert. "Pulling the Plug on Culture." *Time,* August 7, 1995, 62.

Hull, David. *Science as a Process.* Chicago: University of Chicago Press, 1988.

Hume, David. "Enquiry Concerning Human Understanding." In *Enquiries,* edited by L. A. Selby-Bigge. Oxford: Clarendon, 1894.

———. *A Treatise of Human Nature.* Edited by L. A. Selby-Bigge. Oxford: Clarendon, 1888.

Hylton, Peter. *Russell, Idealism and the Emergence of Analytic Philosophy.* Oxford: Clarendon, 1990.

Jameson, Fredric. *The Political Unconscious: Narrative as a Socially Symbolic Act.* Ithaca, N.Y.: Cornell University Press, 1981.

———. *Postmodernism: The Cultural Logic of Late Capitalism.* Durham, N.C.: Duke University Press, 1991.

Janik, Allan, and Stephen Toulmin. *Wittgenstein's Vienna.* New York: Simon and Schuster, 1973.

Jordan, Cynthia S. " 'Old Words' in 'New Circumstances': Language and Leadership in Post-Revolutionary America." *American Quarterly* 40 (December 1988): 491–513.

Kant, Immanuel. *Critique of Pure Reason.* Translated by Norman Kemp Smith. New York: St. Martin's Press, 1965.

Kettle, Michael. *Salome's Last Veil: The Libel Case of the Century.* London: Granada, 1977.

Kirk, G. S., and J. E. Raven. *The Presocratic Philosophers.* Cambridge: Cambridge University Press, 1960.

Kisiel, Theodore. *The Genesis of Heidegger's Being and Time.* Berkeley: University of California Press, 1993.

Lakoff, George. *Women, Fire, and Dangerous Things.* Chicago: University of Chicago Press, 1987.

Lazarsfeld, Paul, and Wagner Thielens Jr. *The Academic Mind.* Glencoe, Ill.: Free Press, 1958.

Lentricchia, Frank. "On Behalf of Theory." In *Criticism in the University,* edited by Gerald Graff and Reginald Gibbons, 105–10. Evanston, Ill.: Northwestern University Press, 1985.

LePore, Ernest, ed. *Truth and Interpretation: Perspectives on the Philosophy of Donald Davidson.* Oxford: Blackwell, 1986.

Lewis, Lionel. *Cold War on Campus.* New Brunswick, N.J.: Transaction Press, 1988.

Lipset, Seymour Martin, and David Riesman. *Education and Politics at Harvard.* New York: McGraw-Hill, 1975.

Locke, John. *An Essay concerning Human Understanding.* Edited by Alexander Campbell Fraser. 2 vols. New York: Dover, 1959.

Lynch, Michael. "Detoxifying the 'Poison Pen Effect.' " In *Science Wars,* edited by Andrew Ross, 242–58. Durham, N.C.: Duke University Press, 1996.

Lyotard, Jean-François. *The Postmodern Condition.* Minneapolis: University of Minnesota Press, 1984.

MacIntyre, Alasdair. *After Virtue.* 2d ed. Notre Dame, Ind.: University of Notre Dame Press, 1984.

McCarthy, Thomas. "Private Irony, Public Decency: Richard Rorty's New Pragmatism." *Critical Inquiry* 16 (1990): 355–70.

McCumber, John. *The Company of Words: Hegel, Language, and Systematic Philosophy.* Evanston, Ill.: Northwestern University Press, 1993.

———. *Metaphysics and Oppression.* Bloomington: Indiana University Press, 1999.

———. *Philosophy and Freedom: Derrida, Rorty, Habermas, Foucault.* Bloomington: Indiana University Press, 2000.

———. *Poetic Interaction.* Chicago: University of Chicago Press, 1989.

———. "Reconnecting Rorty: The Situation of Discourse in Richard Rorty's *Contingency, Irony, and Solidarity,*" *diacritics* 20 (1990): 2–19.

Melden, A. I. *Rights in Moral Lives.* Berkeley: University of California Press, 1988.

Merleau-Ponty, Maurice. *Consciousness and the Acquisition of Language.* Translated by Hugh J. Silverman. Evanston, Ill.: Northwestern University Press, 1973.

Mill, John Stuart. *A System of Logic.* London: Longman, 1970.

Moore, Willis. "Causal Factors in the Current Attack on Education." *AAUP* 41: 623–24.

Morton, Andrew. *Monica's Story.* New York: St. Martin's Press, 1999.

Moutsopoulos, Evanghelos A. "The Idea of False in Proclus." In *The Structure of Being: A Neoplatonic Approach,* edited by R. Baine Harris, 137–39. Albany: SUNY Press, 1982.

Nash, Gary, et al. *The American People.* 2d ed. New York: Harper and Row, 1990.

Paine, Thomas. *The Complete Writings of Thomas Paine.* Edited by Philip S. Foner. New York: Citadel Press, 1945.

Pells, Richard. *The Liberal Mind in a Conservative Age.* New York: Harper and Row, 1985.

Popper, Karl. *Conjectures and Refutations.* New York: Basic Books, 1965.

———. "What Is Dialectic?" In *Conjectures and Refutations,* 312–35. New York: Basic Books, 1965.

Prauss, Gerold. "Zum Wahrheitsproblem bei Kant," *Kant-Studien* 60 (1969): 166–82.

Proctor, Robert. *Value-Free Science: Purity and Power in Modern Knowledge.* Cambridge, Mass.: Harvard University Press, 1991.

Pusey, Nathan M. *American Higher Education: A Personal Report.* Cambridge, Mass.: Harvard University Press, 1978.

Putnam, Hilary. *Reason, Truth and History.* Cambridge: Cambridge University Press, 1981.

———. "Two Conceptions of Rationality." In *Reason, Truth and History,* 103–26. Cambridge: Cambridge University Press, 1981.

Quine, W. V. O. *From a Logical Point of View.* New York: Harper Torchbooks, 1953.

———. "A Letter to Mr. Ostermann." In *The Owl of Minerva: Philosophers on Philosophy,* by Charles J. Bontempo and S. Jack Odell, 227–30. New York: McGraw-Hill, 1975.

———. *Methods of Logic.* 2d ed. Cambridge, Mass.: Harvard University Press, 1959.

———. "Necessary Truth." In *The Ways of Paradox and Other Essays,* 68–76. Rev. and enlarged ed. Cambridge, Mass.: Harvard University Press, 1976.

———. *Pursuit of Truth.* Cambridge, Mass.: Harvard University Press, 1990.

———. "Two Dogmas of Empiricism." In *From a Logical Point of View,* 20–46. New York: Harper Torchbooks, 1953.

———. *The Ways of Paradox and Other Essays.* Rev. and enlarged ed. Cambridge, Mass.: Harvard University Press, 1976.

Rawls, John. *A Theory of Justice.* Cambridge, Mass.: Harvard University Press, 1971.

Reichenbach, Hans. *The Rise of Scientific Philosophy.* 2d ed. Berkeley: University of California Press, 1957.

Rescher, Nicholas. "American Philosophy Today." *Review of Metaphysics* 46 (1993): 717–45.

Robertson, K. G. *Public Secrets: A Study in the Development of Government Secrecy.* New York: St. Martin's Press, 1982.

Rorty, Richard. *Consequences of Pragmatism.* Minneapolis: University of Minnesota Press, 1982.

———. *Contingency, Irony, and Solidarity.* Cambridge: Cambridge University Press, 1989.

———. *Essays on Heidegger and Others.* Cambridge: Cambridge University Press, 1991.

———. *Philosophy and the Mirror of Nature.* Princeton, N.J.: Princeton University Press, 1979.

———. "Philosophy in America Today." In *Consequences of Pragmatism,* 211–30. Minneapolis: University of Minnesota Press, 1982.

Rosovsky, Henry. *The University: An Owner's Manual.* New York: Norton, 1990.

Ross, Andrew, ed. *Science Wars.* Durham, N.C.: Duke University Press, 1996.

Russell, Bertrand. *Why I Am Not a Christian.* New York: Simon and Schuster, 1957.

Santayana, George. *The Life of Reason.* Vol. 1. New York: Scribner's, 1905.

Sayer, Jamie. *Einstein in America.* New York: Crown, 1985.

Schiffrin, Andre, ed. *The Cold War and the University.* New York: New Press, 1997.

Schrecker, Ellen. *No Ivory Tower.* New York: Oxford University Press, 1986.

Schürmann, Reiner. "De la philosophie aux États-Unis." *Le temps de la réflexion* 6 (1985): 303–21.

Scruton, Roger. *Modern Philosophy.* Allen Lane: Penguin, 1994.

Searle, John. *The Campus War: A Sympathetic Look at the University in Agony.* New York: World, 1971.

——. *Speech Acts.* Cambridge: Cambridge University Press, 1969.

Shils, Edward A. "Do We Still Need Academic Freedom?" *American Scholar* 62, no. 2 (1993): 187–209.

——. *The Torment of Secrecy: The Background and Consequences of American Security Policies.* Glencoe, Ill.: Free Press, 1956.

Shook, Lawrence K. *Étienne Gilson, 1884–1978.* Toronto: Pontifical Institute of Medieval Studies, 1984.

Simpson, Christopher, ed. *Universities and Empire.* New York: New Press, 1998.

Smolin, Lee. *The Life of the Cosmos.* Oxford: Oxford University Press, 1997.

Spinoza, Benedict de. *The Collected Works of Spinoza.* Edited and translated by Edwin Curley. Princeton, N.J.: Princeton University Press, 1985.

Stevenson, C. L. *Ethics and Language.* New Haven, Conn.: Yale University Press, 1944.

Stewart, George R. *The Year of the Oath.* Garden City, N.Y.: Doubleday, 1950.

Tarski, Alfred. "The Semantic Conception of Truth." *Philosophy and Phenomenological Research* 4 (1943–44): 342–67.

Tyrrell, Ian. *The Absent Marx: Class Analysis and Liberal History in Twentieth-Century America.* New York: Greenwood Press, 1986.

Wasserstrom, Jeffrey N. "Are You Now or Have You Ever Been . . . Postmodern?" *Chronicle of Higher Education,* September 11, 1998, B4.

Weinberg, Stephen. *Dreams of a Final Theory.* New York: Pantheon, 1992.

Wills, Garry. *Inventing America: Jefferson's Declaration of Independence.* New York: Random House, 1978.

Wilshire, Bruce. "The Pluralist Rebellion in the American Philosophical Association: Eastern Division, 1978–1985." Unpublished manuscript, 1985.

——. "Pragmatism, Neopragmatism, and Phenomenology: The Richard Rorty Phenomenon." *Human Studies* 26 (1997): 95–108.

Wittgenstein, Ludwig. *Philosophical Investigations.* 3d ed. Translated by G. E. M. Anscombe. New York: Macmillan, 1958.

Zion, Sidney. *The Autobiography of Roy Cohn.* Secaucus, N.J.: Lyle Stuart, 1988.

Index

Vespucci, Amerigo, 103
Vienna Circle, 69
Vietnam War, 17, 90, 98, 107

Wasserstrom, Jeffrey, 97
Watergate affair, 14
Weinberg, Stephen, 118
Westphal, Merold, 181n36
Whitehead, Alfred North, 51
Wiggins, Forrest, 22, 35

Wilshire, Bruce, 44, 50–51, 52, 53, 72,
    131
Wittgenstein, Ludwig, 38, 71, 99, 107,
    140–41, 144; *Philosophical Inves-
    tigations,* 70
World Spirit, 153
World War II, xviii; effect of, 15

Yale University, 64
Young, Iris Marion, xx, 59